The Grace of the Spirit

The Grace of the Spirit

A Guide to the Mysteries of the Orthodox Church

The Fathers of Saint Edward Brotherhood

King Edward Orthodox Trust
2017

First Edition 2017.

ISBN 978-0-947935-04-7

Published by
King Edward Orthodox Trust
St. Cyprian's Avenue
Brookwood
SURREY
GU24 0BL
UK

Contents

Acknowledgements

We are grateful to Bishop Ambrose of Methone for his advice and for giving his blessing for publication.

We would also like to thank Alexei Merritt for his work in producing the line-drawings of clergy vestments and monastic clothing. We are, as always, indebted to Jon Davies of Knaphill Print for his help and advice.

The Pentecost icon was kindly donated by Mother Elizabeth of the Convent of Saint Elizabeth, Etna, California, www.conventofsainteliza-beth.org. All other icon photographs are of originals venerated at the Shrine Church of Saint Edward the Martyr, Brookwood, Surrey, UK. The Kazan icon of the Theotokos and the icons of Prophet David, St. Cassiane, St. Mary of Egypt, SS. Zacharias and Elizabeth and St. Philaret were painted at the Convent of Saint Elizabeth; the icon of St. Varus was painted by the sisters of the Lesna Icon Convent, France.

Preface

We have tried to cover the theology and practice of the mysteries in as much detail as possible without sacrificing readability. To this end, in order to keep footnotes to a minimum, we have not referenced works in the public domain. Unfamiliar foreign words are italicized on first use, but not on every subsequent use. All these words are explained in the Glossary.

We have abbreviated the most familiar prayers to avoid needless repetition. The abbreviation 'Holy God to Our Father' is used to represent the full sequence of prayers recited at the beginning of morning and evening prayers. The abbreviation 'glory…' is used for 'Glory to the Father, and to the Son, and to the Holy Spirit' and 'both now…' for 'both now and ever, and unto the ages of ages. Amen.' The audible prayers of the priest and deacon are highlighted in bold in order to make the discussion on the services easier to follow.

The names of the Old Testament righteous, with the exception of Noah, follow the Septuagint usage: Jonas, Elias, Elisseus and Esaias instead of Jonah, Elijah, Elisha and Isaiah. We have used the King James Version of the New Testament, corrected where necessary.

The Kazan Icon of the Theotokos

Introduction

The ultimate aim of the Christian life is for us to become inheritors of the Kingdom of Heaven and dwell with Christ in eternity. The mysteries of the Orthodox Church prepare us for eternal life because they unite us with Christ's Body, the Church.

The mysteries regenerate us. The mysteries strengthen us in our spiritual struggle as we work together with the grace of God to purify our souls by repentance. St. Paul says 'that we speak the wisdom of God in a mystery, the hidden wisdom which God ordained before the ages for our glory' (1 Cor. 2:7), and through this hidden wisdom, according to St. John Chrysostom, the Old Testament types and prefigurings have been transformed into life-giving mysteries:

> *Instead of the Jerusalem below we have received that Heavenly Jerusalem which is above; and instead of a material temple, we have seen a spiritual temple; instead of tablets of stone, we have tablets of flesh; instead of circumcision, baptism; instead of the manna, the Lord's body; instead of water from a rock, blood from His side; instead of Moses' or Aaron's rod, the Cross; instead of the promised land, the kingdom of heaven; instead of a thousand priests, One High Priest; instead of the irrational lamb, a Spiritual Lamb.*

All these things are of God, by His free gift, and through these mysteries we are united to each other within the Church; we are fused by grace into a single body with Christ as our Head as Archimandrite Justin Popovic explains:

> *So we being many, are one Body in Christ, only in Christ. Through the holy mysteries and the living of the holy virtues, we become of one body in Christ, so that there is no separation, no gulf between us. We are enlivened by one another and bound together in one life, as the members of the human body are bound together.* [1]

The Church, therefore, is not a human organisation, but a divine-human organism: the Body of Christ. We are united to this one Body through our Orthodox baptism. St. Paul proclaims:

[1] J. Popovic, *The Orthodox Church and Ecumenism* (Birmingham: Lazarica Press, 2000) p.12.

Ye are all the children of God by faith in Christ Jesus. For as many of you as have been baptized into Christ have put on Christ. There is neither Jew nor Greek, there is neither slave nor free, there is neither male nor female; for ye are all one in Christ Jesus. (Gal. 3: 26-28)

In every mystery, an outward sign and the inward grace of the Holy Spirit are combined. The mysteries of the Church are not 'mysterious' in the sense that they are 'unreal' or 'magical'; they are real because in Orthodox mysteries physical matter is transformed by the power and grace of the Holy Spirit; the bread and wine of the Eucharist are transformed into the Body and Blood of Christ; the water of the baptismal font is transformed and we are born again in it. St. John Chrysostom describes a mystery as follows: 'in a mystery, what we believe is not the same as what we see, but we see one thing and believe another.'

The Orthodox Church is the all-encompassing mystery and source of all the mysteries; prayer, making the sign of the Cross, and everything in the Church is a mystery. Although a mystery is always grace-filled regardless of the worthiness of the recipient, it is not 'magic'. The mysteries of the Church cannot be separated from the ascetical life of the Church which encompasses all Christian disciplines: fasting, prayer and spiritual struggle. In other words, a true Christian life cannot be lived without partaking of the mysteries, nor can the mysteries be partaken of worthily without at least attempting to keep the ascetical life of the Church.

Through the mysteries and the ascetical life of the Church we are guided towards unity with God; we move from being in God's image towards God's likeness. Without this practice of the Orthodox faith, we cannot be 'made conformable to the Son of God' (Eph. 1:5). In addition, because we are all 'servants of Christ and stewards of the mysteries of God' (1 Cor. 4:1), it is our responsibility as members of the Church to partake of the mysteries reverently and to spread the Christian faith by our example of piety and holiness.

To this end, we are called to become gods by grace in a real transformation in which we partake of the grace of God through the mysteries of the Church. This transformative path is called *theosis* and by it, according to St. Maximus the Confessor, Orthodox Christians become 'in no way inferior to Him, as far as that is humanly possible and attainable for man. Consequently, by adoption and grace, it is possible for them to be, and to be called, gods, because all of God completely fills them, leaving nothing in them empty of His presence.'[2]

Theosis is also called 'deification', but the saints do not become gods by nature but by grace – they do not partake of God's essence but of His energies. St. Maximus the Confessor and St. Gregory Palamas both teach that God is unknowable in His essence, but He is revealed to us by His uncreated energies – the same uncreated light that dazzled the disciples at the Transfiguration. These uncreated energies are called grace.

In the Roman Catholic Church, grace is believed to be created, and this has far-reaching implications. For example, in Roman Catholicism, sacraments are given out; the priest distributes the sacrament, and the people merely happen to be present. In Orthodoxy, the mysteries are 'partaken of' and the people, as the fullness of the Body of Christ, celebrate the mystery together with the priest. Christos Androutsos explains further:

> The officiating priest in the Orthodox Church is lost to sight, so to speak, under the mysteries which he performs and their operation is ascribed directly to God. In the Latin form, the priest appears as achieving and administering the divine grace, in which the sharp separation of clergy from laity is apparent.

Although the word 'sacrament' is used extensively by the Orthodox instead of 'mystery' it does have some unwanted connotations, being a term meaning 'solemn oath' borrowed from Roman Catholicism. For example, most Orthodox catechisms, following the Roman Catholic practice, list seven sacraments: baptism, chrismation, eucharist, confession, ordination, unction, marriage. However, according to Metropolitan Kallistos (Ware) this list is by no means universally accepted in Orthodoxy:

---

2 J. Stead, (trans.), *The Church, the Liturgy and the Soul of Man* (Still River: St. Bede's Publications, 1982) p. 96.

Only in the seventeenth century, when Latin influence was at its height, did [the list of sacraments] become fixed and definite. Before that date Orthodox writers vary considerably as to the number of the sacraments: John of Damascus speaks of two; Dionysius the Areopagite of six; Joasaph, Metropolitan of Ephesus (fifteenth century), of ten; and those Byzantine theologians who in fact speak of seven sacraments differ as to the items which they include in their list. Even today the number seven has no absolute dogmatic significance for Orthodox theology, but is used primarily as a convenience in teaching.[3]

St. Dionysius the Areopagite numbers the mystery of burial with the other mysteries, and we also include it, together with the mystery of monastic tonsure and a chapter covering the daily services of the Church.

There are significant variations between national Churches which we have only been able to touch upon briefly. Hopefully, traditionalist Orthodox Christians will recognize much from our work, even though their parish practice might be slightly different.

---

[3] T. Ware, *The Orthodox Church* (Harmondsworth: Penguin Books Ltd., 1969) p. 282.

1

The Mystery of Baptism

Know ye not, that so many of us as were baptized into Jesus Christ were baptized into His death? Therefore we are buried with Him by baptism into death: that like as Christ was raised up from the dead by the glory of the Father, even so we also should walk in newness of life.

Romans 6: 3-4

The mystery of baptism is called the 'door into the Church' because it opens the door to the other mysteries and participation in the Holy Eucharist. Through being baptized into Christ, we 'put on Christ' (Gal. 3:27), and we become 'partakers of Christ' (Heb. 3:14), and heirs of eternal life (cf. Titus 3:7).

Although Christians are received into the Church by the service of baptism this is not the first time that the Church prays for those who are going to be joined to Her. There are prayers appointed to be read on the first, eighth and fortieth days after childbirth; through these prayers, and those that the Church offers for the mother and baby before birth, She is preparing the way for the mystical joining of the child to the Church through baptism. In addition, there are prayers in the Liturgy for those adults (called catechumens) who are preparing for baptism.

Holy Baptism is a spiritual rebirth, through which we become members of the Body of Christ, His Church, and are conformed to the image of God (cf. Rom. 8:29), putting on the new man and being renewed after the image of Christ (cf. Col. 3:10). In our descent into the waters of the baptismal font, we are buried with Christ so that just as Christ was raised from the dead through the glory of the Father, we too may live a new life (cf. Rom. 6:4).

The mystery of baptism is inextricably linked with the mystery of the Incarnation through which Christ took upon Himself our nature and healed it. St. John of Damascus describes this connection below:

> *In His compassion He came down to His servants and became like us; He redeemed us from corruption through His own Passion.*

He caused the fountain of remission to well forth for us out of His holy and immaculate side; water for our regeneration and the washing away of sin and corruption; blood as a drink producing eternal life. He gave us the command to be born again of water and the Spirit; the Holy Spirit descending on the water through prayer and entreaty. For since man's nature is twofold, consisting of soul and body, He gave us a twofold purification by water and the Spirit, the Spirit renewing that which is after His image and likeness, and the water, by the grace of the Spirit, cleansing the body from sin and delivering it from corruption. The water expressing the image of death, but the Spirit guaranteeing us life.

Through baptism our sins are washed away in the waters as we read in the Scriptures: 'Get up, be baptized and wash your sins away, calling on His name' (Acts 22:16), and in the writings of St. Justin the Martyr:

By reason, therefore, of this bath of repentance and the knowledge of God, which has been ordained on account of the transgression of God's people, as Esaias cries, we have believed, and testify that this same baptism which he announced is alone able to purify those who have repented; and this is the water of life.

The mystery of baptism is more than a washing away of sin, however, because we are regenerated in the baptismal font and renewed by the Holy Spirit (cf. Titus 3:5-7) as St. John Chrysostom teaches:

And why, someone will say, if the bath takes away all our sins, is it not called the bath of forgiveness, or the bath of cleansing, rather than the bath of regeneration? The answer is that the bath does not simply forgive our sins, nor does it just cleanse us of our faults, but we are born again in this bath; it creates us anew and fashions us again, not moulding us from earth, but recreating us from a different element, the nature of water.

Orthodox baptism renews and illumines us with the light of the Holy Spirit, which is why the newly-baptized Christian is referred to as 'newly-illumined' and clothed in the new white garment to which St. John Chrysostom refers:

Christ said: 'Let your light so shine before men so that they may see your good works and glorify your Father who is heaven.' Do you see how He urges us to let the light within us shine forth, not by clothes but by works? This light does not stop with your bodily senses but illumines the soul and understanding of those who see it. After it chases away the darkness of evil, it draws those who find it to shine with their own light and to imitate the life of virtue.

St. Symeon the New Theologian likewise explains that this illumining in the font is not just an adding of knowledge to our human nature, but a complete refashioning of it:

By Holy Baptism He regenerates and refashions us, completely sets us free from the condemnation, and places us in this world wholly free instead of being oppressed by the tyranny of the enemy. By honouring us with our original free will He gives us strength against our enemy, so that those who are willing may overcome him more readily than could all the saints who lived before Christ's coming.[4]

Through this regeneration we are made into members of the Church (a member, in this sense, is a body part), and we are united by the Orthodox Faith which transcends all barriers of race and gender. St. Paul teaches:

For as many of you as have been baptized into Christ have put on Christ. There is neither Jew nor Greek, there is neither slave nor free, there is neither male nor female; for ye are all one in Christ Jesus. (Gal 3:27-28)

Also, by this regeneration we join, in the words of St. Peter, 'a chosen generation, a royal priesthood, a holy nation, a peculiar people' (1 Pet. 2:9). Spiritually, we become kings and priests according to the words of St. Leo the Great: 'All who have been regenerated in Christ are made kings by the sign of the Cross and consecrated priests by the anointing of the Holy Spirit.'[5]

---

[4] Saint Symeon the New Theologian, *The Discourses* (trans. C. J. de Catanzaro) (New York: Paulist Press, 1980) p. 100.

[5] T. L. Humfries Jr., *Ascetic Pneumatology from John Cassian to Gregory the Great* (Oxford: OUP, 2013) p. 66.

Even though our faith unites us, there are many different roles within the Church corresponding to our spiritual gifts. St. Paul teaches that 'there are many members, but one body. And the eye cannot say to the hand, "I have no need of thee", nor again the head to the feet, "I have no need of you"' (1 Cor. 12: 20-21). St. John Chrysostom comments on this epistle:

> *It is as if Christ were saying that all the trees in a park are watered from the same source and by the same water. Here he says that we have all drunk the same Spirit, we have all enjoyed the same grace. If, then, the Spirit has formed us and has brought us all together into one body – that is, we were baptized into one body – and has given us a single table, he also gave the same watering to all, that is, we were all given one Spirit to drink.* [6]

We are united by our baptism because we are re-born in the water, so the Orthodox Church is our mother, and the baptismal waters are both our grave and our mother as St. Cyril of Jerusalem explains:

> *In that same moment you were dying and being born, and that saving water was at once your grave and your mother. What Solomon said in another context is applicable to you: 'A time for giving birth, a time for dying'; although for you it is a case of a 'time for dying and a time for being born'. One time brought both, and your death coincided with your birth.* [7]

St. Gregory the Theologian links together our physical birth, our re-birth in the baptismal font and our resurrection from the grave on the Last Day:

> *The Word recognizes the following three births for us: the natural birth, that of baptism, and that of the resurrection. Of these, the first is by night, and is servile, and passionate; the second is by day, and destroys the passions, breaking through the veil that is inherited from birth, and leads to a higher life; the third is more terrible and shorter, bringing together in a moment all mankind, to stand before its Creator, and to give an account of its*

[6] J. L. Kovacs (Ed.), *1 Corinthians* (Grand Rapids: Wm. B. Erdmans, 2005) p.206.
[7] R. M. Jensen, *Baptismal Imagery in Early Christianity* (Grand Rapids: Baker Academic, 2012) p.140.

service and conversation here; whether it has followed the flesh, or whether it has mounted up with the spirit, and worshipped the grace of its new creation.

Through baptism we are freed from the law of sin because we are no longer under the law, but under grace (cf. Rom. 6:14); baptism is not an end but a beginning. By baptism we are cleansed and illuminated, so that we can be deified by partaking of the uncreated energies of God as Clement of Alexandria explains:

> *Being baptized, we are illuminated; being illuminated, we become sons; being made sons, we are made perfect; being made perfect, we are made immortal as God Himself says through the Prophet David: 'I have said that ye are gods and sons of the Most High.' This work has different names: grace, illumination, perfection, and washing; washing, by which we cleanse away our sins; grace, by which the debts accumulated by our transgressions are forgiven; illumination, by which that holy light of salvation is beheld and by which we see God clearly.*

However, our re-creation in the font does not remove our ability to sin because it does not remove our free will. We 'all have sinned, and come short of the glory of God' (Rom. 3:23), but through the grace given us through baptism, with the help of our guardian angel, through living our lives according to the teachings of the Orthodox Church we strive to die unto sin and live unto righteousness (cf. 1. Peter 2:24).

Foreshadowing of Baptism in the Old Testament

1) Ritual Washings

St. Paul, in writing to the Hebrews, mentions the ritual washing of the Old Testament (Heb. 9:10), and St. Ambrose of Milan compares this washing with the regenerating effect of Christian baptism:

> *There are many kinds of baptisms, but the apostle cries: 'one baptism'. Why? The baptisms of the heathen are not baptisms; they are baths, and cannot be called baptisms. In them, the body is washed, but guilt is not washed away. No, it is contracted in that*

> *bath. There were, however, baptisms of the Jews, some superflu-ous, others figurative, and the mere figure helps us, since it fore-shadows the reality.*

The water needed for Jewish ritual washings was held in cisterns dug in the ground that were used for whole body cleansing. Some historians argue that this washing was required, during the Second Temple peri-od, of those wishing to convert to Judaism. Below, St. Justin the Martyr compares the Old Testament ritual washing in cisterns with baptism:

> *But the cisterns which you have dug for yourselves are broken and profitless to you. For what is the use of that baptism which cleanses the flesh and body alone? Nor do we receive that useless baptism of cisterns, for it has nothing to do with this baptism of life. Where-fore also God has announced that you have forsaken Him, the living fountain, and dug for yourselves broken cisterns which can hold no water. Even you, who are the circumcised according to the flesh, have need of our circumcision; but we, having the latter, do not require the former.*

The inadequacy of this cistern washing for salvation was foretold by the Prophet Jeremias (Jer. 2:13), and is recalled during the Matins of Great Friday:

> *Two evils hath Israel my first-born Son committed: he hath for-saken Me, the fountain of the water of life, and dug for himself a broken cistern. Upon the Cross he hath crucified Me, but asked for Barabbas and released him. Heaven was amazed at this and the sun hid its rays; yet, thou, O Israel, was not ashamed, but hast delivered Me unto death. Forgive them, Holy Father, for they know not what they have done.*

2) Circumcision

The circumcision of males was a sign of the covenant between God and Abraham (Gen. 17: 9-14), but this circumcision has been super-seded by the 'circumcision made without hands' of baptism that St. Paul speaks of in his letter to the Christians at Colossae:

> *In Him also ye are circumcised with a circumcision made with-out hands, by putting off the body of flesh in the circumcision of*

Christ, buried with Him in baptism, wherein also ye are risen with Him through faith in the operation of God Who hath raised Him from the dead. (Col. 2:11-12)

St. Justin the Martyr, in his *Dialogue with Trypho*, refers to the righteous in the Old Testament that did not receive physical circumcision and likens their spiritual circumcision to baptism:

Circumcision began with Abraham: the Sabbath, sacrifices, offerings and feasts with Moses. It has been proved that they were ordained on account of the hardness of your people's heart, so it was fitting, in accordance with the Father's will, that they should have an end in Him who was born of a virgin, of the family of Abraham, of the tribe of Judah, and of David. This is Christ the Son of God, who was proclaimed by the prophets as He that was to come into the world to be the everlasting law and covenant. We, who have approached God through Him, have received not a bodily, but a spiritual circumcision which Enoch and those like him observed. We have received it through baptism since we were sinners. By the mercy of God, it is granted to all of us, equally.

3) The Saving of Noah through the Flood

The saving of Noah from the flood is mentioned several times in the baptism service because the font symbolizes the ark in which the righteous were saved from the flood of waters. St. John of Damascus, starting with Noah, contrasts the purifying action of water in the Old Testament, with the regenerating action of the baptismal water:

In the time of Noah, God washed away the sin of the world by water. By water every impure person is purified, according to the Law, and even their clothes were washed with water. Elias showed forth the grace of the Spirit mingled with the water when he burned the sacrifice by pouring on water. And almost everything is purified by water according to the law: for the things of sight are symbols of the things of thought. The regeneration, however, takes place in the soul, for faith has the power of making us sons, creatures as we are, by the Spirit, and of leading us into our former state of blessedness.

4) The Crossing of the Red Sea

The account of the crossing of the Red Sea by the Israelites is a common subject in Orthodox hymnography because it is a figure of Christian baptism. St. Gennadius of Constantinople explains:

> *The cloud was a figure standing for the grace of the Spirit. For just as the cloud covered the Israelites and protected them from the Egyptians, so the Spirit's grace shields us from the wiles of the devil. Likewise, just as the crossing of the sea protected them from their enemies and gave them real freedom, so baptism protects us from our enemies.*[8]

St. Paul, in his First Letter to the Corinthians, compares the Crossing of the Red Sea with baptism and the Eucharist: 'And all in Moses were baptized, in the cloud, and in the sea: and did all eat the same spiritual meat; and did all drink the same spiritual drink; for they drank of a spiritual Rock that followed them: and the Rock was Christ' (1 Cor. 10:2-4). St. John Chrysostom describes how St. Paul links the foreshadowing (the figure) of baptism even more closely to the mystical truth of baptism by saying that the Hebrews were 'baptized' in the sea:

> *What does 'they were baptized into Moses' mean? Just as we, once we have confessed Christ and his resurrection, are baptized so that we may partake of these mysteries…in the same way the Israelites, because they had confidence in Moses – that is, because they had seen him cross over first – also braved the waters of the sea. But since Paul wants to relate the figure closely to the truth [of its Christian fulfilment], he does not explain this as I have done but instead described it in terms of the fulfilment of the figure. The crossing of the sea is a symbol of the washing [i.e. baptism], and the event that follows is a symbol of the Holy Table. Just as you eat the Body of the Lord, so they ate the manna; just as you drink the Blood, so they drank water from the rock. Although the events were physical, Paul presents them in a spiritual way, not as events that followed in the natural order but as gifts of grace, as events that nurtured the soul along with the body and moved it toward faith.*[9]

---

[8] T. Oden, G. Bray, *1-2 Corinthians* (Chicago: Fitzroy Dearborn Publishers, 1999) p.91.

[9] Kovacs, *1 Corinthians* p. 161.

5) The Sweetening of the Waters of Marah

After the crossing of the Red Sea to escape from Pharaoh, the Israelites fled into the wilderness of Sur, but the only water they could find was at a place called Marah, but this water was bitter and undrinkable (Marah means 'bitter' in Hebrew). The Prophet Moses threw a piece of wood into the water and it became drinkable. St. Ambrose compares the bitter font of the waters of Marah with the sweet font of baptism:

> The font of Marah was most bitter; Moses cast wood into it, and it was made sweet. Without the blessing of the Lord's Cross, water serves no purpose of future salvation; but when it has been consecrated by the mystery of the saving Cross, then it becomes fit for both a spiritual bath and the cup of salvation. Just as the Prophet Moses cast wood into that font, so also the priest casts the proclamation of the Lord's Cross into this font and the water becomes sweet unto grace.

The wood used by Moses is a type of the Cross. The account of the sweetening of the waters of Marah is therefore read during the vigil of the Exaltation of the Cross: 'In days of old Moses transformed with wood the bitter wells in the wilderness, prefiguring the bringing of the Gentiles to the true faith through the cross.'[10] It is for this reason that the priest signs the baptismal waters three times with the sign of the Cross.

6) The Sacrifice Made by Elias

The burning of the sacrifice offered by Prophet Elias with fire from heaven (1 Kings 18:34-35) was initiated by his prayer and the threefold pouring of water on the altar:

> The Prophet said: 'Fill four pitchers with water and pour it on the burnt offering and on the wood.' And he said, 'Do it a second time,' and they did it a second time. And he said, 'Do it a third time,' and they did it a third time. The water flowed around the altar and he also filled the trench with water.

---

[10] M. Mary, K. Ware, The Festal Menaion (London: Faber & Faber Ltd., 1969) p. 146.

The account of this sacrifice is one of the thirteen Old Testament Readings of the Vespers on Great Saturday, the traditional time for baptizing converts. St. John Chrysostom says that 'baptism is a cross and death', and this death, and the resurrection that follows, is brought about by the mystic waters of baptism, sanctified by the Holy Spirit as St. Gregory of Nyssa teaches:

> *By that wondrous sacrifice Elias clearly proclaimed to us the sacramental rite of baptism that should afterwards be instituted. For the fire was kindled by the water thrice poured upon it, so that it is clearly shown that where the mystic water is, there is the kindling, warm and fiery Spirit, that burns up the ungodly and illuminates the faithful.*[11]

7) *The Cleansing of Naaman from Leprosy*

The leper Naaman the Syrian was cured of leprosy when he dipped himself seven times in the River Jordan at the command of the Prophet Elisseus (2 Kings 5:14). St. Irenaeus of Lyons compares this cleansing from disease with the spiritual cleansing of baptism:

> *It was not for nothing that Naaman of old, when suffering from leprosy, was purified upon his being baptized, but [it served] as an indication to us. For as we are lepers in sin, we are made clean, by means of the sacred water and the invocation of the Lord, from our old transgressions; being spiritually regenerated as new-born babes, even as the Lord has declared: 'Unless a man be born again through water and the Spirit, he shall not enter into the kingdom of heaven.'*

8) *The Recovering of the Axe-head from the Jordan River*

The recovering of the lost iron axe-head from the waters of the Jordan by the Prophet Elisseus (2 Kings 6: 4-6), is a prefiguration of both baptism and the power of the Cross. The Prophet Elisseus, in order to recover the axe-head threw in a piece of wood, and the iron axe-head rose out of the water and floated. Below, St. Ambrose links the heaviness of iron to the weight of our sins:

> *Elisseus called on the name of the Lord, and the axe-head that had sunk came up out of the water. Here is another kind of bap-*

[11] Jensen, *Baptismal Imagery in Early Christianity* p. 130.

tism. Why? Because every man before baptism is weighed down like iron, and sinks: when he has been baptized he is no longer like iron, but now rises like the fruit-bearing wood, which is a lighter substance.

We hear this link between the Cross and baptism in the canon for the Feast of the Exaltation of the Cross: 'Jordan received into its deep bosom a sharp axe, and then was forced by a stick of wood to give it back again, thereby foreshadowing the severing of error by the Cross and baptism.'

9) The Baptism of Christ by John the Baptist

We celebrate the baptism of Christ by John the Forerunner on the Great Feast of Theophany. Christ did not need to be baptized, but chose to 'fulfil all righteousness' (Matt. 3:15), and in doing so He sanctified the waters of the Jordan. Christ sanctified the water by His descent into it, and in the mystery of baptism the water is sanctified by the descent of the Holy Spirit as St. Ambrose explains;

> *What then does it mean? You saw water, but not all water heals, but only that water which has the grace of Christ. The element is one thing, the consecration another; the work is one thing, the working another. Water does not heal, unless the Spirit has descended and consecrated that water; as you have read that, when our Lord Jesus Christ was giving us the example of baptism, He came to John and John said to him, 'I have need to be baptized of thee and comest thou to me?' Christ answered him, 'Suffer it to be so now: for thus it becometh us to fulfil all righteousness.'*

Christ entered the water and the Trinity was made manifest by the voice of the Father and the descent of the Holy Spirit in the form of a dove; when we descend into the water of baptism, we confess our faith in the Trinity. Christ sanctified the nature of water in the Jordan and the demons were scattered; in our baptism, the sins we have committed are washed away by the bath of the Spirit.

Preparations for Baptism

The Catechumenate

In the Early Church, and in traditional Orthodox Churches today, adults who wished to be baptized were formally catechized and made 'catechumens'. When they neared baptism, catechumens received daily teaching: in Alexandria and Rome this lasted thirty days, in Jerusalem it lasted the whole of Great Lent.[12] The Early Church viewed a change of life before baptism as important because after baptism the devil plots more strongly against us as St. Paul teaches: 'call to remembrance the former days, in which, after ye were illuminated, ye endured a great fight of afflictions' (Heb. 10:32).

Change of life before baptism makes the struggle to change our way of life after baptism easier. In the era of mass conversion to Christianity, catechumens had to prove that they were serious about living a Christian life and had not chosen to convert for social or financial advantage. The fourth century saint, Gregory of Nyssa, goes so far as to assert that unless baptism is followed by spiritual struggle, the rite is effectively meaningless, not on a mysteriological, but a personal level:

> *If, when the washing of baptism is applied to the body, the soul does not cleanse itself from the stains of the passions, but our life after initiation continues to be the same as it was before – then, though it may be a bold thing to say, yet I will say it without shrinking: in such cases the water remains water, since the gift of the Holy Spirit is nowhere manifested in what has taken place.*[13]

We can see exactly this problem today when children are brought for baptism as a kind of 'rite of passage' after which they receive little guidance or teaching from their godparents or parents. They are baptized, and this cannot be repeated, but are they growing in the Church?

---

[12] A. Kreider, *The Change of Conversion and the Origin of Christendom* (Eugene: Wipf and Stock Publishers, 2006) p.41.

[13] K. Ware, 'The Sacrament of Baptism and the Ascetic Life in the Teaching of Mark the Monk' *Studia Patristica* (1970) Vol. 10, p. 448.

The Godparents

Godparents are responsible for a child's spiritual development, so they must be conscientious Orthodox Christians. Being a godparent (also called a 'sponsor') is an honour, but it is primarily a responsibility. A godchild will need guidance throughout life to make good use of the grace of baptism as St. Mark the Ascetic states: 'Holy Baptism is perfect, but it does not make perfect him who does not perform the commandments… Faith consists not only in being baptized into Christ but also in performing His commandments.'[14]

St. John Chrysostom calls godparents 'spiritual fathers' and those whom they sponsor at the font 'spiritual sons'. St. Caesarius of Arles also reminds godparents of the duty they have to teach the faith to both their natural and their spiritual sons:

> Remember the Creed and the Lord's Prayer yourself and teach it to your children. I do not know with what boldness a man says he is a Christian, if he refuses to learn a few lines of the Creed and the Lord's Prayer. Remember that you stood surety before God for the sons you received in baptism, so always reprove and rebuke those whom you adopted at the font just as you do those who were born of you.[15]

The Prayers for the Reception of Catechumens

The service of baptism starts in the narthex with the candidate being received as a catechumen and ends in front of the iconostasis signifying the candidate's journey from unbelief to the true faith.

The priest breathes three times in the face of the candidate and signs him or her three times with the sign of the Cross on his forehead and chest saying the prayer: **'In Thy name, O Lord God of truth…'** This breathing on the candidate indicates the re-creation of man, recalling the first creation, when the Lord 'breathed into the face of man the breath of life' (Genesis 2:7).

We hear in the first epistle of St. John that 'the Son of God was manifested, that He might destroy the works of the devil' (I John 3:8).

---

[14] Ibid., p. 446.

[15] Kreider, *The Change of Conversion and the Origin of Christendom* p. 76.

Following this teaching, the Church reads prayers over the catechumen to expel evil spirits from him. These prayers are called exorcisms and there are four, in total, in the baptism service. In these prayers, and throughout the baptism service, the relevant personal pronouns 'him' or 'her' are used as appropriate. In order to improve readability, we have omitted these changes here and used 'him' throughout.

During the fourth prayer, the priest breathes on the mouth, forehead and chest of the candidate and says, three times:

> **Expel from him every evil and impure spirit which hides and makes its lair in his heart.**

At the end of the fourth prayer, the catechumen and his sponsors turn to face the west (so they have their back to the iconostasis). Because the sun sets in the west, it is seen as the personification of darkness and evil. The priest then asks the candidate three times:

> **Dost thou renounce Satan and all his angels, and all his works and all his service, and all his pride?**

The candidate replies, 'I do,' showing that he is prepared to renounce his former life together with all the powers of darkness. The renunciation of Satan is completed by the candidate (or the child's godparent) breathing and spitting on Satan.

The candidate then turns to the east as a sign that he accepts faith in Jesus Christ, the 'Dayspring from on high' (Luke 1:78) and the 'Sun of Righteousness' (Mal. 4:2). He then affirms his desire to be united to the Body of Christ, the Orthodox Church, and confirms it by reciting the Creed; when infants are baptized it is read for them by the godparent.

Fifth Century Neonian Orthodox Baptistery, Ravenna, Italy

Newly discovered Sixth Century Byzantine Font from Bekalta, Tunisia.
The inscription around the font is 'Glory to God in the Highest, and on
earth peace, good will among men.'

Original colour photograph by Habib M'henni

Fifth Century Lateran Baptistery, Rome

The Baptism Service

The baptism service begins with the same blessing used at the beginning of the Divine Liturgy: '**Blessed is the Kingdom of the Father, and of the Son, and of the Holy Spirit.**' The deacon intones the Great Litany, with the following additional petitions:

> That this water may be sanctified with the power, and effectual operation, and descent of the Holy Spirit.

> That there may be sent down into it the grace of redemption, the blessing of Jordan.

The next petition links the forthcoming immersion of the candidate in the purifying water with the 'purifying waters' of the Jordan in which the Trinity was manifest to us.

> That there may come upon this water the purifying operation of the super-substantial Trinity.

> That we may be illumined by the light of understanding and piety, and by the descent of the Holy Spirit.

The litany asks that 'we may be illumined' because a baptism is not a private matter between the priest and candidate but involves the whole Church; this is why private baptisms in homes are not permitted except during times of persecution.

> That this water may be effective for the averting of every snare of enemies, both visible and invisible.

> That he who is baptized in it may be made worthy of the kingdom incorruptible.

> For him who is now come unto Holy Baptism, and for his salvation; that he may prove himself a child of the light, and an heir of eternal good things.

> That he may be a member and partaker of the death and resurrection of Christ our God.

> That he may preserve his baptismal robe and the pledge of the Spirit pure and undefiled unto the dread day of Christ our God.

> That this water may be to him a bath of regeneration, unto the remission of sins, and a robe of incorruption.

At the end of the Great Litany, the priest reads, out loud, a long prayer which ends:

> Wherefore, O King Who lovest mankind, come Thou now and sanctify this water, by the indwelling of the Holy Spirit. *(thrice)* Grant unto it the grace of redemption, the blessing of Jordan. Make it the fountain of incorruption, the gift of sanctification, the remission of sins, the remedy of infirmities; the final destruction of demons, unconquered by hostile powers, filled with angelic might.

The priest then signs the water in the font three times with the sign of the cross, and breathing on it he says:

> Let all adverse powers be crushed beneath the sign of the image of Thy Cross. *(thrice)*

> Do Thou, O Master of all, show this water to be the water of redemption, the water of sanctification, the purification of flesh and spirit, the loosing of bonds, the remission of sins, the illumination of the soul, the bath of regeneration, the renewal of the Spirit, the gift of adoption to sonship, the garment of incorruption, the fountain of life. For thou hast said O Lord: Wash ye, be ye clean; put away evil things from your souls (cf. Is. 1:16).

The priest breathes three times over a vessel of olive oil, and makes the sign of the cross over it three times. He then says the following prayer:

> O Lord and Master, the God of our fathers, Who didst send a dove unto them that were in the ark of Noah, bearing in its beak a twig of olive, the token of reconciliation and of salvation from the flood, and the foreshadowing of the mystery of grace. Thou didst grant the fruit of the olive for the fulfilling of Thy Holy mysteries, thereby filling them that were under the Law with Thy Holy Spirit, and perfecting them that are under grace. Bless also this holy oil with the power, operation and indwelling of Thy Holy Spirit, that it may be an anointing unto incorruption, an armour of righteousness, the renewing of soul and body, the averting of every assault of the devil. Do Thou deliver from all evil those that are to be anointed with it in faith.

The Anointing with Oil

Before immersion in the font, the candidate is anointed with this blessed olive oil. Below, St. Ambrose of Milan links the anointing of the athletes in the Greco-Roman world with the Christian anointing before baptism:

> *The anointing with oil is similar to that undergone by athletes in the ancient world. You are anointed as Christ's athlete and have agreed to fight against your opponent in the contest of this world. He who wrestles has something to hope for because where there is a contest, there is also a crown. You wrestle in the world, but you are crowned by Christ; for, though the reward is in heaven, yet it is earned here on earth.*

St. John Chrysostom emphasizes that God, the Judge of our contest, is not only the Judge, but also our helper:

> *In the Olympic combats the judge stands impartially aloof from the combatants, favouring neither the one nor the other, but awaiting the outcome. He stands in the middle because his judgment is impartial. But in our combat with the devil, Christ does not stand aloof but is wholly on our side. How true it is that Christ does not stand aloof but is entirely on our side you may see from this: He anointed us as we went into the combat, but He fettered the devil; He anointed us with the oil of gladness, but He bound the devil with fetters that cannot be broken to keep him shackled hand and foot for the combat. But if I happen to slip, He stretches out His hand, and lifts me up from my fall, and sets me on my feet again.*[16]

The anointing, according to St. Cyril of Jerusalem, also symbolizes that the candidate is a 'good soldier for Christ Jesus' (2 Tim. 2:3), and that he who was formerly wild and barren must become a fruitful olive tree in Christ:

> *When you were stripped, you were anointed with exorcized oil, from the very hairs of your head to your feet, and were made sharers in the good olive-tree Jesus Christ. For you were cut from the wild olive tree, and grafted into the good one, and were made to share the richness of this true olive-tree. The exorcized oil is a symbol of the participation in the richness of Christ, a blessing which drives away all trace of the influence of the hostile powers. For as the breathing of*

---

[16] St. John Chrysostom, *Baptismal Instructions* (trans. P. W. Harkins), (New York: Newman Press, 1963) p. 58.

the saints, and the calling upon the name of God, like fiercest flame, scorches and drives out evil spirits, so also this exorcized oil receives such virtue by the invocation of God and by prayers. It receives powerer not only to burn and cleanse away the traces of our sins, but also chases away all the invisible power of the evil one.

In the Early Church candidates removed all their clothes and were baptized naked, the women being anointed by deaconesses. Nakedness is viewed differently now than in earlier centuries, so adults and older children are baptized wearing swimwear; babies are still baptized naked. Women (and men if they wish) wear a knee length white robe when they enter the water (this is not the baptismal robe: that is given later in the ceremony).

The priest pours some of the olive oil onto the water in the form of the Cross and makes the sign of the Cross with the oil on the candidate's forehead:

> **The servant/handmaid of God [*Name*] is anointed with the oil of gladness in the Name of the Father, and of the Son, and of the Holy Spirit. Amen.**

He then anoints the candidate's chest and back as he says, '**unto the healing of soul and body**', and the ears, hands and feet as he says the following verses:

> **Unto the hearing of faith; Thy hands have made and fashioned me; that he may walk in the paths of Thy commandments.**

In the Greek usage, the priest pours the remainder of the oil into the cupped hands of the godparent who rubs the oil onto the exposed parts of the candidate's body.

The Threefold Immersion

After the anointing the catechumen is fully immersed in the water three times as the priest says:

> **The servant/handmaid of God [Name] is baptized in the Name of the Father, Amen. And of the Son, Amen. And of the Holy Spirit, Amen.**

The immersions occur as the priest says the words 'Father', 'Son' and

'Holy Spirit'. This immersion is a bath of grace that removes the real uncleanness of the body: that which defiles the soul. The descent into the water is a death unto sin, and the rising out of the water is the resurrection of the man unto a holy, spiritual life with Jesus Christ, as St. Paul teaches: 'Therefore if any man be in Christ, he is a new creature: old things are passed away; behold, all things are become new. And all things are of God, who hath reconciled us to Himself by Jesus Christ' (2 Cor. 5:17-18). St. John Chrysostom, in his instructions to catechumens, teaches:

> *After this anointing, the priest makes you go down into the sacred waters burying the old man and at the same time raising up the new, who is renewed in the image of his Creator. It is at this moment that, through the words and the hand of the priest, the Holy Spirit descends upon you. Instead of the man who descended into the water, a different man comes forth, one who has wiped away all the filth of his sins, who has put off the old garment of sin and has put on the royal robe.* [17]

In Italy and France, baptisms were performed in free-standing baptistery buildings that often resembled mausolea. Indeed, for many years archeologists thought that Rome's Constanza mausoleum was an early Christian baptistery. Those descending into the waters must have had a real sense of entering a tomb, an experience on which St. Ambrose of Milan reflects: 'We are received and plunged into the font, whose appearance is somewhat like that of a tomb in shape, believing in the Father, and the Son, and the Holy Spirit. We then emerge; that is, we are raised up.'

The Neonian Baptistery at Ravenna is one of the best surviving examples of an Orthodox Baptistery (*see page 27*). A fine sixth century Byzantine font for full immersion has been recently discovered in Tunisia (*see page 28*). The Lateran Basilica in Rome (*see page 28*) has an octagonal shaped baptistery attached to it, the foundations of which date back to the time of Constantine the Great in the third century and which was used for baptisms by total immersion. This original baptistery was almost one metre deep, but was rebuilt in

---

[17] St. John Chrysostom, *Baptismal Instructions* p.52.

the fifth century in its present octagonal shape which is over eight metres wide. On each of the eight sides there is a different Latin inscription, recently attributed to Pope Leo the Great when he was a deacon under Pope Sixtus:

> *From a life-giving seed, a people consecrated to the heavens is here born whom the Spirit bringeth forth from the fertile waters.*
>
> *Plunge in, O sinner, and be thou cleansed by the holy flood; those whom it receiveth as old, the wave returneth as new.*
>
> *No difference remaineth among the reborn, whom one font, one Spirit, and one faith make one.*
>
> *By a virginal birth, the Mother Church, beareth these children; those whom she conceiveth by God's breathing, she bringeth forth by this stream.*
>
> *Those who wish to be innocent are made clean by this washing, whether from the weight of the ancestral sin or their own.*
>
> *This is the fountain of life that cleanseth the whole world; its ultimate source is the side of Christ wounded.*
>
> *Reborn in this font for the kingdom of heaven; that blessed life doth not receive those who are only once-born.*
>
> *Let neither the number, nor the kind, of your sins terrify you, for, once reborn in this water, ye are made holy.*

Keeping to this ancient and theologically important practice, traditional Orthodox Christians baptize by threefold immersion in the name of the Trinity. Unfortunately, most Orthodox Churches today do not immerse candidates but simply pour, or sprinkle, water over them. The motives for this are not clear, but are probably a mixture of laziness and a desire to be more western and ecumenical as both the Roman Catholic and Anglican Churches baptize by sprinkling. The position of the Orthodox Church, however, is quite clear: baptism (the word means 'dipping' in Greek) consists of a threefold immersion in the name of the Trinity.

The Reading of Psalm 31

Immediately after the immersion, Psalm 31 is read which begins 'Blessed are they whose iniquities are forgiven and whose sins are covered,' and in which the Psalmist speaks of the blessed state of people who are cleansed of their sins. During this time, the newly-illumined is taken to a side room to be dried.

The Putting-on of the Baptismal Robe

The newly-illumined is clothed in a long white robe as the choir sings: 'Vouchsafe unto me the robe of light, O Thou who clothest Thyself with light as with a garment, Christ our God, plenteous in mercy.' The clothing of the newly-baptized in a white robe dates back to the earliest years of Christianity; it is mentioned by St. John Chrysostom, but is rarely seen in early Christian art, because these depictions tend to be of the immersion, during which the person was naked. The white robe is a symbol of purity and of cleansing, as St. Ambrose of Milan explains:

> You received white garments as a sign that you had exchanged your covering of sins for the chaste robe of innocence, of which the prophet said: 'Thou shalt sprinkle me with hyssop and I shall be made clean; Thou shalt wash me and I shall be made whiter than snow.' For the one baptized is clearly cleansed both according to the law and according to the Gospel; according to the law, because Moses, using a bunch of hyssop, sprinkled the blood of the lamb, and according to the Gospel because the garments of Jesus were white as snow, when in the Gospel He showed the glory of His resurrection (Matt. 17:2). As the Lord said through the Prophet Esaias: Even though your sins are scarlet, I will make them as white as snow (Is. 1:18).

The robe, however, is not just a symbol of purity, but reminds us of our actual re-birth in the waters when we become members of 'a chosen generation, a royal priesthood, a peculiar people' (1 Pet. 2:9), and recalls the linen ephod of King David, the priestly vestments of Aaron and the cloak of Elias. According to St. John Chrysostom: 'In baptism we become king, priest and prophet and this robe signifies all these three.' He continues:

> Only yesterday and the day before, these were slaves of sin, with no freedom to speak, subject to the domination of the devil; like captives, they were led to this place and that. To-day they have been received into the rank of sons. They

*have put off their burdens of sin and put on the royal robe;
they vie in brilliance with heaven itself. We see them shine more
brightly than the stars, as they light up the faces of those
who look on them.*[18]

The Anointing with Chrism

The priest then anoints the newly illumined Christian with chrism,
so as to grant him the fullness of the gift of the Holy Spirit. The forehead, eyelids, nostrils, lips, ears, chest, hands, feet, and between the
shoulders are anointed with chrism. The mystery of chrismation is
explained in more detail in the next chapter.

The Presentation of the Candle and Cross

The newly-illumined is given a lighted candle that symbolizes the illumination of the soul through baptism. St. Gregory the Theologian,
compares the baptismal candle with the lamps held by the virgins in
the Gospel parable (Matt. 25:1-13):

> *The place in which you shall presently stand after your bap-
> tism before the Great Altar is a prefiguring of the future glory.
> The chanting with which you will be received is a prelude to the
> chanting of Heaven; the lights which you will hold are a symbol of
> the illumination with which we shall meet the Bridegroom; with
> shining and virgin souls, with the lamps of our faith shining, not
> sleeping through our carelessness, so that we do not miss Him that
> we look for if He arrives unexpectedly. Let us not be unprepared,
> without oil, and destitute of good works. Let us not be cast out of
> the Bridal chamber.*

The newly-illumined is then given a cross to wear. The Fathers liken
the wearing of the cross to the branding of livestock to signify own-
ership. Below, Saint Basil explains that our baptismal cross is a sign
of our brotherhood in Christ and compares the protection given by
the cross to that afforded the Israelites (Ex. 12:23) by painting their
doorposts with blood:

> *When preparing for battle the generals give a password to the sol-
> diers, so that they can recognize one another and more easily call
> on each other for help, should they become mixed up with others*

---

[18] St. John Chrysostom, *Baptismal Instructions* pp. 66-67.

in the conflict. No one can know whether you belong to us, or to our adversaries, if you don't show your brotherhood by the mystic sign of having the light of the countenance of the Lord signed upon you. How can the angel claim you? How can he rescue you from the enemy, unless he recognize the seal? How can you say: 'I am of God,' if you do not bear the mark? Do you not understand that the destroying angel passed by the houses that were marked with blood, while he slew the first born in those that were not marked? A treasure unsealed is easily laid hold of by robbers; a sheep without a mark is carried away with ease.

The Procession around the Font

After this, the newly-illumined and the godparents are led by the priest around the font three times. The priest holds the Gospel book and the newly-illumined holds the priest's *epitrachelion* as they process. During the procession, the choir sings the hymn:

All ye that in Christ have been baptized; Christ have ye put on (cf. Gal. 3:27).

The leading around the font signifies that the newly-baptized has become a member of the royal priesthood (priests are led around the Holy Table three times during the service of ordination).

The Prokeimenon and Epistle

The Epistle (Rom. 6: 3-11) is also read at the Liturgy of Great Saturday, and is introduced by the Prokeimenon in the Third Tone:

The Lord is my light and my Saviour, whom then shall I fear? *Verse*: The Lord is the strength of my life: of whom then shall I be afraid?

Brethren, so many of us as were baptized into Jesus Christ were baptized into his death. Therefore we were buried with Him by baptism into death: that like as Christ was raised up from the dead by the glory of the Father, even so we also should walk in newness of life. For if we have been planted together in the likeness of His death, we shall be also in the likeness of His Resurrection, knowing this, that our old man is crucified with Him, that the body of sin might be destroyed, that henceforth we should not serve sin. For he that is dead is freed from sin. Now if we be dead with Christ, we believe that we shall also live with Him, knowing that Christ, being raised from the dead, dieth no more; death hath no more dominion over Him. For in that He died, He died unto sin once: but in that He liveth, He liveth unto God. Likewise reckon ye also yourselves to be dead indeed unto sin, but alive unto God through Jesus Christ our Lord.

The mystery of baptism washes away our sins, but it does not remove our free will. For grace to become effective in us, we need to work in synergy with the Holy Spirit, which is why St. Paul commands that we should be 'dead unto sin' (Rom. 6:11). St. Symeon the New Theologian explains further:

> We receive the remission of our sins at our divine baptism and we are freed from the ancient curses and sanctified by the presence of the Holy Spirit. But this is not yet that perfect grace of which the Scripture speaks: 'I shall dwell in them and walk therein.' This applies only to those who are strong in faith and show it in their works, for if we fall back into evil and shameful deeds after our baptism, we completely throw away this very sanctification.[19]

The perfect grace of baptism manifests itself in our lives as we make progress in dying unto sins as St. Mark the Ascetic makes clear:

> Everyone who has been baptized in an Orthodox manner has received secretly the fullness of grace; and if he then goes on to perform the commandments, he will become consciously aware of this grace within him. However far a man may advance in faith, however great the blessings that he attains, he never discovers, nor can he ever discover, anything more than what he has already received secretly through baptism. Christ, being perfect God, bestows upon the baptized the perfect grace of the Spirit. We for our part cannot possibly add to that grace, but it is revealed and manifests itself to us increasingly in proportion to our fulfilment of the commandments. Whatever, then, we offer to Him after our regeneration, was already within us and came originally from Him.[20]

---

[19] St. Symeon the New Theologian, *The Theological and Practical Treatises and the Three Theological Discourses* (trans. P. McGuckin) (Kalamazoo, Cistercian Publications, 1982) p. 84.

[20] K. Ware, *The Orthodox Way* (Crestwood: SVS Press, 1995) p. 103.

The Gospel Reading

The Gospel reading is taken from the final chapter of the Gospel of Saint Matthew (Matt. 28: 16-20):

At that time, the eleven disciples went away into Galilee, to a mountain where Jesus had appointed them. And when they saw Him, they worshipped him: but some doubted. And Jesus came and spake unto them, saying, All power is given unto me in heaven and in earth. Go ye therefore, and teach all nations, baptizing them in the name of the Father, and of the Son, and of the Holy Spirit, teaching them to observe all things whatsoever I have commanded you: and, lo, I am with you always, even unto the consummation of the age. Amen.

The Threefold Litany and Washing

After the Gospel, a short threefold litany is intoned with the following special petitions:

Again we pray for mercy, life, peace, health, salvation and forgiveness of sins for the servant of God, the sponsor [*Name*].

Again we pray for the newly-illumined servant of God [*Name*].

That he may be kept in the faith of a pure confession, in all godliness, and in the fulfilling of the commandments of Christ all the days of his life.

After a short prayer, the priest, using a small sponge (or a ribbon in the Romanian tradition), sprinkles the newly-baptized with water as he references the words of St. Paul: 'Thou art justified; thou art illumined; thou art sanctified; thou art washed in the name of the Lord Jesus, and by the Spirit of our God' (cf. 1 Cor. 6:11). The priest then washes off the chrism using the sponge as he says:

Thou art baptized; thou art illumined; thou hast received anointment with the holy Chrism; thou art sanctified; thou art washed in the Name of the Father, and of the Son, and of the Holy Spirit. Amen.

The Tonsure

A tonsure is the cutting of the hair from the front, back, right and left sides of the head thus making the form of the Cross. The tonsure demonstrates that the newly-illumined has become a member of the royal priesthood; a tonsure is performed on those who become readers – the most junior rank before the ordained clergy. In addition, the tonsure signifies an offering to God and that the person offers himself to God out of obedience – hair being the symbol of strength (cf. Judges 16:17). Monastics are also tonsured as a sign of their willing obedience to their abbot and, of course, the Church. During the first prayer of the baptismal tonsure, the priest makes reference to the offering of the harvest gifts in the Temple in the Old Testament (cf. Deut. 26: 2-4).

The Dismissal and Removal of the Baptismal Robe

The mystery of baptism ends with the priest giving the appointed dismissal. The prayer for the removal of the baptismal robe is read on the eighth day after baptism; in other words, if a child is baptized on a Sunday, the robe is removed on the following Sunday.

Frequently Asked Questions

How do we prepare for our child's baptism?

The first step is to arrange a suitable time with the priest. Don't arrange a time for the baptism and automatically expect the church to be available on that date.

Godparents should be chosen carefully because they undertake the responsibility for bringing up the child in the Orthodox faith. Godparents should be Orthodox Christians who attend church regularly; ideally, they should be members of the same parish as the child.

In addition, it is a good idea to consider the age of the child and the sex and age of the godparent's own children because an adult cannot marry a person to whom he, or she, is related by baptism. In other words, a boy cannot marry a girl if her father is the boy's godfather – they are viewed as brother and sister in the eyes of the Church. On a practical level, godparents need to provide the baptismal cross, candle and the olive oil to be used at the baptism.

Did the first Christians baptize children or only adults?

In the time of the apostles adult baptism was extremely common as people responded to the Gospel. Children were baptized though, as we read in the Book of Acts: 'At that hour of the night the jailer took them and washed their wounds; then immediately he, and all his household, were baptized' (Acts 16:33). The word 'household' implies the jailer had a wife and children. St. Peter is also clear that baptism should not be denied to anyone, regardless of age, when he says:

> *Repent, and be baptized every one of you in the name of Jesus Christ for the remission of sins, and ye shall receive the gift of the Holy Spirit. For the promise is unto you, and to your children, and to all that are afar off, even as many as the Lord our God shall call (Acts 2:38-39).*

What happens if a child needs to be baptized in an emergency?

If a child is born and not expected to survive, then baptism should be performed immediately. It is very important for Orthodox parents to note that they should perform the baptism if their priest is unable to attend in time. In no circumstances should a non-Orthodox minister be allowed to perform it. In emergency baptisms, tap water or bottled water can be used. The formula is identical to that used in a regular baptism: '**The servant/handmaid of God [***Name***] is baptized in the Name of the Father, Amen. And of the Son, Amen. And of the Holy Spirit, Amen.** Instead of the immersions, a little water is poured or sprinkled on the head of the child at the words 'Father', 'Son' and 'Holy Spirit'. If the child dies, this baptism is considered entirely valid, but if the child recovers, the service of baptism is performed in its entirety in church.

Are there any days that we cannot be baptized?

Baptisms can be carried out on most days of the Church year; emergency baptisms, of course, are performed on any day regardless of circumstances. Baptisms are not performed on weekdays in Great Lent or between Great Monday and Great Friday. Women cannot be baptized if they are in their period of menstruation.

The Descent of the Holy Spirit at Pentecost

2

The Mystery of Chrismation

*Grieve not the Holy Spirit of God, in whom ye were sealed for the
day of redemption.*

Ephesians 4:30

In the apostolic era, the apostles themselves laid hands on each person that was baptized into the Faith, as described in the Acts of the Apostles:

> *Now when the Apostles which were at Jerusalem heard that
> Samaria had received the word of God, they sent unto them Peter
> and John, who, when they were come down, prayed for them,
> that they might receive the Holy Spirit (for as yet He was fallen
> upon none of them; only they were baptized in the Name of the
> Lord Jesus.) Then laid they their hands on them, and they received the Holy Spirit (Acts 8:14).*

This laying on of hands by an apostle or bishop became increasingly impractical as the Early Church grew and more converts were made. As a result, the Church began to bless chrism with which to anoint converts in place of the laying on of hands of the bishop. Chrism is a mixture of oil and spices which is blessed periodically by the Synod of Bishops; the old chrism is added to the new, thus preserving the chain of blessing uninterrupted from the Early Church.

In the mystery of chrismation, we receive the gift of the Holy Spirit by the anointing with chrism. The Holy Spirit, as we read in our daily prayers, is the 'Comforter, the Spirit of Truth Who is everywhere present and fills all things, a Treasury of every good and the Giver of life.' The Holy Spirit is united with the Father and the Son in a perfect unity of Essence, but also a perfect distinction of Persons as we hear in the service of Pentecost:

> *The Holy Spirit hath ever been, and is, and shall be, neither beginning nor ending; but He is ever ranked and numbered together*

> *with the Father and the Son. He is Life, and life-creating; Light,*
> *and light bestowing; by nature good, and the source of goodness;*
> *through Him the Father is known, and the Son is glorified; and*
> *thereby all men acknowledge a single sovereignty, single cove-*
> *nant, one adoration of the Holy Trinity.*[21]

The Holy Spirit descended on the apostles at Pentecost in the form of tongues of fire (Acts 2:3), but this was not the first time, by any means, that the Holy Spirit was manifested to the world. The Holy Spirit descended in the form of a dove at Christ's Baptism in the Jordan, and the Holy Spirit hovered over the waters at the Creation; the prophets of the Old Testament spoke by the power of the Holy Spirit.

The anointing with chrism is a calling to a higher ministry, and both St. Cyril of Jerusalem and St. Ambrose of Milan compare the chrismation of the newly baptized to the anointing of Aaron, as well as to that of the kings David and Solomon. The mystery of chrismation was prefigured by the bathing of Aaron and then his anointing by Moses (Lev. 8:12). The high priest also anointed Solomon after he had bathed in Gihon (1 Kings. 1:39). St. Cyril says that both Moses and Solomon are called 'christs' because they were both anointed: the word 'christ' means 'anointed one'.

Priests and kings were anointed in the Old Testament, and now Christians are anointed into the spiritual priesthood and the spiritual kingdom. By baptism we become priests of the royal priesthood mentioned by St. Peter: 'you are a chosen generation, a royal priesthood, a holy nation, His own special people, that you may proclaim the praises of Him who called you out of darkness into His marvellous light' (1 Peter 2:9).

Unlike a normal anointing, chrismation sanctifies our souls with the gift of the Holy Spirit. Below, St. Cyril of Jerusalem links our anointing with Christ's:

> *Christ was in reality crucified, buried, and raised, and you are*
> *accounted worthy, in baptism, of being crucified, buried, and*

---

[21] Holy Transfiguration Monastery (trans.), *The Pentecostarion* (Brookline: Holy Transfiguration Monastery, 1990) p. 416.

raised together with Him in a likeness. Correspondingly, we are anointed in likeness. Christ was anointed with an ideal oil of gladness, that is, with the Holy Spirit, who is so called because He is the author of spiritual gladness, so you were anointed with ointment, having been made partakers and fellows of Christ… But beware of supposing this to be ordinary ointment. For as the Bread of the Eucharist, after the descent of the Holy Spirit, is mere bread no longer, but the Body of Christ, so also this holy ointment is no longer simple or common ointment, after the invocation, but it is Christ's gift of grace, and, by the coming of the Holy Spirit, is made fit to impart His Divine Nature. This ointment is symbolically applied to your forehead and other sense organs, and whilst your body is anointed with this visible ointment, your soul is sanctified by the Holy and life-giving Spirit.

Chrismation is our personal Pentecost that 'seals' or confirms us as members of the Church, the Body of Christ. Only in the Orthodox Church can we make the fullness of the Holy Spirit our own (cf. John 1:16), and this grace is given to us 'according to the measure of the gift of Christ' (Eph. 4:7). We receive the grace of the Holy Spirit in chrismation, but we need to 'live by the Spirit and walk by the Spirit' and show forth the fruit of the Spirit: love, joy, peace, patience, kindness, goodness, faithfulness, gentleness and self-control (cf. Gal. 5:22-25). St. Ambrose of Milan links the Gifts of the Spirit prophesied by Esaias (Is. 11:3) with the Gifts of the Holy Spirit received in baptism and chrismation:

After the font, it remains for the perfecting to take place, when at the invocation of the priest, the Holy Spirit is bestowed: the spirit of wisdom, and understanding, the spirit of counsel and strength, the spirit of knowledge and godliness, the spirit of the fear of God, as it were the seven virtues of the Spirit.

Through chrismation we are sealed with the gift of the Holy Spirit, but this marks the beginning of our journey and not the end. We are born again and renewed by the Spirit, but, following the teaching of St. Gregory Palamas, we must persevere in Orthodoxy of faith and repentance to receive the crown:

*The bishop, having clothed the person who has been bap-
tized in a radiant white garment, and anointed him with holy
chrism, and having made him a communicant of Christ's Body
and Blood, then sends him on his way, showing that he has
thenceforth become a child of light, both united in one body
with Christ and a partaker of the Holy Spirit. For we are born
again and become heavenly sons of God instead of earthly beings, eternal instead of transient. God has mystically implanted
heavenly grace in our hearts and set the seal of adoption by
means of the all-Holy Spirit for the day of redemption provided
we keep this confession firm to the end and fulfil our promise
through deeds, though we may renew it through repentance if it
drifts a little off course.*[22]

The Holy Spirit is that 'one spirit' in the Body of the Church to
which St. Paul refers (Eph. 4:4), and He guides us to the knowledge
of Christ, binding together the whole institution of the Church in
the manner Archimandrite Justin Popovic describes:

*The Holy Spirit keeps all the faithful, who have been baptized
by Him and who constitute the Body of the Church, in unity
within the theanthropic Body of the Church, by the grace of the
holy mysteries and virtues. The Holy Spirit, who is ever one, is
instrumental in the relationship and unity of each member of
the Church with the others. All vocations in the Church, all the
ministries, all the servants of the Church: apostles, prophets,
teachers, bishops, priests and laity, all constitute one body, the
Body of the Church. All are necessary to each, and each to all.
All are bound into one conciliar, theanthropic Body by the Holy
Spirit, the Unifier and Architect of the Church.*[23]

The mystery of chrismation is normally an intrinsic part of the baptism service; the anointing with chrism is carried out straight after the
newly-baptized is clothed with the white robe. Before the anointing,
the priest reads the following prayer:

---

[22] St. Gregory Palamas, *The Homilies* (trans. C. Veniamin) (Dalton: Mount Thabor
Publishing, 2014) p. 488.

[23] Popovic, *The Orthodox Church and Ecumenism* p. 15.

Blessed art Thou, O Lord God Almighty, the source of all good things, the Sun of Righteousness, who shonest upon them that were in darkness the light of our salvation, through the revelation of Thine Only-begotten Son and our God, Who hast given us, the unworthy, blessed purification through blessed water, and divine sanctification through life-giving chrismation. Thou hast now also been pleased to regenerate Thy newly-illumined servant by water and the Spirit, granting unto him forgiveness of sins, both voluntary and involuntary. Do Thou, the same Master, the compassionate King of kings, seal him with the gift of Thy holy, almighty and heavenly Spirit, and grant him to participate in the Holy Body and precious Blood of thy Christ. Keep him in Thy holiness, confirm him in the Orthodox faith, deliver him from the evil one, and all his devices. Preserve his soul in purity and honesty, through the saving fear of Thee, that he may please Thee in every deed and word and may be a child and heir of Thy heavenly kingdom. For Thou art our God, the God who showeth mercy and saveth, and unto Thee do we send up glory, to the Father, to the Son and to the Holy Spirit, now and ever, and unto the ages of ages.

The newly-baptized is then anointed with chrism on the forehead, eyelids, nostrils, lips, ears, chest, hands, feet, and between the shoulders using a small brush kept especially for this purpose. As each part of the body is anointed, the priest says: 'the seal of the gift of the Holy Spirit. Amen.' The chrism is washed off using the chrism sponge at the appointed part of the service.

Frequently Asked Questions

What is 'confirmation'?

The Roman Catholic sacrament of confirmation consists of an anointing with chrism on the forehead, preceded by a laying on of hands by the bishop. Roman Catholics receive their 'first communion' around the age of eight, but are confirmed when they are teenagers. Confirmation, therefore, is not a prerequisite for receiving communion; baptism is all that is needed, provided the child is old enough. Recently some Catholic dioceses have reverted to a more traditional and logical order: baptism, confirmation and first communion.

In the Anglican Communion, confirmation is traditionally performed by the laying on of hands by the bishop before first communion. The anointing with chrism may, or may not, accompany confirmation depending on the beliefs of each particular bishop. In recent years, modernist parts of the Anglican Church have allowed children (and the non-baptized) to receive communion without being confirmed.

Roman Catholic and Anglican confirmation has become a 'rite of passage' before which teenagers can decide, for themselves, whether they want to carry on being a Christian or not. It becomes, therefore, a personal decision replacing that made by the godparents at baptism.

The Orthodox Church, on the other hand, does not debar Orthodox children from receiving Holy Communion because this would mean, in effect, that baptism and chrismation are somehow deficient or incomplete because of age. Christ Himself teaches: 'Suffer the little children, and forbid them not, to come unto me: for of such is the kingdom of heaven' (Matt. 19:14).

3

The Reception of Converts

Go ye therefore, and teach all nations, baptizing them in the name of the Father, and of the Son, and of the Holy Spirit.

Matthew 28: 19

The Orthodox Church calls all to Herself whether from unbelief in God, or from another religion. We mentioned earlier that those who wish to become Orthodox are first made catechumens, signalling their desire to learn about the Orthodox Faith: this is part of the teaching that Christ calls us to perform (cf. Matt 28: 19).

Baptism is the traditional method of receiving converts because the Orthodox Church does not accept the existence of baptism outside Orthodoxy. Converts from Judaism, Islam and other non-Christian faiths are baptized because they have not received any baptism. Converts from other Christian faiths are asked publicly to renounce their previous errors and are then baptized because the Orthodox Church does not accept their baptism as valid.

This form of reception does not amount to 're-baptism' because heterodox baptism is not a 'baptism' in the Orthodox sense of the word; it is unable to regenerate by water and the Spirit. The 'one baptism' that we confess in the Creed is not an acknowledgment that any 'baptism' is equivalent to Orthodox baptism, but a confession that one Orthodox baptism unifies us within the Church.

True baptism, which grants forgiveness of sins and rebirth in Christ, is only possible when it is linked perfectly with the Orthodox Faith as Saint Basil the Great teaches:

> *Faith and baptism are two related and inseparable modes of salvation; faith is perfected through baptism, while baptism is founded through faith…. first comes the confession, introducing us to salvation, and baptism follows, setting the seal upon our assent.*

In general, anyone who has not been baptized by three immersions in the name of the Trinity must be baptized when being received into the Orthodox Church. In addition to considering this correct 'form' of baptism, the previous faith of the convert is also taken into account. For example, Coptic Christians, and most other Monophysites, are received by chrismation and not baptism because not only is their faith much closer to Orthodoxy than any western Christian denomination, but also their baptism is correct in form, in that it retains the threefold immersion and invocation of the Trinity. This relaxation in the strictness of the rules of the Church is known as 'economy'.

Economy was applied in the Early Church when receiving Arians and Macedonians into the Church; both groups baptized by triple immersions in the name of the Trinity and were sufficiently close to Orthodoxy for their deviations from the faith to be annulled by a written confession of faith and chrismation. Eunomians, on the other hand, who practiced a single immersion only, were always received by baptism.[24] The QuiniSext Oecumenical Council (The Council in Trullo) confirmed this in its 95th Canon:

> We receive those who come from the heretics to Orthodoxy and the portion of the saved in accordance with the following order and custom. In the case of Arians and Macedonians and Novatians…. we receive them when they present a document certifying that they hold as anathema every heresy which does not hold the same beliefs as the holy Catholic and Apostolic Church; and they are sealed, that is, we first anoint them with holy chrism, on the forehead, eyes, the nose, mouth, and the ears, and then sealing them we say: 'The seal of the Gift of the Holy Spirit'… In the case of Eunomians, who are baptized with one immersion… as well as all the other heretics… we receive those from amongst them who wish to embrace Orthodoxy as we do pagans; on the first day we make them Christians, on the second Catechumens, and on the third we exorcize them by blowing thrice on their faces and their ears; then we give them instruction, requiring

---

[24] G. Metallinos, *I Confess One Baptism* (Holy Mountain: St. Paul's Monastery, 1994) p. 57

them to attend Church for a year and to attend the reading of the Scriptures; thereupon we baptize them.[25]

The Orthodox Church therefore does not 're-baptize' people: She baptizes those who have not received baptism. Non-Orthodox baptism is not capable of making someone a member of the Orthodox Church and so is not saving because, as St. Cyprian of Carthage affirms, 'outside the Church there is no salvation.' In proclaiming the uniqueness of Orthodox baptism, we are not, of course, saying the non-Orthodox are 'going to hell'. In Orthodoxy we never, ever, say this because it shows contempt for God who is the Judge - not us!

Unfortunately, most Orthodox Churches do not baptize converts because they accept the baptism of any group outside Orthodoxy as equivalent to Orthodox baptism regardless of its deficiencies in form and the non-Orthodox faith of the celebrant. This position is clearly contrary to traditional Orthodox practice as summarized in the 46th Apostolic Canon: 'a bishop or priest that has recognized the baptism or sacrifice of heretics should be defrocked, for "what accord has Christ with Belial? Or what has a believer in common with an unbeliever?"'

If we acknowledge the existence of true Christian baptism outside the Orthodox Church we are actually supporting the heterodox in their errors and not helping them. St. Cyprian of Carthage expresses this position clearly when he says:

If the heretics see that their baptism is approved of, and accepted by us as true and legitimate, they will think that they are justly and legitimately in possession of the Church also, and the other gifts of the Church. Why would they then come to us for baptism, when they seem to have everything else?

As we have discussed above, baptism must be by threefold immersion in the name of the Trinity. A threefold sprinkling, or pouring, is unacceptable, as is the single immersion in the 'name of Jesus'

---

[25] G.Nedungatt, M. Featherstone (Eds.), *The Council in Trullo Revisited* (Rome: Pontifico Istituto Orientale, 1995) p. 175.

favoured by some Protestant groups. In general, most baptisms outside Orthodoxy are deficient in form with the exception of the various Monophysite Churches who baptize using the correct form.

Chrismation has, in some historical periods, been used to receive members of other Christian denominations into the Orthodox Church whose baptism is somehow lacking in form (most often consisting of sprinkling rather than immersion). Chrismation can fill up what was lacking in the original 'baptism', but this use of economy is not in accordance with the strictness of Orthodox tradition. Moreover, as we have already mentioned, receiving converts by economy in exceptional circumstances does not imply that their original 'baptism' was valid. If we acknowledge that the heterodox have a valid baptism they must also have the priesthood and the Eucharist and so there would be no need to receive them into Orthodoxy at all!

Chrismation is also used to receive back into the Church those Orthodox Christians who have joined another religion. Baptism cannot be repeated, but as these people have formally left the Church, they are formally received back into Her by renouncing heresy and anointing with chrism.

We confess 'one baptism' within the Orthodox Church. In the words of Saint Basil the Great:

> *What makes us Christians? 'Our faith', everyone would answer. How are we saved? Obviously through the regenerating grace of baptism. How else could we be? We are confirmed in our understanding that salvation comes through Father, Son and Holy Spirit. Shall we cast away the standard of teaching that we received? This would surely be grounds for great sorrow; if we now reject what we accepted at baptism, we will be found to be further away from our salvation than when we first believed. We would be no different from someone who died without baptism, or who had been baptized with an unacceptable form.*[26]

[26] Saint Basil the Great, *On the Holy Spirit* (trans. D. Anderson) (New York: SVS Press, 1980) p. 46.

It is our duty as Orthodox Christians to preserve the Orthodox Faith, to witness to it in our personal lives so that the heterodox will see our good works and glorify God (cf. 1 Peter. 2:12). Those who have received non-Orthodox baptism and live according to the Gospels, do this, as St. Maximus the Confessor says, by grace. However, because they are not part of the Church, they cannot make this grace their own, and they cannot be transformed by the mysteries of the Church. The attitude of the Orthodox Church to heretics is summed up by Saint Maximos the Confessor:

> *I write these things not wishing to cause distress to the heretics or to rejoice in their ill-treatment – God forbid! – I take the greatest joy and pleasure in their conversion. For what is more pleasing to the faithful than to see the scattered children of God gathered together again? I am not so insane as to suggest that harshness should be valued above love for man. On the contrary, I advise that we should, with care and experience, do good to all men, becoming all things to all men according to their need. I desire and advise that you should be implacable with heretics only in regard to cooperating with them in their senseless beliefs. To give support to error leading to the ruination of those who hold it, I do not call love, but hatred and a falling-away from divine love.*

Prophet, King and Psalmist David

4

Daily Services

*Rejoice always, pray without ceasing, give thanks in all circumstances;
for this is the will of God in Christ Jesus for you.*

1 Thessalonians 5: 16-18

The daily services of the Orthodox Church are the foundation on
which the services of the various mysteries of the Church are based.
Indeed, as we have discussed already, these services themselves are
mysteries in which the Orthodox Church fulfils the commandment
of St. Paul to 'pray without ceasing' (1 Thess. 5:16).

The Church is constantly being renewed by the Holy Spirit, and services to the saints are still being written today. Nevertheless, most
of the hymns and prayers that make up the fixed parts of the Daily
Services are extremely old. For example, part of the text of the theotokion 'Under thy compassion do we flee O Theotokos…' that is
sung at Orthodox Vespers can be seen on the papyrus fragment,
Rylands 470; the writing on this fragment dates from the middle of
the third century.

The services of the Church are appointed to be read at set times of
the day and night, and in the following order.

- Vespers
- Compline (Small or Great depending on the Church season)
- Midnight Office
- Matins
- First Hour
- Third Hour
- Sixth Hour
- Ninth Hour

In most monasteries and parishes, this order is modified slightly and
the services are abbreviated to a greater, or lesser extent. For example,
the service of Midnight Office is normally served just before Matins

rather than at midnight. The Divine Liturgy may be served after the reading of the Third and Sixth Hours or directly after Matins. The Russian Church follows the former practice; Vespers and Matins are sung together on the previous evening as the 'All-night Vigil' service.

A number of different books are needed to read the Daily Services in their entirety, and the sheer number of these can seem formidable to converts to Orthodoxy. Confusion can also arise because the Orthodox Church has a fixed calendar and a movable (Paschal) calendar which means that the date of Pascha moves every year, and so do all the feasts associated with it such as Ascension and Pentecost. The fixed calendar is unaffected by the date of Pascha; Christmas day is always on the 25th December whatever the date of Pascha.

The daily services of the Church begin with the blessing: 'Blessed is our God, always now and ever, and unto the ages of ages.' The Divine Liturgy, and the mysteries of baptism and marriage begin: 'Blessed is the Kingdom, of the Father, and of the Son, and of the Holy Spirit, both now and ever, and unto the ages of ages;' immediately after this blessing the priest or deacon intones a litany. The word 'litany' is taken from the Greek verb 'to ask' because in all litanies the deacon petitions God for mercy on our behalf and on behalf of the whole world. A number of different litanies are used in the services of the Orthodox Church.

Great Litany: This is also called the 'Litany of Peace' because it begins, 'In peace let us pray to the Lord'. To each of the petitions, the choir replies, 'Lord have mercy,' but in many Greek monasteries the choir answers 'Amen' to the final petition, 'Help us, save us, have mercy on us, and keep us, O God, by Thy grace.'

Little Litany: This is often called the 'Small Litany'. It begins: 'Again and again, in peace let us pray to the Lord,' to which the choir answers, 'Lord have mercy'.

Litany of Fervent Supplication: This litany starts with the petition, 'Have mercy on us, O God, according to Thy great mercy, we pray Thee, hearken and have mercy,' to which the choir answers 'Lord have mercy' three times.

Augmented Litany of Fervent Supplication: The Litany of Fervent Supplication is sometimes lengthened by adding the following petitions at the beginning:

- Let us all say with our whole soul and with our whole mind, let us say:
- O Lord Almighty, the God of our fathers, we pray Thee, hearken and have mercy.

Litany of Supplication: This litany begins, 'Let us complete our evening prayer to the Lord,' when it is used at Vespers, but for morning services such as Matins the phrase 'morning prayer' is used instead. After the first two responses, the choir answers 'Grant this O Lord' to the remaining petitions. At the end of each litany there is an exclamation by the priest, which varies according to the type of litany and whereabouts in the service it is used.

The Dismissal given by the priest at the end of the service is different on every day. On Sundays, it begins: 'May Christ our true God Who is risen from the dead…'; this beginning is also used during the Paschal period. The dismissal is always preceded by a dialogue between the deacon, priest and choir.

Service Books of the Orthodox Church

General Service Books

General service books are used throughout the year; details of all these books can be found in the 'Further Reading' chapter.

Prayer Book: An Orthodox Prayer Book contains all the necessary daily prayers for every Orthodox Christian: morning and evening prayers, the prayers before and after Holy Communion, and a selection of *akathists* and canons.

Holy Bible: The Orthodox Church uses the Septuagint version of the Old Testament which dates from the third century BC. The word 'Septuagint' comes from the Latin word for 'seventy' because the work was carried out by seventy translators. The Septuagint is more reliable than the Hebrew Old Testament text used by most English-speaking Bible translators. The King James Version (KJV) Bible is reasonably reliable for the New Testament, but it lacks some of the books of the Old Testament known in Orthodoxy as the '*Anagignoskomena*' (lit. 'profitable reading') or 'deutero-canonical books'. Unfortunately, the translators of the KJV mistranslated some important verses so that they would appear to support Protestantism. It still remains, however, the best of the English language versions of the Bible.

Psalter: The Orthodox Psalter contains all the Psalms of Old Testament and is divided into sections called 'kathismas'; each kathisma is further divided into three sections, each of which is called a 'stasis'. We have used the translation of the Psalter published by Holy Transfiguration Monastery for all the psalms quoted in this book.

Epistle and Gospel Book: The Epistle Book or '*Apostolos*' contains all the Epistle readings for the Divine Liturgy and the other mysteries of the Church. The Gospel Book contains all four Gospels in their entirety, but like the Epistle Book, these Gospels are divided into sections according to the usage of the Church. Over the course of the Church year, the entire New Testament, apart from the Apocalypse, is read in church. The Gospel Book is always kept on the Holy Table when not in use.

Horologion: A standard *Horologion* or 'Book of Hours' contains all the daily services of the Church. The *Great Horologion* is the most complete, and contains, in addition to the text of the daily services, hymns and brief lives of the saints for every day of the year.

Service Books of the Paschal Calendar

Triodion: The complete *Triodion* contains all the feasts from the Sunday of the Publican and Pharisee through to the Midnight Office of Pascha morning. The *Lenten Triodion* translated by Bishop Kallistos (Ware) and Mother Mary contains the Sunday services and the most important weekday services of the Triodion period.

Pentecostarion: The *Pentecostarion* contains the complete services for Pascha night to the Sunday of All Saints, and includes the Great Feasts of Ascension and Pentecost.

Service Books of the Fixed Calendar

The complete versions of the following service books are normally only found in churches because of their size and expense, but there are abbreviated versions available containing only the most important feasts of the year.

Octoechos: Octoechos means 'eight tones' in Greek, and a 'tone' is roughly equivalent to a western musical scale. The Octoechos contains all the Sunday and weekday hymns of each tone. These hymns are not just sung differently in the different tones: the words are different too. There is a slight variation in the naming of the tones: the Slavic Churches name the tones from one to eight; in the Greek Church, Tone Five is called the Plagal First Tone; Tone Six, Plagal Second; Tone Seven, Grave Tone; Tone Eight is known as the Plagal Fourth Tone.

A new tone starts on Sunday (actually, as we shall see later, on Saturday evening Vespers), and the tones change every week in ascending numerical order. Tone Eight is followed, the next week, by Tone One and the sequence begins again. Each day of the week has a special commemoration in the *Octoechos*: on Monday, the angels; on Tuesday, the Forerunner; on Wednesday and Friday, the Cross, and on Thursday the apostles and St. Nicolas of Myra. On Saturdays, hymns are sung in honour of all saints and for those Orthodox Christians who have reposed in the faith.

Menaion: This twelve volume compilation contains the services for the feasts of every day of every month; the word 'Menaion' is derived from the Greek word for 'month'. In addition to containing the Great Feasts of the fixed calendar such as Christmas and Theophany, a complete *Menaion* has at least one service to a saint for every day of the year. An abbreviated English version called *The Festal Menaion* contains the services for all the Great Feasts of the year on the fixed calendar.

The days before any Great Feast of the fixed calendar are called the forefeast, during which hymns are sung from the Menaion in expectation of the Feast. The days following a Great Feast are called the afterfeast. The length of the forefeast and afterfeast period can vary depending upon the Feast and the Church season. The last day of the afterfeast period is called the *apodosis* or 'leavetaking'; on this day all the hymns of the Great Feast are sung again.

The Hours

In the Old Testament, a new day began at sunset and daytime was divided into hours which roughly equate to the following times. The first hour is at sunrise, the third hour is about 9 a.m., the sixth hour is about noon and the ninth hour is about 3 p.m. The 'hours' of the Orthodox Church are appointed to be read at these hours of the day, but normally the First Hour is read directly after Matins, the Ninth Hour before Vespers and the Third and Sixth Hours together just before the Divine Liturgy.

The hours also have a theological significance:

- Christ was led before Pilate at the first hour of the day.
- The Holy Spirit descended at the third hour on the apostles.
- Christ was nailed to the Cross at the sixth hour.
- Christ died on the Cross at the ninth hour.

In Great Lent, the First, Third, Sixth and Ninth hours are elongated, and are referred to as 'Lenten Hours'. The first three psalms of the hours are identical, but a kathisma is normally appointed to be read, and the priest and choir chant specially appointed verses for each hour; the Prayer of St. Ephraim is read at the end of the hour.

The 'Royal Hours' are so called because they were attended by the Emperor in Constantinople. There are only three sets of Royal Hours: Nativity, Theophany and Great Friday. The three psalms of each hour are selected for their relevance to the Feast, and the choir sings festal antiphons which are followed by a prokeimenon, an Epistle and a Gospel Reading. The Royal Hours of Christmas and Theophany are said altogether, as one service, on the eve of the Feast and are followed by the Liturgy of St. Basil the Great. On Great Friday, the Royal Hours are read on that morning followed by the Typica.

The Paschal Hours are sung during Bright Week in place of the hours, morning and evening prayers and the thanksgiving prayers after Holy Communion. In the forty days of Pascha, all services begin with the Paschal troparion, 'Christ is risen from the dead by death hath He trampled down death…' three times and then 'Holy God to Our Father'. When a service would normally begin with 'O come let us worship…' this is replaced with the Paschal troparion said three times.

Saturday Evening Vespers

Vespers is the evening service of the Orthodox Church and marks the beginning of the new Church day, and is served on its own or together with Matins as part of the All-night Vigil.

- During the reading of Psalm 103 we recall the Paradise from which Adam and Eve fell, and which has now been opened again unto us, and calling to mind the creation of the world, we glorify God for all the blessings that He has given us.

- The first kathisma is now read. The word *kathisma* means 'sitting' so during kathisma readings we sit, and stand up between each stasis.

- The four psalms (140, 141, 129 and 116) that make up the 'Lord I have Cried' section of Vespers are a lamentation for our fallen state caused by our exile from Paradise. The censing of the church recalls the offering of incense in the Old Testament.

- After the psalm verse 'Bring my soul out of prison…', the choir sings the first *sticheron* of the Octoechos followed by the other stichera of the Resurrection and those of the saint of the day from the Menaion between the remaining psalm verses. Usually, stichera for saints are sung to special melody called a *prosomion*, and in the Greek usage the text of each stichera is metred to fit the music of the prosomion. On the twelve Great Feasts, and on the feasts of major saints, the stichera are sung to a longer, unique melody called an *idiomelon*.

- The dogmatic theotokion which follows expresses the dogma of the incarnation of the Son of God from the Virgin and is sung in the Tone of the Week.

- The entrance represents the foreshadowing of the incarnation of Christ revealed to the prophets in the Old Testament.

- The lighting of a lamp at sunset is based on an Old Testament ritual (Ex. 30:8), but this custom, and the singing of the hymn 'O Joyous Light' are ancient Christian traditions that were already old in the time of Saint Basil the Great (fourth century): 'It seemed fitting to our fathers that they should welcome the gift of the evening light with something better than silence, so they gave

The Structure of Saturday Evening Vespers

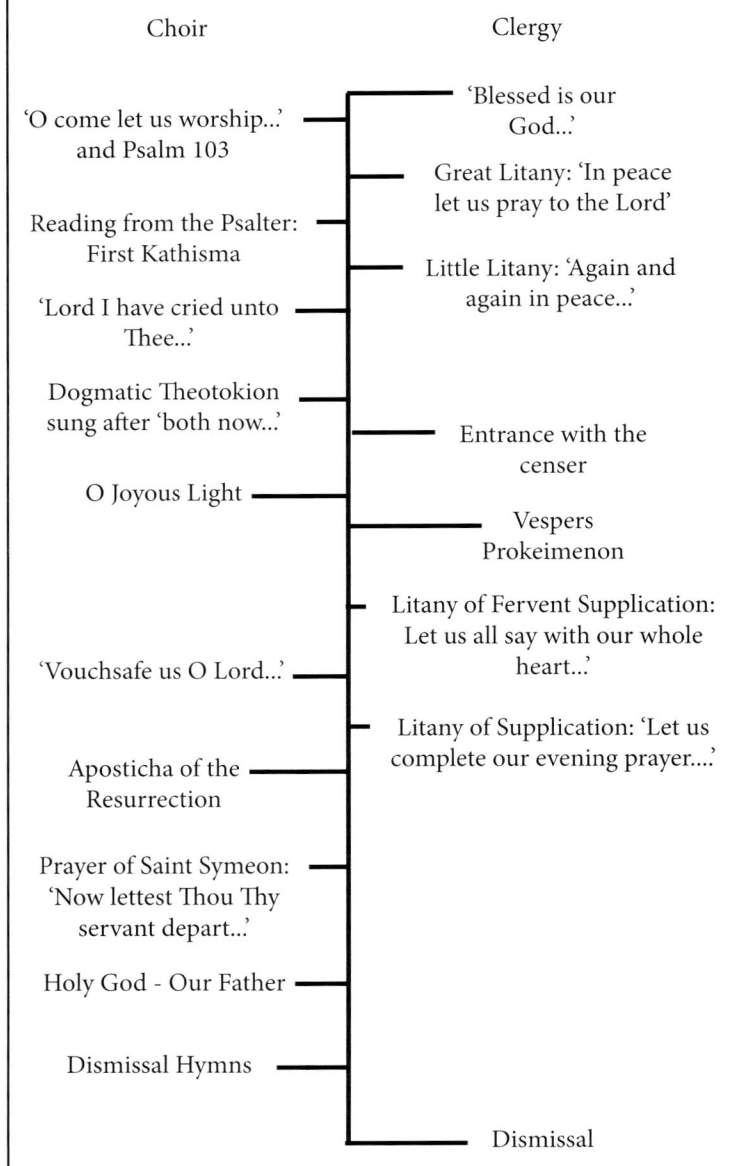

Choir	Clergy
'O come let us worship...' and Psalm 103	'Blessed is our God...'
	Great Litany: 'In peace let us pray to the Lord'
Reading from the Psalter: First Kathisma	Little Litany: 'Again and again in peace...'
'Lord I have cried unto Thee...'	
Dogmatic Theotokion sung after 'both now...'	
	Entrance with the censer
O Joyous Light	Vespers Prokeimenon
	Litany of Fervent Supplication: Let us all say with our whole heart...'
'Vouchsafe us O Lord...'	
	Litany of Supplication: 'Let us complete our evening prayer....'
Aposticha of the Resurrection	
Prayer of Saint Symeon: 'Now lettest Thou Thy servant depart...'	
Holy God - Our Father	
Dismissal Hymns	
	Dismissal

thanks as soon as it appeared. We are not able to say who composed these words of thanksgiving at the lighting of the lamps, but the people use these ancient words, and no one accuses them of blasphemy for singing: "we praise Father, Son, and Holy Spirit, God." The Light is Christ Himself the 'Light of the World' (John 8:12), the 'brightness of the Father's glory' (Heb. 1:3) who enlightens every man coming into the world (cf. John 1:9).

- Vespers portrays how the promise of the coming of Christ was revealed in the Old Testament, and the Prayer of St. Symeon, 'Now lettest thou Thy servant depart…', brings this revelation to its completion.

- A dismissal hymn (*apolytikion*) is a short hymn so-called because it is sung just before the dismissal of Vespers and Matins. Every Great Feast, all the Sundays of the Octoechos and many saints have a unique dismissal hymn.

Sunday Matins

The Greek word for Matins is 'orthros' which means 'daybreak'. Matins is the morning service of the Orthodox Church. In most Greek parishes, the Divine Liturgy follows immediately after Matins, but on days when a Liturgy is not appointed, it is followed by the First Hour.

- During the reading of the Six Psalms (3, 37, 62, 87, 102, 142) we stand still and do not make the sign of the Cross, calling to mind the Final Judgement when, according to tradition, the same Six Psalms will be read.

- In the hymn 'God is the Lord and hath appeared unto us…' we give thanks for the incarnation of the Son of God and recall the praise of the Hebrew children when they sang 'Blessed is He that cometh in the Name of the Lord' (Luke 19:38).

- The *Polyeleos* consists of Psalms 134 and 135 and in many Greek monasteries a twelve-lamped chandelier is swung during the singing. This chandelier is itself called the polyeleos, a word which means 'many mercies' because of the refrain sung during Psalm 135: 'For His mercy endureth forever. Alleluia'.

- The *Evlogitaria* of the Resurrection is sung on every Sunday of the year (except when a Great Feast of the Saviour falls on a Sunday) and consists of hymns to the Resurrection separated by the refrain 'Blessed art Thou O Lord, teach me Thy statutes' (Ps. 118.12).

- The verses that make up the Hymns of Ascent (also called Hymns of Degrees) are taken from the Psalms of the eighteenth kathisma, each of which has the title 'a hymn of ascent'.

- A Gospel is always read on Sunday Matins recounting the events immediately following the Resurrection of Christ. There are eleven of these Gospels, read over a period of eleven weeks: the sequence starts on Thomas Sunday with the reading of the First Matins Gospel. The resurrectional Matins Gospel is read by the priest from the south side of the Holy Table.

- During the singing of the hymn 'Let us who have beheld the Resurrection of Christ…', the priest holds the Gospel aloft signifying the appearance of the risen Christ.

- The Matins canon is made up of nine odes, each of which consists of a series of verses introduced by short refrains. Each ode is based on the following sections of the Old Testament:

  Ode One (Exodus 15: 1-9) The hymn of Moses, which he sang when the Israelites had passed through the Red Sea on foot to escape from Pharaoh.

  Ode Two (Deut. 32: 1-43) Moses' exhortation to the Jews. Ode Two is only found in the Triodion, and it is read on Tuesdays during Great Lent.

  Ode Three (1 Kings 2: 1-10) The thanksgiving hymn offered up by Hannah, the mother of the Prophet Samuel. She is a foreshadowing of the Church, which before was childless but now rejoices in a multitude of children.

  Ode Four (Abb. 3: 2-19) The prophecy of Abbacum (Habbakuk) who in fear foresaw the manifestation of the Lord on earth.

  Ode Five (Is. 26: 9-20) In the Fifth Ode, the Church prays in the words of the Prophet Esaias that the faithful might be enlightened by grace.

  Ode Six (Jon. 2: 3-10) The hymn of Jonas. The irmoi contain supplications for our deliverance from the waves of life and from every danger.

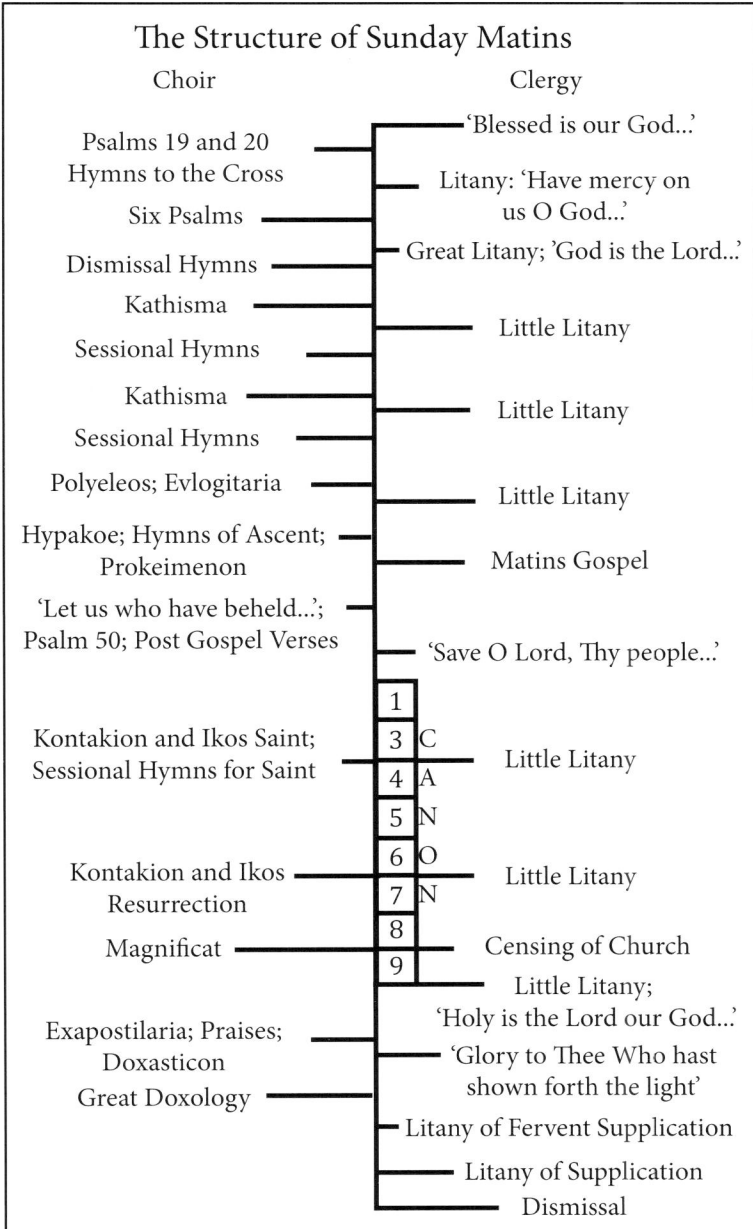

The Structure of Sunday Matins

Choir	Clergy
Psalms 19 and 20 Hymns to the Cross	'Blessed is our God...'
Six Psalms	Litany: 'Have mercy on us O God...'
Dismissal Hymns	Great Litany; 'God is the Lord...'
Kathisma	
Sessional Hymns	Little Litany
Kathisma	Little Litany
Sessional Hymns	
Polyeleos; Evlogitaria	Little Litany
Hypakoe; Hymns of Ascent; Prokeimenon	Matins Gospel
'Let us who have beheld...'; Psalm 50; Post Gospel Verses	'Save O Lord, Thy people...'
Kontakion and Ikos Saint; Sessional Hymns for Saint	Little Litany
Kontakion and Ikos Resurrection	Little Litany
Magnificat	Censing of Church
	Little Litany; 'Holy is the Lord our God...'
Exapostilaria; Praises; Doxasticon	'Glory to Thee Who hast shown forth the light'
Great Doxology	Litany of Fervent Supplication
	Litany of Supplication
	Dismissal

(Canon numbered 1, 3, 4, 5, 6, 7, 8, 9 with letters C A N O N)

Ode Seven (Dan. 3:26-56) and Ode Eight (Dan. 3: 57-88)
The hymn of the Three Children in the Babylonian furnace. At the end of Ode Eight the choir sings the Magnificat with the refrain: 'More honourable than the Cherubim, and beyond compare more glorious than the Seraphim, thee who without corruption gavest birth to God the Word, the very Theotokos, do we magnify.'

Ode Nine (Luke: 1-46-55) The Ninth Ode is dedicated to the Theotokos, and continues on from the Magnificat with the prophetic hymn of Zacharias regarding his son, the Forerunner. On Great Feasts, the Magnificat is omitted and Ode Nine is sung instead of being read.

- These biblical odes are not read in full outside of Great Lent, but they are referenced in the hymn sung by the choir at the beginning of every ode called an '*irmos*' (pl. *irmoi*). At the end of each ode, the choir sings a hymn called a *katavasia* which changes according to the calendar. A short hymn called a *kontakion* is sung after Ode Six followed by the reading of a stanza called an *ikos* which is modelled on the kontakion.

- The 'Praises' consist of Psalms 148, 149 and 150. On Sundays, the Resurrectional stichera from the Octoechos are sung between the verses of Psalm 150 followed by the stichera of the saint, or the feast. On most Sundays of the year, a special doxasticon is chanted relating to the Resurrectional Matins Gospel.

- The 'light' referred to in the exclamation 'Glory to Thee Who hast shown forth the light,' is both the physical light of the sun and Christ the Light of the World (cf. John 8:12). The Great Doxology is sung immediately after this exclamation.

The All-night Vigil

The All-night Vigil consists of Vespers followed by Matins and joined together by a section called the 'Lity' which takes place in the narthex. A Vigil is served on the eve of Great Feasts, and, in the Slavic Churches, on Saturday evenings.

- The Vigil begins with the curtain and Royal Doors open and starts with the exclamation: 'Glory to the holy, consubstantial and life-creating Trinity...'. Whilst Psalm 103 is being read the priest and deacon cense the altar and the body of the church.

- The Lity is served in the narthex so that the catechumens, who in earlier times were not permitted to enter the church itself, can participate in the prayers. It represents the Church's out-reach and ministry to those not yet joined to Her.

- The word 'Lity' means 'earnest supplication', which is why the choir sing 'Lord have mercy' many times in response to the deacon's petitions. During the Lity we pray for our Synod of Bishops and for all Orthodox Christians, both living and re-posed, the sick and those in prison, the government of our country and all those in lawful authority over us. At the end, the priest makes the exclamation: 'Hearken unto us, O God our Saviour, the hope of all the ends of the earth and of them that be far off at sea...'

- The clergy re-enter the nave of the church, as the choir sings the apos-ticha of Vespers, in order to bless the five loaves, wheat, wine and oil (*right*). This part of the service is known as the *artoklasia* (lit. blessing of loaves). After the 'Holy God to Our Father' sequence and the dismissal hymns, the priest reads the prayer of the artoklasia, 'O Lord Jesus Christ our God Who didst bless the five loaves and sat-isfy the five thousand....' and blesses the loaves, wheat, wine and oil. Psalm 33 is read, followed, after the exclamation by the priest, by the reading of the Six Psalms which begins Matins.

Frequently Asked Questions

On what days do we not make full prostrations in Church?

There are some local customs in which prostrations are made out of piety, but we should not, strictly speaking, make prostrations:

- on Sundays (except on the Sunday of the Cross in Great Lent and when the Feast of the Exaltation of the Cross falls on a Sunday).

- from Pascha to the Vespers of Pentecost Sunday
- from Christmas to Theophany
- on Great Feasts of the Saviour and Mother of God.

Should we make the sign of the Cross when the priest blesses us?

No. The blessing is the 'peace' that the priest blesses us with, and so there is no need to make the sign of the Cross as well. At 'Peace be unto all' we bow our heads; we do the same when we are censed and do not make the sign of the Cross.

If the Church day begins at Vespers, why don't we fast from after Vespers?

The fasting day begins at midnight, even though the Church day begins at Vespers. This might seem confusing, but consider the following example: The Triodion appoints that wine, figs and dates are blessed after the Great Saturday Liturgy, but this Liturgy is combined with Vespers. In other words, we have already celebrated the first Paschal service: Great Saturday Vespers. We don't bless cheese and eggs at this time, because the Lenten fast is broken after the midnight Paschal Liturgy rather than after Vespers. Perhaps some of the confusion arises because of the modern Russian practice of blessing Paschal foods on Great Saturday. In traditional Orthodox parishes, these foods are blessed after the Paschal Liturgy early on Sunday morning.

What is a moleben?

The word *moleben* means 'prayer service' in Slavonic and a moleben is often served in Slavic churches after the Liturgy at the request of parishioners for a particular need, or as a thanksgiving for prayers that have been answered. There is also a special moleben appointed to be served on Church New Year (1st September). In a moleben we ask for the prayers of a saint to God, and it is quite different from a *Panikhida* in which we pray for the souls of the departed. In the Greek Church, an artoklasia is often served instead of a moleben in honour of a saint or to ask for intercessions for a particular need.

When is the Typica used?

The Typica is a short service that is read when a Divine Liturgy is not celebrated. The characteristic features of this service are the reading of the Typical Psalms (Psalms 102 and 145) and the Beatitudes, the Creed, the kontakion of the day and Psalm 33. Outside Great Lent, the Typica is read immediately following the Sixth Hour.

The Typica of Great Lent is read immediately after the Ninth Hour and is substantially different in structure; in the Lenten Typica, the Typical Psalms are omitted, the Beatitudes are sung with a refrain, and the Prayer of St. Ephraim is read. On Wednesdays and Fridays in Great Lent the Typica is followed immediately by the Presanctified Liturgy.

What is the Prayer of St. Ephraim?

The Prayer of St. Ephraim the Syrian is only said in Great Lent and on Wednesday and Friday of Cheesefare Week. The text of the prayer is as follows:

> **O Lord and Master of my life, a spirit of idleness, curiosity, ambition and idle talking give me not.**
>
> **But a spirit of chastity, humility, patience and love, bestow upon me Thy servant.**
>
> **Yea, O Lord and King, grant me to see mine own failings and not to judge my brother, for blessed art Thou unto the ages of ages. Amen.**

At the end of each petition we make one full prostration. Most often, we then make twelve bows from the waist whilst saying quietly: 'God be merciful to me a sinner.' The whole prayer is then read again with one prostration only at the end. This practice is known in the typicon as 'the Prayer of St. Ephraim read twice'. At certain times, for example at the end of the Ninth Hour, the twelve bows and the second reading of the prayer are omitted; in other words, the prayer is read once. There is no simple explanation as to when the Prayer is read once or twice. The easiest solution is to copy the priest and prostrate when he prostrates; the prayer of St. Ephraim is always read by the priest either in front of the Royal Doors or the Holy Table so it is easy to see.

*The Three Great Hierarchs: Saint Gregory the Theologian,
Saint John Chrysostom and Saint Basil the Great.*

5

The Mystery of the Eucharist

Christ is the victim; He is the priest; He is the altar; He is God; He is man; He is King; He is High Priest; He is the sheep; He is the lamb. For our sake He becomes everything for each of us, so that in every way He may become our life.[27]

Saint Epiphanius of Cyprus

The mystery of the Eucharist is a thanksgiving, a sacrifice of praise to God; the word 'Eucharist' itself is derived from the Greek word for 'thanksgiving'. This mystery was inaugurated at the Mystical Supper, which the Church commemorates every year on the Thursday of Great Week:

> *When Christ had washed the feet of His disciples, He took bread, blessed it, broke it and gave it to the disciples, saying Take, eat: this is My body, which is broken for you; do this in remembrance of Me'(1 Cor. 11:24). Then He took a cup of wine, and giving praise to God, gave it to them, saying: Drink ye all from it: for this is My blood of the new testament, which is shed for many for the remission of sins.' (Matt. 26:27)*

After the descent of the Holy Spirit on Pentecost, the apostles assembled with the faithful in Jerusalem to celebrate the mystery of the Eucharist. The order set up by the apostles can still be seen within the ancient Liturgy of the Apostle James which is still used in the Orthodox Church. The apostles ordered that every Christian community should also celebrate the mystery of the Eucharist – the service we call the Divine Liturgy. The word 'Liturgy' means 'the work of the people', because the Church as a community participates in this mystery. Indeed, the word 'communion' is derived from the Greek word for 'participation'.

The mystery of the Eucharist is not a commemoration of the Mystical Supper, but it is the Mystical Supper held again for us. Jesus Christ is at the same time both what is offered as the Holy Lamb, and the One

---

[27] Hieromonk Gregorios, *The Divine Liturgy: A Commentary in the Light of the Fathers* (Mount Athos: Cell of St. John the Theologian, 2009) p. 188.

Who as the Heavenly High Priest makes the offering. St. Symeon of Thessalonika summarizes this paradoxical mystery within the mystery of the Eucharist:

> *Communion, then, is God's union with us, our deification, sanctification, fullness of grace, enlightenment, prevention of everything against us, and granting of every good. What else is both a commingling and communion with God? This is the mystery of mysteries, the sanctification of saints, truly the holy of holies, the rite of all rites, both the beginning, author and final completion of the rites. Since the originator of the rite, the Word, alone established it and passed it on, He Himself is the rite; and in order that He remain with us, He has passed it on.*[28]

The Eucharist is a sacrifice offered to God by the people for the sins of all, whether living or dead. Moreover, the sacrifice in the Divine Liturgy is identical to Christ's sacrifice on Golgotha as we hear in the Divine Liturgy of Holy Saturday: 'Behold, the king of kings and Lord of Lords cometh to be slain and to be given as food for the faithful.'

By His incarnation, Christ put on our nature, our flesh and blood, to heal it through His Passion and Resurrection, and by partaking of the Body and Blood of Christ, we receive healing and nourishment for our souls and are united with Christ as St. Gregory Palamas explains:

> *Christ became our brother, partaking of the same flesh and blood with us, and through them became like us. Through this blood He has redeemed us for Himself as true servants. He has made us His friends by bestowing upon us the revelation of these mysteries. Through the partaking of this Blood, He has bound and betrothed us to Himself as a bridegroom his bride, and become one flesh with us. But He has also become our Father through Holy Baptism in His name, and nourishes us with His own breast as a loving mother feeds her babies. And what is better and more wondrous still, He feeds us not only with blood instead of milk, but with His own Body, and not only His Body but also His Spirit.*[29]

---

[28] St. Symeon of Thessalonika, *The Liturgical Commentaries* (trans. S. Hawkes-Teeples) (Toronto: Pontifical Institute of Medieval Studies, 2011) p. 169.

[29] St. Gregory Palamas, *The Homilies* p. 464.

The mystery of the Eucharist is truly the work of the people because we all take part in this mystery. In fact, a priest cannot serve the Liturgy on his own, there must be at least one other Orthodox Christian present to chant the responses. The choir in the Liturgy represents the people but it does not take the place of the people.

The oldest of the commonly used Liturgies is that of Saint James the Brother of God; St. Basil the Great and St. John Chrysostom also have Liturgies named after them because of the work each did in writing and formulating the traditions passed down from the apostles.

In the Orthodox Church, the Liturgy has always been celebrated, and it will always be celebrated until the end of time. Through Holy Communion we are cleansed of our sins and joined with Christ as He says 'He that eateth My Flesh, and drinketh My Blood, dwelleth in Me and I in him' (John 6:56).We are also joined with our fellow Orthodox Christians 'for we being many, are one bread, and one body: for we are all partakers of that one bread' (1 Cor. 10:17).

The Liturgy of St. John Chrysostom

The Divine Liturgy of St John Chrysostom is divided into three parts:

- The Service of Preparation
- The Liturgy of the Catechumens
- The Liturgy of the Faithful

In order to understand more clearly the structure of the Liturgy it is necessary to have some understanding of the structure of the church and of the various sacred objects needed to celebrate the Divine Liturgy.

The area behind the iconostasis is called the altar and the raised area behind the Holy Table is the 'High Place'. The double doors in the middle of the iconostasis are the 'Beautiful Gates', but most English translations call them the 'Royal Doors' and we will do that too even though it is not strictly correct. The raised area in front of the iconostasis is called the *soleas* and the semi-circular area in the middle of it is the *ambon.* The curtain across the Royal Doors is always kept closed except during Bright Week (the week after Pascha) and those times during the services when it is appointed to be opened.

Every Liturgy is served on a cloth called an *antimension* (*below*) that is laid out on the top of the Holy Table; outside the Divine Liturgy the antimension is folded up. Each antimension is signed by the bishop of the diocese as a sign that the Eucharist is celebrated with his permission and has the relics of a martyr sewn into it: a remembrance of the times when the Early Christians would celebrate the Liturgy on the tombs of the martyrs.

The antimension should not be confused with the *epitaphios* (Slavonic: *plashchanitsa*) which is brought out in procession on Great Friday and laid on the Holy Table from Great Saturday until the Ascension.

The bread used for the Divine Liturgy is called a *prosphoron*; this is derived from the Greek word for 'offering'. A prosphoron is made from pure flour and the dough is allowed to rise in contrast to the unleavened wafers used in most heterodox churches. Leavened bread (in other words 'risen bread') rather than unleavened bread is used in the Divine Liturgy because the Gospels record that Christ used leavened bread at the Mystical Supper. The Greek word 'artos' used in the Gospels means 'risen bread'. In addition, the use of risen bread, rather than the unleavened bread of the Jewish Passover, is theologically significant as St. Symeon of Thessalonika teaches:

> For [Christ] deified His whole humanity, and made it equally God by the ultimate union. He maintained, however, His own nature, and is perfect man, just as He is also perfect God, but in a given place and everywhere and above all things, and yet He bears the qualities of the body. For, because of this, after his rising and according to His incorruption, He was both seen and touched, and He entered closed doors. Do you see that He was incorruptible and preserved His own qualities? That He is uncreated and created? And that He is of two natures, even if He is perfectly one in His hypostasis? Therefore, follow Orthodoxy, and do not offer either dead or inanimate things; do not renew the customs of the Jews, or introduce Jewish law, or celebrate with unleavened bread.[30]

A *prosphoron* (*right*) has two layers, representing the two natures of Jesus Christ: God and Man; on the top, there is a seal made by pressing a carved stamp into the dough before baking. The seal is a cross with the initials, IC, XC, NI, KA, in the four corners of the cross. These letters stand for 'Jesus Christ conquers' in Greek. The central portion of the prosphoron is called the Lamb because, until its consecration, it represents Christ, Who was foreshadowed in the Old Testament by the Passover lamb.

There are some variations in the number and size of prosphoras used in different national churches. Greek parishes use a single large prosphoron, but Slavic parishes use five smaller prosphoras; on Mount Athos, two prosphoras are used. The prosphoras in the time of Saint Symeon of Thessalonika (fifteenth century) were square in shape, but the seal itself was round. Sweet, red wine is needed for the Eucharist; white wine, sherry or non-alcoholic wines are not permitted to be used under any circumstances.

Before beginning the Liturgy, the priest and deacon stand before the Royal Doors and read the preparation prayers in which they ask that

---

[30] St. Symeon of Thessalonika, *The Liturgical Commentaries* p. 191.

they be strengthened for the service. They then kiss the icons of the Saviour and the Mother of God and turn and bow to the congregation, asking their forgiveness and prayers. The clergy then enter the altar and prostrate or bow before the Holy Table; then they kiss the Gospel Book and the Holy Table. The priest then greets the deacon by saying, 'Christ is in our midst,' to which the deacon replies: 'He is and ever shall be.'

Both priest and deacon then put on their vestments, reading the appointed verse from the psalms as they do so, reflecting the spiritual significance of each vestment and the virtues which should adorn the clergy. Having vested, they wash their hands, as they say Psalm 25.

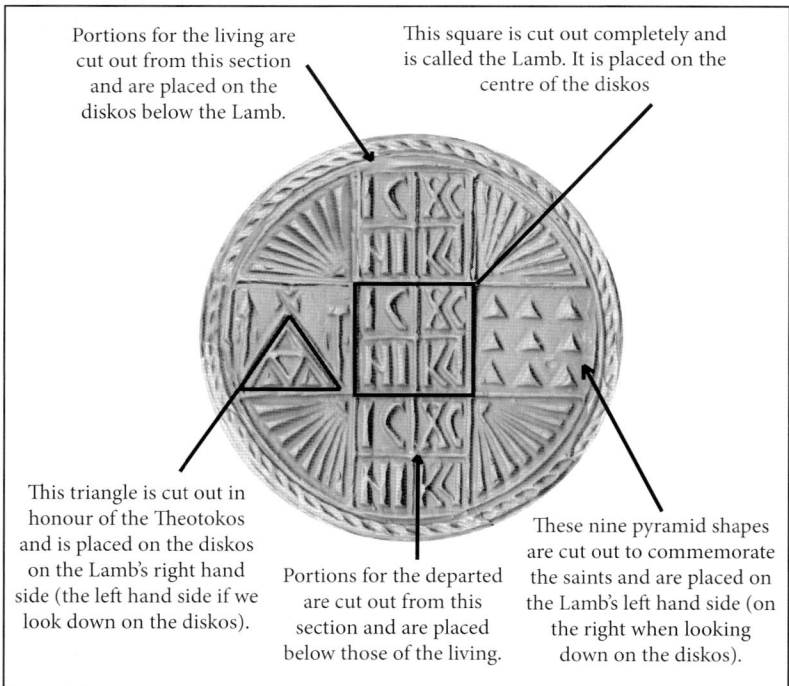

Portions for the living are cut out from this section and are placed on the diskos below the Lamb.

This square is cut out completely and is called the Lamb. It is placed on the centre of the diskos

This triangle is cut out in honour of the Theotokos and is placed on the diskos on the Lamb's right hand side (the left hand side if we look down on the diskos).

Portions for the departed are cut out from this section and are placed below those of the living.

These nine pyramid shapes are cut out to commemorate the saints and are placed on the Lamb's left hand side (on the right when looking down on the diskos).

Diagram showing how the particles are cut out of the prosphoron during the Service of Preparation

The Service of Preparation

The first part of the Liturgy, during which the bread and wine are prepared on the Prothesis Table, is called the Service of Preparation or *Proskomedia*. *Prothesis* is a Greek word meaning 'preparation', and *proskomedia* means 'offering'. The Prothesis Table is smaller than the Holy Table and is normally situated in the north-east corner of the altar. The structure of the Service of Preparation is outlined below:

- Using the lance (*right*), the priest makes four cuts on each side of the Lamb, and at each cut he repeats the words of the Prophet Esaias: 'He was led as a sheep to the slaughter; As a blameless lamb dumb before his shearer, so opened He not His mouth; In His humiliation His judgment was taken away; and who shall declare His generation?'

- The Lamb is taken out of the prosphoron, as the priest says, 'For His life is taken up from the earth.' It is then almost completely cut into four quarters from the underside and then placed upright on the *diskos* (*left*). The priest then pierces the Lamb on the right side with the lance, in remembrance of our Saviour being pierced with the lance when He was crucified.

- Wine and water are poured into the chalice, just as blood and water flowed from the Saviour's pierced side.

- A triangular portion is cut out in honour and memory of the Theotokos, and is placed on the diskos on the right side of the Lamb, in accordance with the prophecy in the Psalms: 'At Thy right hand stood the Queen, arrayed in a vesture of inwoven gold, adorned in varied colours' (Ps. 44:9).

- Nine small triangular portions are removed to commemorate the Saints and placed in three rows of three to the left of the Lamb.

- Portions are removed to commemorate the bishop of the diocese, and all Orthodox Christians.

- Portions to commemorate the Orthodox faithful departed are taken from the fifth section of the seal.

- The priest blesses the incense, censes the asterisk (*right*) and then places it on the diskos; he censes the veils for the diskos and chalice. After having covered them both with the veils, he censes the *aer* and places it over the covered diskos and chalice.
- The priest then prays that the Lord will accept the offering upon His altar above the heavens, and that He will remember those who have made the offering and those for whom they have made it, and that He preserve those serving 'uncondemned in the priestly ministry'. After this prayer, he gives the dismissal and the Service of Preparation is completed.

The Lamb in the centre of the diskos represents Christ the Head of the Church. It is surrounded by portions representing all the members of the Church: the choirs of the saints in heaven and the Orthodox members of the Church here below, both the living and the departed.

The prosphoron also represents the All-holy Virgin Mary, and its placing on the Prothesis Table represents the journey of the Holy Virgin and St. Joseph to Bethlehem. The taking of the Lamb out of the prosphoron represents the birth of Jesus Christ from the Virgin Mary. The Prothesis Table, at this moment, represents the cave where Christ was born, and the diskos the manger, in which He was laid. The chalice veils represent the swaddling bands in which Christ was wrapped, the asterisk is the star which appeared to the Wise Men, and the censer and the incense represent the gifts which they offered to Christ.

Christ was born so that by becoming man, the Son of God might destroy death and sin by the Cross and His Resurrection. It is for this reason that the Church remembers in the Service of Preparation not only Christ's birth in Bethlehem but also His Passion, death and burial.

The priest pierces the Lamb with the lance commemorating the piercing of Christ's side by a spear at the Crucifixion and at this moment the prothesis table represents Golgotha where Christ was crucified, the diskos the tomb, and the chalice veils the cloths that were used to wrap the body of Christ.

There are a number of variations in how the Service of Preparation is served. In the Slavic churches, five small prosphoras are used: the Lamb is taken from one; the triangle for the Mother of God from the second, and particles for the saints, the living and the reposed from the other three. On Mount Athos, two large prosphoras are used: the Lamb is taken from one, and the triangle honouring the Mother of God and the particles for the Saints are taken from the other. In the Slavic practice, members of the congregation bring small prosphoras and submit lists of names to be commemorated. Particles are taken from these prosphoras, placed on the diskos and the used prosphoron is returned as a blessing for those requesting prayers.

Only Orthodox people may be commemorated in the Service of Preparation because as St. Symeon of Thessalonika explains:

> *It is also not at all right for a priest to make an offering for a heterodox or make a commemoration of him; neither is he permitted to do so for those openly sinning and unrepentant. For the offering is to their condemnation, just as it is also for the unrepentant who receive communion of the awe-inspiring mysteries, as the divine Paul says.*[31]

When submitting names for commemoration, make sure that everyone on the list is Orthodox, and that the names are clearly divided into dead and living.

---

[31] St. Symeon of Thessalonika, *The Liturgical Commentaries* pp.231-233.

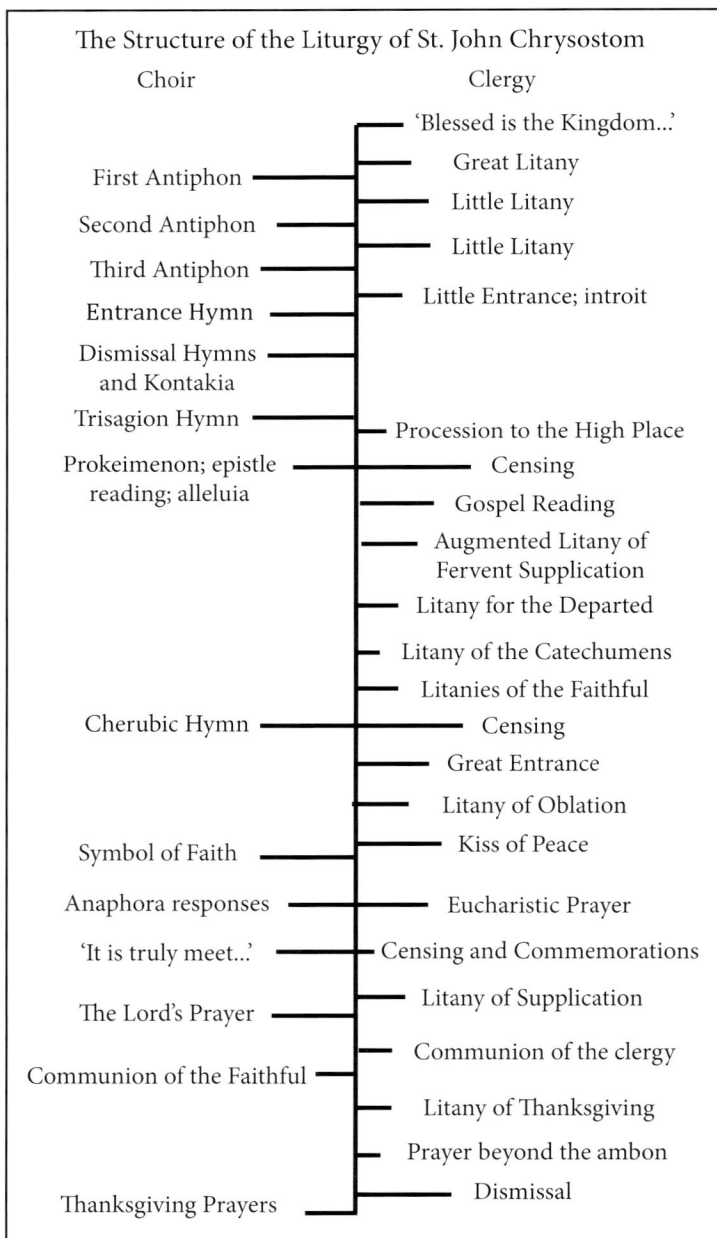

The Structure of the Liturgy of St. John Chrysostom

Choir	Clergy
	'Blessed is the Kingdom...'
First Antiphon	Great Litany
	Little Litany
Second Antiphon	
	Little Litany
Third Antiphon	
Entrance Hymn	Little Entrance; introit
Dismissal Hymns and Kontakia	
Trisagion Hymn	
	Procession to the High Place
Prokeimenon; epistle reading; alleluia	Censing
	Gospel Reading
	Augmented Litany of Fervent Supplication
	Litany for the Departed
	Litany of the Catechumens
	Litanies of the Faithful
Cherubic Hymn	Censing
	Great Entrance
	Litany of Oblation
Symbol of Faith	Kiss of Peace
Anaphora responses	Eucharistic Prayer
'It is truly meet...'	Censing and Commemorations
The Lord's Prayer	Litany of Supplication
Communion of the Faithful	Communion of the clergy
	Litany of Thanksgiving
	Prayer beyond the ambon
Thanksgiving Prayers	Dismissal

The Liturgy of the Catechumens

The second part of the Liturgy, which consists of prayers, hymns and Scripture readings from the New Testament, is called the Liturgy of the Catechumens, and is primarily a service of teaching and instruction.

The priest, standing before the Holy Table, raises his hands in prayer to the Lord, and quietly reads the prayer 'O Heavenly King, Comforter…' and the following verses: 'Glory to God in the highest, and on earth peace good will among men (*twice*); O Lord, Thou shalt open my lips and my mouth shall declare Thy praise.' He then exclaims aloud: **'Blessed is the Kingdom of the Father, and of the Son, and of the Holy Spirit, now and ever, and unto the ages of ages,'** as he makes the sign of the Cross with the Gospel Book over the antimension which lies folded up on the Holy Table.

The Antiphons

After the Litany of Peace, the choir sings three antiphons separated by Little Litanies. The word 'antiphon' is used for verses that are sung alternately by two choirs, or that consist of a verse followed by a response. On most Sundays, the First Antiphon is Psalm 102 and the Second Antiphon is Psalm 145; these 'Typical Psalms' are so called because they describe the blessings that will come upon us through the mystery of the Liturgy: such prefigurings are called 'types' in theology. In his commentary on the Divine Liturgy, St. Nicolas Cabasilas explains that the antiphons are sung at the beginning of the Liturgy because, like the prophets, they prefigure both the Incarnation and the mystery of the Eucharist:

> *The sacrifice commemorates the death, resurrection, and ascension of our Lord, since the precious gifts are changed into the very Body of the Saviour, that Body which rose from the dead and ascended into heaven. Those acts which precede the sacrifice recall the events which took place before His death – His coming, His first appearance, and His perfect manifestation.*[32]

---

[32] St. Nicholas Cabasilas, *A Commentary on the Divine Liturgy* (trans. J.M. Hussey, P.A. McNulty) (London: SPCK, 1977) p.52.

The hymn 'Only-begotten Son and Word of God…' is always sung at the end of the Second Antiphon in which we confess our belief in the incarnation, crucifixion and resurrection of the Son of God, Who, even after the incarnation, was not separated from the Father and the Holy Spirit. St. Maximus the Confessor teaches:

> In becoming incarnate, the Word of God teaches us the mystical knowledge of God because He shows us in Himself the Father and the Holy Spirit. For the full Father and the full Holy Spirit are essentially and completely in the full Son, even the incarnated Son, without being themselves incarnate. Rather, the Father gives approval and the Spirit cooperates in the incarnation with the Son who effected it, since the Word remained in possession of His own mind and life, contained in essence by no other than the Father and the Spirit, while hypostatically realizing out of love for man the union with the flesh.[33]

After another Little Litany, the Beatitudes from the Gospel of St. Matthew (Matt. 5:3-12) are chanted with the appointed troparia from the canon of Matins between them.

The Typical Psalms and the Beatitudes are not sung on Great Feasts, but are replaced by antiphons specific to the Feast in which psalm verses that foretell New Testament events are alternated with refrains. Together, these show that the festal celebration is a fulfilment of ancient prophesies concerning the Saviour, and indicate the essential message of the feast as St. Symeon of Thessalonika explains:

> The choir sing the antiphons, typifying the choir of the prophets. They divide these in three, honouring the Trinity, saying first the psalm verses and then adding on the hymns of grace. Through the psalmic verses they were proclaimed in advance, and to the ancients they announce the incarnation of the Word of God, while the hymns of praise set forth the accomplished grace itself and the incarnate Son of God and everything done for us.[34]

---

[33] St. Maximus the Confessor, *Selected Writings* (trans. G. Berthold) (Mahwah: Paulist Press, 1985) p. 103.

[34] St. Symeon of Thessalonika, *The Liturgical Commentaries* p. 113.

The Little Entrance

At the beginning of the Beatitudes or the Third Antiphon, the Royal Doors are opened, indicating that the Kingdom of Heaven is now opened to the people.[35] After kissing the Holy Table, the priest takes the Gospel Book and gives it to the deacon. Led by a candle-bearer, they leave through the north door of the altar and stand before the Royal Doors. The deacon, after asking the priest to bless the entrance, raises the Gospel Book and making the sign of the Cross with it, exclaims: **Wisdom, Upright!** The deacon enters the altar through the Royal Doors and places the Gospel book on the Holy Table as the choir chant:

O come let us worship and fall down before Christ. O Son of God, risen from the dead, save us who chant to Thee, Alleluia.

This hymn is used on Sundays and during the Paschal Season. On weekdays the entrance hymn is:

O come let us worship and fall down before Christ. O Son of God, wondrous in Thy saints, save us who chant to Thee, Alleluia.

Great Feasts of the Saviour have their own entrance hymns. For example the hymn sung on the Nativity of Christ is:

O Son of God, born of a Virgin, save us who chant to Thee: Alleluia.

The Little Entrance symbolizes the Saviour's preaching. The candle which is carried in front of the Gospel Book represents John the Forerunner who went before Jesus Christ as 'a burning and shining light' (John 5:35); the opening of the Royal Doors shows us that the Kingdom of Heaven is now opened to the people, and the Gospel Book signifies the coming of the Son of God and His entrance into the world.

After the Little Entrance, while the choir chants the appointed hymns of the day, the priest, standing before the Holy Table, silently prays

---

[35] Senior priests by rank are permitted to serve with them open from the beginning of the Liturgy.

that the Lord will accept the chanting of the Trisagion Hymn; this silent prayer ends with the exclamation: '**For holy art Thou, O our God, and unto Thee do we send up glory, to the Father, and to the Son, and to the Holy Spirit, now and ever.**'

The deacon, coming out through the Royal Doors, exclaims '**O Lord, save the pious and hearken unto us,**' which the choir repeat. Then facing the people, holding up his *orarion*, he completes the priestly exclamation by saying '**and unto the ages of ages**'.

The Chanting of the Trisagion

The choir now sings the Trisagion Hymn sequence:

H oly God, Holy Mighty, Holy Immortal, have mercy on us (thrice)

 Glory to the Father and to the Son and to the Holy Spirit, both now and ever and unto the ages of ages. Amen.

 Holy Immortal have mercy on us.

 Holy God, Holy Mighty, Holy Immortal, have mercy on us.

The word Trisagion means 'three holies' (the Greek word for 'holy' is agios) so this hymn is often referred to as the 'thrice holy hymn' and is inspired by the words of the Prophet Esaias who describes the hymn of the angels as 'Holy, Holy, Holy, Lord of Sabaoth' (Is. 6:3). The Trisagion hymn, as it is used today, dates from the time of Emperor Theodosius II. During a powerful earthquake in Constantinople, a small child reported that he had heard the Angels in the Heavens chanting: Holy God, Holy Mighty, Holy Immortal. The people, recognizing this as a divine revelation immediately began to chant this hymn, added their own supplication, 'Have mercy on us', and the earthquake ceased.

By singing the Trisagion, we confess our belief in the Trinity together with the angels as St. Germanos of Constantinople explains:

> *[In heaven] the angels say, 'Glory to God in the highest'; here, like the Magi, we bring gifts to Christ – faith, hope and love like gold, frankincense and myrrh – and like the bodiless hosts we cry in faith: 'Holy God', that is the Father; 'Holy Mighty', that is the Son and Word, for He has bound the mighty devil and made him who*

had dominion over death powerless though the cross and He has given us Life by trampling on him; 'Holy immortal', that is the Holy Spirit, the giver of life, through whom all creation is made alive and cries out 'have mercy on us'.[36]

On the feasts of Pascha, the Nativity of Christ, the Baptism of the Lord, Pentecost, Lazarus Saturday and Great Saturday, the Trisagion Hymn is replaced by 'All ye that in Christ have been baptized, Christ have ye put on. Alleluia.' On the feast of the Exaltation of the Cross (14th September) and on the Sunday of the Cross in Great Lent, we sing: 'Thy Cross do we worship, O Master, and Thy holy Resurrection do we glorify.' The structure of the sequence remains exactly the same.

The Trisagion sequence is elongated when a bishop serves the Liturgy. There are differences between the Greek, Slavic and Romanian usages, but in each tradition one of the repetitions of the Trisagion is divided up. As the choir sings 'Holy God', the bishop leaves the altar through the Royal Doors and blesses the people with the *dikirion* and *trikirion* whilst saying: 'Lord, O Lord, look down from heaven and behold and visit this vine which Thy right hand hath planted' (cf. Ps. 79:15-16). The choir then sings 'Holy Mighty' and the bishop blesses again and repeats the same verse and does so again after the choir sings 'Holy Immortal'; the choir then completes the Trisagion with 'have mercy on us'.

The Prokeimenon, Epistle Reading and Alleluia

The reader and choir chant the appointed prokeimenon, during which the deacon censes the altar and people, symbolizing the grace which is spread abroad like incense by the Gospel teaching which is soon to be heard. During the Epistle reading, the priests sit in the High Place, indicating that, like the apostles, they have been given authority to preach.

At the end of the Epistle reading, the choir and the reader sing the Alleluia a word which is based on the Hebrew for 'Praise God'. St. Germanos of Constantinople explains further that AL means 'He comes, He appears'; EL means 'God' and OUIA means 'praise and sing hymns' to the living God. The Alleluia is sung three times to honour and praise the Godhead of three persons.

---

[36] St. Germanos of Constantinople, *On the Divine Liturgy* (trans. P. Meyendorff) (New York: SVS Press, 1985) p. 75.

The Gospel Reading

The word 'gospel' itself means 'good news' and the Gospels speak to us of the good news brought to us by the Son of God's incarnation. God no longer speaks to us indistinctly through a cloud as He did to Moses, or through thunder and lightning and trumpets, but He has now appeared visibly as God and Man. The reading of the Gospel is actually the second appearance of the Gospel book during the Divine Liturgy, and this signifies the gradual manifestation of the Saviour to the world as St. Nicolas Cabasilas explains:

> *The first appearance of the Gospel [At the Little Entrance], with the book closed, represents the first manifestation of the Saviour, when, while He himself remained silent, the Father bare Him witness; He remained silent, and it was another's voice that proclaimed Him. That which is represented here is the more perfect manifestation, when He mingled with the crowd and made Himself known not only by His own words, but also by that which He taught to His apostles when He sent them to the lost sheep of the house of Israel.*

The Augmented Litany of Fervent Supplication

After the reading of the Gospel, the priest descends from the High Place as the choir chants 'Glory to Thee O God, Glory to Thee'. The Augmented Litany of Fervent Supplication is now intoned, and during it, the *antimension* on the Holy Table is partially unfolded. This is often done as the bishop is commemorated to indicate that the priest is serving on his behalf. On weekdays, there is also a Litany for the Faithful Departed, in which we pray for the remission of sins of those Orthodox Christians who have departed this life. This Litany is also used at memorial services.

The Litany of the Catechumens

In the Litany of the Catechumens we pray that the Lord will grant the catechumens to be worthy of Holy Baptism and we pray more generally for all the non-Orthodox that they may 'come to the knowledge of the truth' (1 Tim. 2:4). During this litany, the antimension is completely unfolded when the deacon says '**reveal unto them the Gospel**

of righteousness'. The catechumens bow their heads as the choir sings 'to Thee O Lord', and the priest reads the following prayer quietly:

> O Lord our God, who dwellest on high and lookest upon the humble, Who didst send forth Thine only-begotten Son and God, our Lord Jesus Christ, for the salvation of the race of men; Look down upon Thy servants the catechumens, who bow before Thee; make them worthy in due season of the bath of regeneration, the forgiveness of sins and the robe of incorruption. Unite them to Thy Holy Catholic and Apostolic Church, and number them with Thy chosen flock.

The 'robe of incorruption', referred to in the prayer above, is the baptismal robe. During the exclamation: **'that they with us also…',** the priest makes the sign of the Cross over the antimension with the sponge that is kept within it. This sponge is used to gather up any crumbs after the communion of the clergy and the placing of the particles from the diskos into the chalice. He then kisses the sponge and places it on the top-right-hand corner of the antimension.

The catechumens are now dismissed because they are not yet worthy to take part in the greatest mystery, the Communion of the Body and Blood of Christ. Below, Saint Maximus the Confessor describes the spiritual significance behind this separation of the catechumens from the faithful:

> *The priest's descent from his special seat, and the dismissal of the catechumens, represents the second coming from heaven of our great God and Saviour Jesus Christ, which is followed by the separation of the sinners from the saints, with just retribution for the deeds of each.*

This dismissal of the catechumens marks the end of the second part of the Liturgy.

The Liturgy of the Faithful

The third part of the Liturgy is called the Liturgy of the Faithful, because only baptized Orthodox Christians (the faithful) are permitted to attend.[37] The Liturgy of the Faithful begins with the deacon intoning a Litany which begins: '**As many as are of the faithful, again and again in peace let us pray to the Lord.**' Before the exclamation by the priest the deacon exclaims '**Wisdom!**' to draw our attention to the importance of the sacred rites to come.

The Cherubic Hymn

After these litanies, the Royal Doors are opened, and the choir begins to chant the Cherubic Hymn:

> **Let us who mystically portray the Cherubim, and chant the thrice-holy hymn unto the life-creating Trinity, lay aside all earthly care: That we may receive the King of all, escorted invisibly by the angelic orders. Alleluia, Alleluia, Alleluia.**

At this moment we should remember that we are members of the Church together with the Seraphim, Cherubim and all the other angels. We should join with them in praising God as St. John Chrysostom says:

> *On high the armies of angels are giving praise. Here below, in the Church, the human choir offers the same doxology. The Seraphim above cry the Thrice Holy Hymn; on earth, crowds of people join together in singing the same hymn. The festival of heaven's citizens is united with the inhabitants of earth in a single thanksgiving, a single upsurge of happiness, a single chorus of joy.*[38]

In the Cherubic Hymn we are reminded to 'lay aside all earthly care' and to follow the advice of St. John Chrysostom: 'As the Magi came out of Persia to go and worship Christ, so let us withdraw from the concerns of everyday life and make our way towards Jesus.'

---

[37] In most parishes, this rule is relaxed somewhat.

[38] Adapted from C.A. Hall, *Worshipping with the Church Fathers* (Downers Grove: Intervarsity Press, 2009) pp.69-70

The Great Entrance

During the chanting, the priest prays silently that he be permitted to offer the prepared gifts, and the deacon censes the church. They then approach the Prothesis Table, and the priest, taking the aer from the gifts, places it on the shoulder of the deacon and gives him the diskos which the deacon holds above his head. The priest takes the chalice, and led by a candle-bearer they leave the altar by the north door, and process into the middle of the church (or in some usages, only to the centre of the ambon). As they leave the altar the deacon exclaims: '**May the Lord God remember you all in His Kingdom, always, now and ever, and unto the ages of ages.**'

In many parishes, instead of the exclamation above, the deacon commemorates the bishop of the diocese in a special petition taken from the hierarchical Liturgy. In many parishes, the priest then commemorates the faithful departed by name, and those of the Orthodox who celebrate on that particular day. At the end of these commemorations the priest exclaims again: '**May the Lord God remember you all in His Kingdom, always, now and ever, and unto the ages of ages.**' The clergy return to the altar through the Royal Doors and the choir completes the Cherubic Hymn:

> That we may receive the King of all, escorted invisibly by the angelic orders. Alleluia, Alleluia, Alleluia.

When they reach the Holy Table, the priest places the diskos and chalice on the opened antimension, and covers them both with the aer; he then censes the gifts that have been offered.

The Great Entrance is an image of the burial of Christ; His Body was taken down from the Cross, wrapped in clean linen and spices and laid for burial in a tomb. The altar is an image of the tomb, the Holy Table is the stone on which the Body of Christ was placed, and the diskos represents the hand of Joseph and Nicodemos who buried Christ and anointed His Body with sweet-smelling spices; the cover on the diskos corresponds to the cloth which lay upon Christ's head; the aer represents the stone which closed the tomb; the incense represents the fragrant spices, myrrh and aloes with which the Body of

Christ was anointed. The closing of the Royal Doors and the drawing of the curtain across them represents the sealing of the stone of the tomb and the soldiers that guarded it.

The Litany of Oblation

After the Great Entrance, the deacon intones the Litany of Oblation, which is similar in structure to the Litany of Supplication but which includes the special petition **'for the precious gifts set forth…'**. After the priest says **'Peace be unto all'**, the deacon exclaims: **'Let us love one another, that with one mind we may confess.'** As the choir chants in response, 'Father, Son, and Holy Spirit, the Trinity one in essence and undivided', the clergy bow down three times before the Holy Table and silently say: 'I will love Thee, O Lord, my strength; the Lord is my foundation, and my refuge, and my deliverer.' They kiss the covered diskos and chalice and the edge of the Holy Table and then greet each other with a threefold kiss, the senior one saying: 'Christ is in our midst,' and the others replying: 'He is and shall be.' The kiss used to be exchanged by all the faithful and has, according to St. Symeon of Thessalonika, a symbolic significance:

> While the sacred creed is recited, the kiss occurs because through the right confession of the Trinity, and of the one of the Trinity who was incarnate, the union with us has occurred. It is this confession which has united us to the angels; and because it is necessary to love one another, since Christ was sacrificed through love, and because the one preparing to receive Him in communion must not approach with anger, and because in the future age all will be friends, and none will be enemies then, for enemies will have been cast out.[39]

The Creed

The Creed, or Symbol of Faith, is a statement of our Orthodox Faith and, as St. Maximus the Confessor makes clear, signifies the 'mystical thanksgiving which we shall offer in the next life for the wondrous events and ways in which the all-wise providence of God has dealt with us, by which we have been saved.'[40]

---

[39] St. Symeon of Thessalonika, *The Liturgical Commentaries* p. 133.
[40] Gregorios, *The Divine Liturgy: A Commentary in the Light of the Fathers* p. 214.

As the deacon exclaims, '**The doors! The doors! In wisdom let us attend!**' the curtain behind the Royal Doors is opened. The Creed is now recited during which the priest lifts the aer from the gifts and gently waves it over them.

The exclamation 'The doors!' refers to the practice of the Early Church when the doors would be closed to secure the church building, and it also reminds us to guard the doors of our hearts and minds from worldly concerns. The opening of the curtain represents the opening of the tomb, and the waving of the aer signifies both the over-shadowing of the Holy Gifts by the power and grace of the Holy Spirit and the earthquake at the time of Christ's Resurrection.

The closing of the doors further represents our progress from simple faith by the guarding of our thoughts; the Great Entrance enacts our initiation into the mysteries, and the kiss of peace our oneness in faith and love with our fellow Christians leading to the pure Orthodox piety summarized in the reciting of the Creed. Saint Maximus the Confessor also links this gradual progress through the Liturgy to the spiritual life itself, in which we progress through the ascetical and mystical life of the Church to the vision of God.

The Anaphora

When the Creed is finished, the deacon exclaims: '**Let us stand well. Let us stand with fear. Let us attend, that we may offer the holy oblation in peace,**' and the choir responds, 'A mercy of peace, a sacrifice of praise', to proclaim our joy in the Resurrection as St. Germanos of Constantinople explains:

> *Thus Christ is crucified, life is buried, the tomb is secured, the stone is sealed. In the company of the angelic powers, the priest approaches, standing no longer as on earth, but attending at the heavenly altar, before the altar of the throne of God, and he contemplates the great, ineffable, and unsearchable mystery of God. He gives thanks, proclaims the resurrection, and confirms the faith in the holy Trinity. The angel wearing white approaches the stone of the tomb and rolls it away with his hand, pointing with his garment and exclaiming with an awed voice through the deacon, who proclaims the resurrection on the third day, raising the veil*

> *and saying 'let us stand aright' – behold the first day! 'Let us stand*
> *in fear' – behold the second day! – 'Let us offer in peace'– behold*
> *the third day! The people proclaim thanks for the resurrection of*
> *Christ: 'a mercy of peace, a sacrifice of praise'.*[41]

This part of the Liturgy is called the *anaphora* (lit. 'offering up') because, during it, bread and wine are offered to God. The priest then
blesses the people and says: 'The grace of our Lord Jesus Christ, and
the love of God the Father, and the communion of the Holy Spirit be
with you all' (2 Cor. 13:14). Below, St. Nicolas Cabasilas shows how
this prayer expounds the Orthodox doctrine of the Trinity:

> *This prayer is taken from the Epistles of St. Paul. It procures for*
> *us the benefits of the Holy Trinity – every perfect gift; and it asks*
> *from each of the Divine Persons His special gift; from the Son*
> *grace, from the Father love, from the Spirit fellowship. For the Son*
> *gave Himself as Saviour to us who not only had bestowed nothing*
> *upon Him, but also were already in His debt…, for 'while we were*
> *yet sinners, Christ died for us' (Rom. 5:8); His care for us then is*
> *in the truest sense a grace. The Father, through the sufferings of*
> *His Son, was reconciled to mankind, and showered His love upon*
> *His enemies, so that His goodness to us is given the name of love.*
> *Finally, the Being 'rich in mercy' (Eph. 2:4) wished to give to His*
> *enemies, who had now become His friends, the best of Himself;*
> *this the Holy Spirit achieved when He descended upon the apos-*
> *tles; that is why His goodness is called fellowship.*[42]

The priest then asks us to free our minds and hearts from everything
earthly, and to raise them up to that which is heavenly by exclaiming: **'Let us lift up our hearts.'** The choir then answers on our behalf:
'We lift them up to the Lord.'

Following the example of the Saviour, Who, at the Mystical Supper,
offered up thanks to God the Father at the breaking of the bread, the
priest exclaims: 'Let us give thanks unto the Lord.' The choir answers
by singing the hymn in which we confess that God is one in essence
and three in persons: 'Meet and right it is to worship Father, Son, and

---

[41] St. Germanos of Constantinople, *On the Divine Liturgy* pp. 89-91.

[42] St. Nicholas Cabasilas, *A Commentary on the Divine Liturgy* pp. 68-69.

Holy Spirit, the Trinity one in essence and undivided.' The Greek word *ousia* is translated as essence in the hymn above, but is often translated as 'nature' or 'substance'; the phrase 'one in essence' is sometimes therefore rendered as 'consubstantial'.

The Church developed its theological vocabulary as a response to various heretical challenges to traditional Christian doctrine. Arius, for example, denied that Christ is also 'consubstantial' or 'one in essence' with the Father and the Holy Spirit - in other words, he did not believe that Christ is perfect God and man.

During this hymn the priest starts to read the Eucharistic Prayer which is divided into three sections. In the first, all God's gifts to man are commemorated: the creation of the world, the restoration of mankind through Jesus Christ, and all the other acts of goodness, both those which are known and those unknown, visible and invisible. This section of the Eucharistic Prayer ends with the priest saying out loud: **'Singing the triumphal hymn, shouting, crying and saying...'** The choir responds by chanting the hymn:

Holy, Holy, Holy, Lord God of Sabaoth! Heaven and earth are full of thy glory. Hosanna in the highest: Blessed is He that cometh in the name of the Lord. Hosanna in the highest.

This hymn is based on the hymn of the angels described by the Prophet Esaias (Is. 6:3), combined with that sung by the people when Christ entered Jerusalem (Matthew 21:9). In this hymn we join with the angels in the present, and in the hope that we will be with them, praising God in the life eternal. St. Maximus the Confessor explains this further when he says:

> *The threefold acclamation of holiness, which all the faithful sing in praise of God, is an intimation of future unity and equality with the incorporeal and spiritual powers; in this unity, mankind will learn to join with one voice in the unchanging perpetual motion about God of the higher powers praising the glory of the one God in three persons with the three acclamations of holiness.*[43]

[43] D.J. Stead, *The Church, the Liturgy and the Soul of Man* (Still River: St. Bede's Publications, 1982) p. 94.

The priest now starts the second part of the Eucharistic Prayer silently. After offering praise to all three persons of the Holy Trinity, he specially refers to the Son of God in particular recalling how Christ initiated the mystery of the Eucharist:

> …on the night He was betrayed, or rather gave Himself up for the life of the world, He took Bread in His holy and immaculate and blameless hands, and when He had given thanks, and blessed, and hallowed, and broken it, He gave it to His holy disciples and apostles, saying **Take, eat: This is My Body, which is broken for you, for the remission of sins.**

The choir responds 'Amen', and the priest continues silently with the Eucharistic Prayer:

> In like manner also, He took the cup when He had supped, saying: **Drink ye all from it: This is My Blood of the new testament, which is shed for you and for many, for the remission of sins.**

The choir answers 'Amen' and the priest continues:

> Having in remembrance therefore, this saving commandment and all those things that have come to pass for us: the Cross, the grave, the Resurrection on the third day, the Ascension into the heavens, the sitting at the right hand, and the second and glorious coming:

At the exclamation, '**Thine own of Thine own we offer unto Thee, because of all and for all,**' the priest (or deacon if there is one) picks up the chalice with his left hand and the diskos with his right, and lifts them above his head. This exclamation emphasizes that God is offered what is already His, because He is the Creator of all. In response the choir chants: 'We hymn Thee, we bless Thee, we give thanks to Thee, O Lord, and we entreat Thee, O our God,' and the priest begins the third part of the Eucharistic Prayer:

> Again, we offer unto Thee this reasonable and unbloody service, and we ask, we entreat, and we supplicate: Send down Thy Holy Spirit upon us, and upon these Gifts set forth* and make

this bread the precious Body of Thy Christ. Amen. And that which is in this Cup the precious Blood of Thy Christ. Amen. Changing them by Thy Holy Spirit. Amen. Amen. Amen.

During this prayer, the priest makes the sign of the Cross over the Lamb on the diskos, then over the chalice, and then over both together. This is the most sacred moment in the Liturgy when the bread and wine are changed into the Body and Blood of the Saviour. The clergy and all those in the church make a deep bow or a prostration to the ground. In the Slavic Churches a prayer of the Third Hour 'O Lord Who at the third hour didst send down Thine All-holy Spirit…' is read three times at the point marked * in the prayer above.

As he censes the Body and Blood of Christ before him on the Holy Table, the priest prays that the mysteries may not be unto condemnation for those that receive them, but for the remission of sins, eternal life, and the inheritance of the Kingdom of Heaven.

The Commemorations

During the Eucharist, the Church prayerfully commemorates all Her members, both the departed and the living, and especially the Mother of God, and it is for this reason that the next exclamation is: **'Especially our all-holy, immaculate, exceedingly blessed, glorious Lady Theotokos and Ever-Virgin Mary.'** The choir responds by chanting this hymn of praise to the Mother of God:

It is truly meet to call thee blest, the Theotokos, the ever blessed and all immaculate and Mother of our God. More honourable than the Cherubim and beyond compare more glorious than the Seraphim, thee who without corruption gavest birth to God the Word, the very Theotokos do we magnify.

The Mother of God is glorified immediately after the consecration of the Holy Gifts because Christ became incarnate from her and she was the first to serve Christ. On Great Feasts, this hymn is replaced by the irmos of the Ninth Ode of the festal canon.

The priest now commemorates, by name, the saints of the day, the faithful departed and the living, and makes special reference to the bishop of the diocese by saying:

> **Among the first, remember, O Lord, our Bishop [*Name*] and grant that he may serve Thy holy Churches in peace, safety, honour, health, length of days, rightly proclaiming the word of Thy truth.**

The Church embraces all Orthodox believers in Her prayers, living and departed, male and female, those in the priestly ministry and those whose priestly ministry is to be laymen (cf. 1. Pet. 2:9), so at this point we silently remember by name our Orthodox relatives and all those whom we wish to call to mind. To the priest's exclamation the deacon adds: '**And all whom each hath in mind, each and every one**', and the choir responds: 'Each and every pious and Orthodox Christian'.

The Litany of Supplication

Through Christ we have become acceptable to the Father, and have obtained boldness through the Blood of Christ to enter into the Holy of Holies (cf. Hebrews 10:19-20). Our preparation for the reception of the Holy Gifts continues with the Supplicatory Litany that begins:

> **Calling to remembrance all the saints, again and again in peace let us pray to the Lord.**
>
> **For the precious Gifts offered and hallowed, let us pray to the Lord.**
>
> **That our man-befriending God, Who hath accepted Them upon His holy and noetic altar above the heavens for an odour of spiritual fragrance, will send down upon us divine grace and the gift of the Holy Spirit, let us pray.**

During these petitions, the priest prays silently that the Lord will grant him, and all the faithful, to be worthy to partake of the Holy Mysteries. The last petition of this litany is a special one emphasizing that we are bound together by our Orthodox faith: '**Having asked for the unity of the Faith and the communion of the Holy Spirit, let us commend ourselves and one another and all our life unto Christ our God.**'

The Lord's Prayer; the Elevation and Breaking of the Lamb

The priest then continues: '**And vouchsafe, O Master, that with boldness and without condemnation we may dare to call upon Thee, the Heavenly God, as Father, and to say**'. The faithful and clergy together then say the Lord's Prayer. This prayer, as St. Maximus the Confessor says, confirms that we are adopted by grace as sons, and are therefore become equal to the angels (Luke 20:36) and inheritors of eternal life (Titus 3:7).

> *We are taught to proclaim the grace of our adoption, since we have been found worthy of addressing our Creator by nature as our Father by grace. Thus, venerating this title of our begetter by grace, we should strive to stamp the characteristics of the Father on our lives, sanctifying His name on earth, taking after Him as our Father, showing ourselves to be His children through our actions, and through all that we think or do glorifying the author of this adoption, who is by nature Son of the Father.*[44]

Through the sacrifice of Christ we are reconciled to God; we call upon Him as our Father, and we ask that we may be communicants of that mystical bread which we receive in the Eucharist. This prayer, as St. Maximus the Confessor explains further, contains things that are openly proclaimed but, at the same time, mysteriously hidden:

> *[This prayer] teaches us to strive for those goods of which only God the Father through the natural mediation of the Son in the Holy Spirit is in all truth the bestower, since according to the divine Apostle, the Lord Jesus is 'mediator between God and men'. Through His flesh He made manifest to men the Father whom they did not know, and through the Spirit He leads the men whom He reconciled in Himself to the Father. For them and on their account, He became man without any change, and He Himself worked and taught many new mysteries whose number and dimension the mind can in no way grasp or meas-*

---

[44] *The Philokalia: The Complete Text Compiled by St. Nikodimos of the Holy Mountain and St. Makarios of Corinth Vol. 2* (trans. G.E.H. Palmer, P. Sherrard, K. Ware) (London: Faber and Faber, 1981) p. 291.

ure. There are seven in number which are more general than the others which He appears to have given to men in his extraordinary generosity.[45]

After the exclamation '**for Thine is the Kingdom…**', the priest blesses the people and all bow their heads whilst the priest reads a prayer quietly:

> We give thanks to Thee, O King invisible, Who by Thy measureless power didst fashion all things, and in the multitude of Thy mercies didst bring all things from non-being into being. Do Thou, O Sovereign Lord, look down from heaven upon them that now bow their heads unto Thee; For they are bowed not before flesh and blood, but unto Thee, O dread God. Bestow on us, therefore, O Lord, these Thy gifts, giving to each according to his need; Sail with them that sail upon the seas; journey with them that travel on dry land; heal the sick, O Thou that art the Physician of souls and bodies.

The prayer ends with the exclamation '**Through the grace and love towards mankind…**' and the priest then reads a second prayer quietly as the choir signs 'Amen'. During the priest's exclamation, '**The Holies are for the holy,**' he raises the Lamb slightly, and the choir sings: 'One is holy, One is Lord, Jesus Christ, to the glory of God the Father. Amen.' This hymn is one of the most ancient in the Liturgy, and in it we hymn Jesus Christ Who is holy by nature, and confirm, as St. Nicholas Cabasilas states, our hope that we can become holy by grace:

> *For no one has holiness of himself; it is not the consequence of human virtue, but comes to all from Him and through Him. It is as if we were to place mirrors beneath the sun; each would shine, and send forth rays of light, so that one would think that there were many suns; yet in truth there is but one sun which shines in all; just so Christ, the only Holy One, pours Himself forth upon the faithful, shines in so many souls, and gives light to many saints; yet He alone is holy, to the glory of God the Father.*[46]

---

[45] St. Maximus the Confessor, *Selected Writings* p. 102.

[46] St. Nicholas Cabasilas, *A Commentary on the Divine Liturgy* p. 89.

St. Maximus the Confessor observes that in singing this hymn we join chorus with the angels:

> *The profession 'One is Holy' and what follows, which is voiced by all the people at the end of the mystical service, represents the gathering and union beyond reason and understanding which will take place between those who have been mystically and wisely initiated by God and the mysterious oneness of the divine simplicity in the incorruptible age of the spiritual world. There they behold the light of the invisible and ineffable glory and become themselves together with the angels on high open to the blessed purity.*[47]

The elevation of the Lamb represents Christ being raised upon the Cross. The priest breaks the Lamb into four pieces and arranges them on the diskos in the form of the Cross. In the breaking of the Lamb, 'the Inseparable One is separated in pieces for our sake, so that we all may partake of Him, and being indivisible He is divided for us, uniting us to Himself, and making us one just as He prayed.'[48]

The priest places one quarter of the Lamb in the Chalice; this union of the Body of Christ with the Divine Blood represents the Resurrection of Christ, just as the flesh of man only becomes living when united with blood. He then pours hot water into the chalice as the deacon says, 'the fervency of faith, full of the Holy Spirit. Amen.' The warmth of the water emphasizes the life-giving energy of the mystery, and the life-giving resurrected Body of the Saviour. The vessel used for the hot water is called a *zeon*, which means 'fervour' or 'boiling' in Greek.

The Communion of the Clergy and Faithful

The curtain is drawn across the Royal Doors and the clergy take Holy Communion within the altar. The priest and deacon receive Holy Communion in their hands, from one quarter of the Lamb; they also drink from the chalice. After this, the deacon or priest (if he is serving alone) prepares the Holy Communion for the lay people by placing

---

[47] Ibid., p. 203.

[48] St. Germanos of Constantinople, *On the Divine Liturgy* p. 257.

the two remaining quarters of the Lamb in the chalice. When this is finished, the curtain and the Royal Doors are opened, and the chalice is brought out as the deacon says, '**In fear of God with faith draw near,**' and the choir replies: 'Blessed is He that cometh in the name of the Lord. God is the Lord and hath appeared unto us.' The drawing back of the curtain symbolizes the rolling away of the stone, and the bringing out of the chalice, the appearing of the Saviour to the myrrh-bearing women after the Resurrection.

Litany of Thanksgiving; Prayer beyond the Ambon

After the Communion of the faithful, the chalice is placed on the Holy Table, and the priest exclaims, facing the people: '**Save O Lord, Thy people and bless Thine inheritance.**' The choir replies with the hymn: 'We have seen the true light…' (on Great Feasts this is replaced by the dismissal hymn of the Feast). As the choir are singing, the asterisk is placed on the diskos, the veils are replaced and the Holy Gifts are censed.

When this is finished, the priest gives the diskos to the deacon who, passing in front of the Holy Table, returns it to the Prothesis Table. The priest, lifting up the chalice says quietly: 'Blessed is our God' and then turning to the people finishes the exclamation aloud: '**always now and ever and unto the ages of ages**'.

The choir answers 'Amen' and then sings the hymn 'fill my mouth with Thy praise…' as the chalice is placed on the Prothesis Table symbolizing the Ascension; the priest censes the chalice, the incense representing the cloud in which Christ was taken up (Acts 1:9). At this moment, the Holy Table represents the Throne of God the Father, and the Prothesis Table the 'place' where the Son of God sits at His right hand.

The deacon then intones the Litany of Thanksgiving. During the exclamation of this Litany, '**For thou art our sanctification, and unto Thee we ascribe glory, to the Father, and to the Son, and to the Holy Spirit,**' the priest takes the Gospel in both hands and makes the sign of the Cross over the folded antimension. This action concludes the Liturgy and is the same action that started it, when the priest made the sign of the Cross when he exclaimed 'Blessed is the Kingdom…'.

The priest then exclaims: '**Let us depart in peace!**' At the beginning of the Liturgy we prayed in peace and so we now leave in peace. We are being sent out into the world having received the gift of the Holy Spirit like the apostles at Pentecost.

The priest then leaves the altar and reads the prayer which begins: '**O Lord, who blessest those who bless Thee and sanctifiest those who put their trust in Thee…**'. This prayer is called the 'Prayer beyond the Ambon' because the priest descends the ambon and then reads the prayer facing the altar.

The Dismissal

The choir then sings, 'Blessed be the Name of the Lord, from henceforth and for evermore' (three times) and the priest gives the appropriate dismissal, after which the prayers of thanksgiving after Holy Communion are read as the faithful come forward to kiss the cross and receive the *antidoron*.

The Liturgy of Saint Basil the Great

The Divine Liturgy of St. Basil is served ten times a year on the following days:

- On the Eves of the Nativity of Christ and Theophany
- On the Feast of the Circumcision which is also the Feast of St. Basil the Great
- The Five Sundays of Great Lent
- Great Thursday and Great Saturday

The Liturgy of St. Basil is similar to that of St. John Chrysostom, but there are some notable differences. In the Liturgy of St. Basil, the secret prayers of the anaphora are longer, and the words that the priest speaks at the time of the consecration are also different; the Prayer beyond the Ambon is also considerably longer. In addition, the hymn 'It is truly meet…' sung after the consecration is replaced by the following:

In thee, O full of grace, all creation – both the company of angels and the race of man – doth rejoice; O hallowed temple and spiritual paradise, boast of virgins; from thee God was incarnate and became a Child, He our God Who existed before the ages; for He made thy womb a throne, and He made thee more spacious than the heavens. In thee O full of grace, all creation doth rejoice; glory be to thee.[49]

On Great Thursday, at the Liturgy of St Basil the Great, the Cherubic Hymn is replaced by the following:

At Thy Mystic Supper, O Son of God, receive me today as a communicant: for I will not speak of the mystery to Thine enemies; I will not give these a kiss as did Judas, but like the thief do I confess Thee: Remember me, O Lord, when Thou comest in Thy kingdom.

On Great Saturday, instead of the Cherubic Hymn we sing:

Let all mortal flesh keep silence, and stand with fear and trembling; and let it take no thought for anything earthly. For the King of kings and Lord of Lords draweth near to be sacrificed and given as food for the faithful. Before Him go choirs of angels with all the Principalities and Powers, the many-eyed Cherubim and six-winged Seraphim, which cover their faces as they sing: Alleluia. Alleluia. Alleluia.

The Liturgy of the Presanctified Gifts

The Liturgy of the Presanctified Gifts is only served on weekdays of Great Lent. The term 'Presanctified' refers to the fact that bread and wine are not consecrated in this Liturgy; Holy Communion is distributed from a Lamb consecrated at the Liturgy on the preceding Sunday. Thus, on a typical Sunday in Great Lent, three Lambs are consecrated in the Sunday Liturgy: one for the Sunday, and one for each of the Presanctified Liturgies on Wednesday and Friday.

The Lamb that is to be consecrated for the Presanctified Liturgy is cut out during the Service of Preparation on the preceding Sunday, and placed on the diskos in the normal manner. After the clergy have taken Holy Communion, the Lamb is prepared for the Presanctified Liturgy by either dipping the underside of the consecrated Lamb into the chal-

---

[49] Holy Transfiguration Monastery (trans.), *A Prayer Book for Orthodox Christians* (Boston: Holy Transfiguration Monastery, 1987) p.110.

ice or by carefully spooning the Blood of Christ onto the Lamb; the Lamb is then placed upside down in the *artophorion* so that the Blood of Christ does not come into contact with the surface of the artophorion.

The Liturgies of St. John Chrysostom and St. Basil are not used on weekdays during Great Lent because the Church regards these as too festive for this fasting period. Unlike these two Liturgies, which as we have seen, are almost indistinguishable to a casual observer, the Liturgy of the Presanctified is very different in structure.

The Presanctified Liturgy is commonly attributed to St. Gregory the Great, the Pope of Rome, but this attribution is probably honorific due to St. Gregory's support for the principle of a special lenten weekday Liturgy in Rome during his tenure.

The Presanctified Liturgy is served on Wednesdays and Fridays, on the first three days of Great Week, and on other weekdays of Great Lent when there is a special commemorated saint; in larger monasteries, it is served on every weekday of Great Lent.

The Structure of the Presanctified Liturgy

The Liturgy of the Presanctified Gifts is integrated into Vespers, so ideally it should be held in the afternoon and not in the morning. Regardless of the timing of the Liturgy, those wishing to take Holy Communion should have fasted from midnight and read the prayers of preparation.

The service begins with the Ninth Hour and Typica read according to the lenten order. During the Typica, at the beginning of the Beatitudes, the curtain is opened; at this point, the clergy leave the altar through the north door and begin the prayers said by the clergy before the Liturgy.

The normal prayers for vesting are not read, but the priest simply makes the sign of the Cross over each vestment and says 'Let us pray to the Lord' as he puts it on. The priest, now fully vested in *sticharion* and *phelonion,* ends the Typica with the usual dismissal. He then re-enters the altar to begin the Presanctified Liturgy with the blessing: **'Blessed is the Kingdom of the Father, and of the Son, and of the Holy Spirit, now and ever and unto the ages of ages.'** As he says this, the priest makes the sign of the Cross with the Gospel Book.

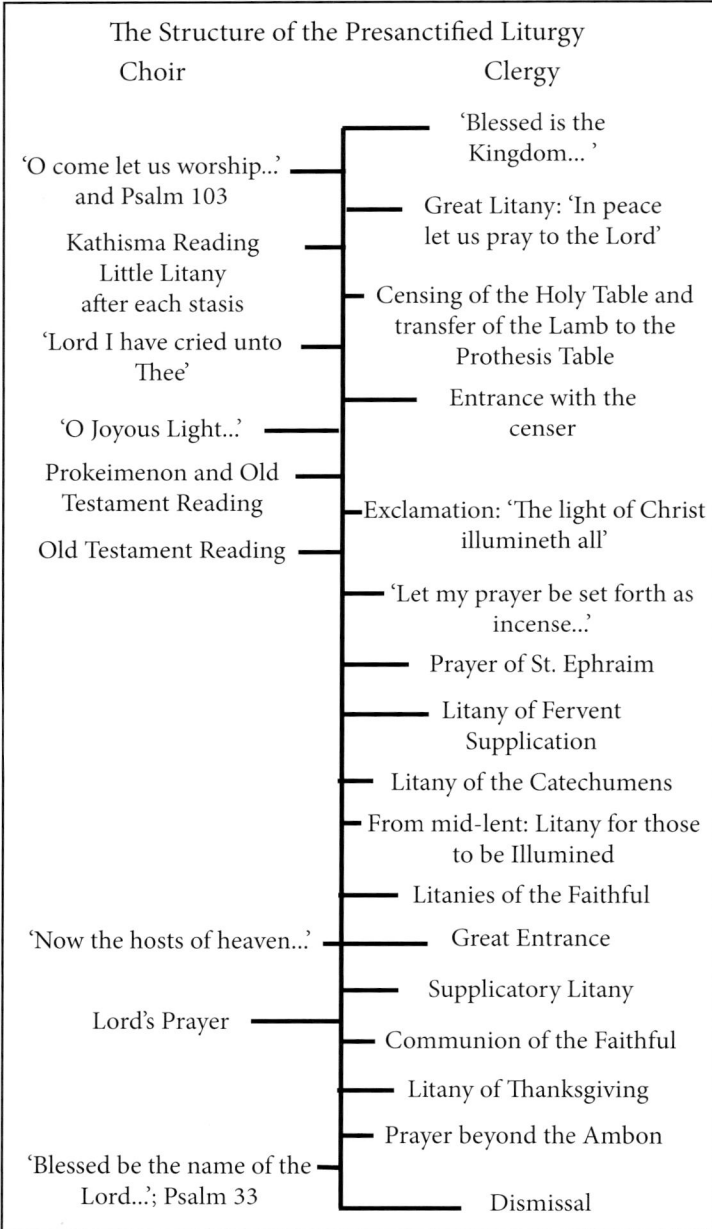

The Structure of the Presanctified Liturgy

Choir	Clergy
	'Blessed is the Kingdom...'
'O come let us worship...' and Psalm 103	Great Litany: 'In peace let us pray to the Lord'
Kathisma Reading Little Litany after each stasis	Censing of the Holy Table and transfer of the Lamb to the Prothesis Table
'Lord I have cried unto Thee'	
'O Joyous Light...'	Entrance with the censer
Prokeimenon and Old Testament Reading	Exclamation: 'The light of Christ illumineth all'
Old Testament Reading	
	'Let my prayer be set forth as incense...'
	Prayer of St. Ephraim
	Litany of Fervent Supplication
	Litany of the Catechumens
	From mid-lent: Litany for those to be Illumined
	Litanies of the Faithful
'Now the hosts of heaven...'	Great Entrance
	Supplicatory Litany
Lord's Prayer	Communion of the Faithful
	Litany of Thanksgiving
	Prayer beyond the Ambon
'Blessed be the name of the Lord...'; Psalm 33	Dismissal

The choir answers 'Amen' and then begins Vespers with 'O Come let us worship….' and Psalm 103. After the Psalm, the deacon intones the Litany of Peace and then the appointed kathisma is read with a Little Litany between each stasis. During Great Lent, with the exception of the fifth week, the eighteenth kathisma is read on every weekday Vespers.

During the kathisma reading the consecrated Lamb is moved from the artophorion on the Holy Table to the Prothesis Table, ready for the Great Entrance. The transfer occurs in three stages carried out during the three sections of the kathisma:

- *First Stasis:* The Gospel is moved off the antimension and the latter is unfolded and opened out. The diskos is placed on it, and the Lamb is removed from the artophorion and placed on the diskos.
- *Second Stasis*: The priest prostrates before the Holy Table, and then censes it from all four sides preceded by the deacon holding his candle.
- *Third Stasis:* The curtain is closed, and all the people in the church prostate. As the deacon censes, the priest, with the diskos raised level with his forehead, processes to the Prothesis Table and places the diskos on it. The curtain is opened and the people arise from their prostration. Wine and water are poured into the chalice, and the asterisk is placed on the diskos. Both chalice and diskos are covered with chalice veils and the aer.

'Lord I have Cried…'

The reading of the kathisma is followed by a Little Litany and then the choir begins to sing the *Lord I have Cried* with ten stichera: seven from the *Triodion* and three from the *Menaion*. If the Presanctified Liturgy is being held on the day of a particularly celebrated saint, the stichera are sung in his or her honour. On Wednesdays and Fridays when there is not a particularly celebrated saint, the stichera chanted are for the saint or saints celebrated on the following day.

As we have explained earlier, the new Church day begins at Vespers, During the 'both now…' there is an entrance with the censer, but on days when a Gospel is to be read during the Liturgy, the entrance is made with the Gospel and not the censer.

After the entrance, the prokeimenon is read by the reader and the choir, followed by a reading from the Book of Genesis and a second prokeimenon. After this, the priest, holding a candle in both hands, faces the people through the Royal Doors and exclaims: '**Wisdom, Upright! The Light of Christ illumines all!**' as all the faithful prostrate. The Royal Doors are then closed and the reader begins the second reading from the Old Testament.

'Let my Prayer be set forth as incense...'

After the second reading is completed, the choir and the priest begin the 'Let my Prayer be Set Forth' sequence which is similar in structure to a prokeimenon, in that the deacon intones a verse to which the choir sings a response. The faithful prostrate themselves to the ground and the priest censes the Holy Table as the choir sings the response.

The Prayer of St. Ephraim

The priest, from within the altar, now reads the Prayer of St. Ephraim with everyone in Church making a full prostration after each petition. At this point, on particularly celebrated feasts, such as the patronal feast of a church, the appointed prokeimenon, Epistle and Gospel for the saint are read – the Gospel sequence is identical to that normally used in the Liturgy of St. John Chrysostom.

Augmented Litany of Fervent Supplication; Litany for the Catechumens; Litany for those Preparing for Illumination.

The Augmented Litany of Fervent Supplication and the Litany of the Catechumens are intoned according to the normal order, but from the Wednesday of the Fourth Week of Lent they are followed by the 'Litany for those Preparing for Illumination'. In this litany, the Church prays for those that are going to be baptised at Pascha. Two Little Litanies are then intoned by the deacon according to the normal order of the Liturgy of St. John Chrysostom.

The Great Entrance

The hymn of the Great Entrance is unique to the Presanctified Liturgy:

Now the hosts of the Heavens invisibly do worship with us; for behold, the King of Glory entereth.

The priest and deacon recite this hymn quietly three times and make three prostrations in front of the Prothesis Table. The priest, his head completely covered by the aer, holding the diskos in his right hand, and the chalice in his left, exits the altar through the north door preceded by the deacon, who censes the Holy Gifts. At this point, all the faithful in the Church prostrate themselves to the ground. The Entrance is made in silence, and the clergy re-enter through the Royal Doors; the people stand up as the choir sings the second half of the entrance hymn:

Behold the accomplished mystical sacrifice is being escorted. In faith and love let us draw nigh that we may become partakers of eternal life. Alleluia, Alleluia, Alleluia.

The priest places the diskos and the chalice on the Holy Table and removes the chalice veils, placing the aer over the diskos and chalice. In the Greek usage, the diskos is placed on the right of the chalice as it already holds the Body and Blood of Christ. At the end of the hymn, in the Russian usage, the priest reads the Prayer of St. Ephraim once and then everyone makes three prostrations according to the normal order. In some churches the three prostrations are made in silence without the prayer being read. The Royal Doors are then closed, and the curtain is drawn half across signifying that the mystery has previously been completed and that the Body of Christ is present on the diskos.

The Litany of Supplication; Our Father; Communion hymn

The deacon then begins the Litany of Supplication which is identical to that used in the Liturgy of St. John Chrysostom except that it begins, 'Let us complete our evening prayer,' and the second petition refers to the 'precious gifts set forth and presanctified'. The Liturgy now proceeds according to the normal order of St. John Chrysostom until the priest exclaims: 'The Presanctified Holies are for the Holy.' As he says this he merely holds the Lamb and does not elevate it. The Presanctified Liturgy has a special communion hymn: 'O taste and see that the Lord is good. Alleluia.'

Communion of the clergy and the faithful; Litany of Thanksgiving; Prayer beyond the Ambon

The priest breaks the Lamb on the diskos and places a portion in the chalice, saying nothing. Hot water is poured into the chalice from the zeon in the normal manner and Holy Communion is distributed in the usual manner to both clergy and people. The Presanctified Liturgy concludes according to the normal order of that of St. John Chrysostom, until the Prayer beyond the Ambon, which is different:

> **O Almighty Master, Who hast made all creation and by Thine inexpressible providence and great goodness hast brought us to these all-revered days, for the purification of soul and body, for the restraint of the passions and for hope of resurrection; O Thou who during the forty days didst give into the hands of Thy servant Moses the tablets of the law divinely inscribed: Enable us also, O Good One, to fight the good fight, to complete the course of the fast, to preserve inviolate the faith, to crush under our feet the heads of invisible serpents, to be accounted victors over sin and to worship the holy resurrection without condemnation. For blessed and glorified is Thine all-honourable and majestic name of the Father, and of the Son, and of the Holy Spirit, now and ever and unto the ages of ages.**

After singing 'Blessed be the Name of the Lord' the choir reads Psalm 33 (the same psalm that is read at the end of the Typica). The Presanctified Liturgy starts with Vespers and finishes with the ending normally used in the lenten Typica, a further indication of the special character of the Liturgy which does not stand on its own, but only in the context of the services of Great Lent.

Frequently Asked Questions

Why, in some parishes, are the priest's silent prayers read audibly?

The Church indicates in Her service books that these prayers should be read quietly, and this is the traditional practice. Although the reading aloud of these Eucharist Prayers might seem to be a small innovation, it is often promoted by supporters of the Orthodox ecumenical movement who support wider-reaching changes in Orthodox theology and practice. Any changes that emanate from a movement that denies that the Orthodox Church is the One Holy Catholic and Apostolic Church cannot, by definition, be traditional.

Tradition is not simply 'oldness' and new traditions are not always inferior to older ones because in Orthodoxy we change nothing solely on the basis of age; the Church as the Body of Christ, is a theanthropic organism and not a museum. For example, in previous centuries lay people were given the Body of Christ in their hands and drank directly from the chalice. This practice died out, and now the more modern practice of being communed from the spoon is traditional.

Finding a practice in the Orthodox historical record, such as the audible reading of the priest's silent prayers, does not itself mean that this practice is superior or more 'traditional' than the present one. Tradition is Orthodoxy, as it is, as it was and as it shall be. We keep traditions, but we also accept innovations as long as they are from within the Church and not from without.

At which points in the Divine Liturgy do we make full prostrations?

There are differences in local customs, but a good rule of thumb is when the priest makes a full prostration we do as well. In the context of the Liturgies of St. John Chrysostom and St. Basil the Great, this means that we make prostrations, on weekdays, at the following places:

- After the consecration at the end of the hymn 'We hymn thee we bless Thee…;
- At the end of the hymn 'It is Truly Meet…'
- Before the Our Father when the deacon says: 'Vouchsafe O Master…'
- When the priest says: 'The Holies are for the Holy'

- When the chalice is brought out when the deacon says: 'In fear of God...'
- If we have not received Holy Communion, when the priest stands in the Royal Doors holding the chalice and says 'always now and ever and unto the ages'.

On Sundays and Great Feast days, we do not make full prostrations, but instead make a deep bow. As we have noted above, in the Presanctified Liturgy, we remain prostrated during the whole of the Great Entrance.

Are there any reasons that a Divine Liturgy cannot be celebrated?

A Divine Liturgy cannot be served without an antimension, and a priest cannot serve the Divine Liturgy without wearing his vestments, and he may only serve the Liturgy once a day; also a Liturgy may only be celebrated once a day on the same Holy Table. A Liturgy is never served on Great Friday except when the Great Feast of the Annunciation falls on that day. In this case, the Divine Liturgy of St. John Chrysostom is served and the Matins of Great Friday and the Annunciation are combined. In the modern Greek practice, when this situation arises, the Feast of the Annunciation is moved to the following Monday.

How often should we receive Holy Communion?

In general, we could say that we should try to receive Communion as often as we can, provided that we have kept the appropriate fasts, have been to Confession, and have no impediment to receiving Holy Communion.

Although we are brothers and sisters within the Church, the partaking of the mysteries of the Church is a personal decision which is why they are always given to us personally by name. In addition, some Orthodox Churches have different customs and practices concerning the frequency of reception of Holy Communion. Often, people do not receive Holy Communion because they feel unworthy to do so, but as St. John Cassian teaches, we are all unworthy of such a great mystery:

> *We should not keep away from the Lord's communion because we know that we are sinners, but we should hasten to it all the more*

avidly for the sake of our soul's healing and our spirit's purifica-
tion, yet with that humility of mind and faith that will cause us,
while judging ourselves unworthy to receive such a grace, to seek it
instead as medicine for our wounds. Otherwise communion may
not be worthily received even once a year, as is the case with some
who live in monasteries and who are so in awe of the dignity and
holiness and worth of the heavenly sacraments that they think that
no one should receive them but the holy and stainless, rather than
that it is they that make us holy and pure by receiving them.[50]

Saint John Cassian criticizes those who only receive Holy Communion when they consider themselves 'worthy' as guilty of an 'arrogant
presumption'. However, there are other reasons why Orthodox Christians do not partake regularly of the Holy Mysteries, and many of
these stem from long-held customs rather than individual conceit.
Most importantly, we should not judge either those who do not receive Communion regularly or those who do.

May we receive Holy Communion in any Orthodox parish?

When we receive Holy Communion we are confirming our unity
of faith with the bishop who is commemorated at the Liturgy so we
should not receive Holy Communion in any parish in which the priest
is not in communion with our bishop and of one faith with him.

Can babies receive Holy Communion at the Presanctified Liturgy?

The wine in the chalice is not changed by the Holy Spirit into the
Blood of Christ during the Presanctified Liturgy. In the modern Russian usage, babies are not given Holy Communion, nor does the deacon drink from the chalice (or the priest when he serves alone). The
reasons for this practice are purely logical, since after every Liturgy,
the Holy Communion remaining in the chalice is consumed by the
deacon, and this must be done without breaking the fast beforehand.
As the wine in the chalice has not been formally consecrated in the
Presanctified Liturgy, drinking it would break the fast. Likewise, in
the Russian Church, because small babies are only given the Blood of

---

[50] St. John Cassian, *The Conferences* (trans. B. Ramsey) (Mahwah: Newman Press,
1997) p. 812.

Christ when they receive Holy Communion, they are not communed at the Presanctified Liturgy because the wine has not been consecrated.

In the more ancient usage, the deacon drinks from the chalice in the normal manner, and babies are communed as normal. The consecrated Lamb has, after all, previously been dipped in the Blood of Christ, which has now diffused through the wine in the chalice.

Should we kiss the Cross after receiving Holy Communion?

In the Greek usage, if we have taken Holy Communion we do not take the blessing of the priest afterwards, or kiss the Cross, although it is the custom to do so in Slavic Churches. In addition, in Slavic Churches, communicants kiss the base of the chalice after receiving Holy Communion, but this is not the custom in most Greek churches.

What is the difference between antidoron and prosphora?

Both antidoron and prosphora are the remnants of the prosphoron from which the Lamb and other portions have been cut out during the Service of Preparation. In the Romanian tradition, antidoron is called 'anaphora'.

The difference between the two is that antidoron is blessed by a three-fold elevation after the consecration of the Holy Gifts. In most Slavic churches this blessing is not carried out, so the bread that is given out at the end of the Liturgy is actually 'prosphora' even though it is called 'antidoron'! Prosphora has not been blessed, so anyone can eat it, but only Orthodox Christians can take antidoron, and they should do so after fasting in the same way that we do before Holy Communion.

Are there any practical tips on how to receive Holy Communion?

Receiving Holy Communion is an awesome responsibility, and we should consider the practical implications for ourselves and for the priest. The priest is responsible for any spillage of Holy Communion and this is a very serious matter. To help the priest, it is worth considering the following:

- Open your mouth wide and keep still. Position your mouth near and level to the chalice.
- Babies should be cradled with their head on the adult's right el-

bow. Older babies should be held tightly in case they kick out and knock the chalice.

- If a baby starts to turn his head, keep it still with your hand. If his mouth is closed, pushing gently on both cheeks will cause it to pop open.
- Small babies are only given a tiny portion of the Blood of Christ, but it is a good idea to place a clean paper towel under the chin of children who are inclined to dribble. This can then be given to the priest to be burnt.
- Teething children and toddlers should not be allowed to put their fingers in their mouths after Holy Communion.
- Toddlers should not be allowed to carry toys with them as they approach the chalice in case of accidents.

Some superstitions have grown up over the centuries regarding Holy Communion, but most have some basis in truth. We should not spit after receiving Holy Communion, nor should we brush our teeth that evening or go to the dentist. The issue of bleeding after receiving Holy Communion exercises many, but the problem here is not straightforward. We should not give blood after receiving Holy Communion, but natural bleeding afterwards is not spiritually significant – otherwise we would not give Holy Communion to the sick in hospital or those suffering from chronic conditions which involve bleeding. Women should not commune if they are menstruating but if this starts unexpectedly after receiving Holy Communion it does not indicate any unworthiness.

Why does the bishop wash his hands before the Great Entrance?

The Service of Preparation is served by the most junior priest before the bishop arrives at church. The bishop washes his hands before the Great Entrance because he immediately proceeds to the Prothesis Table and commemorates those whom he wishes by removing particles from a prosphoron set aside for him. The washing of hands in front of the people also 'represents the purity and incomprehensibility of Christ's sacred service and that it is necessary to approach the Holy One and to serve His most pure mysteries as free as humanly possible from all impurity'.[51]

---

[51] St. Symeon of Thessalonika, *The Liturgical Commentaries* p. 125-126.

Saint Mary of Egypt receives Holy Communion from the Elder Zosimas.

The life of Saint Mary is read on the Thursday of the Fifth Week of Great Lent as an example of complete repentance.

6

The Mystery of Repentance

Amen I say unto you, whatsoever ye shall bind on earth shall be bound in heaven: and whatsoever ye shall loose on earth shall be loosed in heaven.

Matthew 18:18

We are all sinners, because the word 'sin' means 'missing the mark' and we all fall far short of the prize of our high calling, which we have received from God in Christ Jesus (cf. Phil. 3:14). There is, in all of us, a conflict between the good we want to do, and our actual actions as St. Paul teaches:

> *For I delight in the law of God after the inward man: But I see another law in my members, warring against the law of my mind, and bringing me into captivity to the law of sin which is in my members. O wretched man that I am! Who shall deliver me from the body of this death? (Rom. 7:22-24).*

The word 'repentance' in Greek (*metanoia*) literally means a 'change of mind', a turning away from evil. Repentance is essential for salvation, because without it we shall all perish (cf. Luke 13:5). Through the mystery of repentance, also known as the service of confession, we confirm our decision to turn away from evil; this repentance reunites us with the Body of Christ, the Orthodox Church, and grants us the forgiveness of the sins that we have confessed.

The Fathers teach that the Orthodox Church is a hospital for sinners and that the mysteries of the Church are medicine for our souls. It is for this reason that the Fathers compare sins to physical wounds on our bodies. Sins are wounds on our souls, that unless treated through repentance and confession, will become infected and eventually cause the death of our soul. St. John Climacus says that 'when a wound is still fresh and warm it is easy to heal; but old, neglected and festering wounds are hard to cure.'[52]

---

[52] St. John Climacus, *The Ladder of Divine Ascent* (trans. Holy Transfiguration Monastery) (Brookline: Holy Transfiguration Monastery, 1991) p. 64.

We are all sinners, so we are spiritually ill to some degree. The Ortho-dox Church is the true source of the Medicine of Immortality, and it is rightly called a 'hospital for sinners'. Sin is actually a spiritual ill-ness, and we receive treatment for this illness through the mysteries of the Church.

This 'fallen state' in which we find ourselves is not our 'natural state' be-cause, by the suffering and death of Christ the Second Adam, we have been freed from death and corruption. Our natural state is the renewed state into which we are re-created by our baptism. It is this natural state that we are trying to regain as St. Nectarios of Aegina explains:

> *Repentance is a bath that cleanses one of his own sins. It is a return from a state contrary to nature to a state in accordance with na-ture, from the devil to God, through spiritual striving and painful efforts. It is a voluntary return from offences to the good that is opposed to them.*

St. Nectarios refers to repentance as a 'bath' and true repentance is of-ten referred to as a 'second baptism'. The power of repentance is great – great enough to wash away all of our sins and transgressions and to give us strength for the spiritual struggle that we face.

Central to the mystery of repentance is the concept of 'synergy' which means 'cooperation'. Synergy, in the Orthodox context, means 'working with the Holy Spirit'. Our desire to repent and change our way of life is strengthened by the Holy Spirit. The Orthodox Church rejects both the ancient heresy of Pelagius who taught that Christians could be saved by the force of their own works without the need for the Holy Spirit, and the modern heresy of Protestantism which teaches that good works are not necessary for salvation.

Preparing for Confession

Facing up to and admitting our sins is difficult, because we always think ourselves better than we really are. Occasionally people say: 'I do not need to go to confession; I haven't done anything wrong.' But what they mean is that they have not noticed that they have done anything wrong. The Apostle Paul referred to himself as the 'chief of sinners' (1 Tim. 1:15), and the Apostle John teaches:

If we say that we have no sin, we deceive ourselves, and the truth is not in us. If we confess our sins, He is faithful and just to forgive us our sins, and to cleanse us from all unrighteousness. If we say that we have not sinned, we make Him a liar, and His word is not in us (1 John 1:8-10).

Just as a small stone can cause an avalanche, ignoring and justifying sins leads inevitably to more serious sins. A failure to confess these sins will become an obstacle on our path to the Kingdom of Heaven as the ever-memorable Metropolitan Cyprian states:

We should confess, therefore on a regular basis our minor and major spiritual infirmities: Let us ask forgiveness of God, through the Confessor, even for the smallest sins, which however small they may appear, gradually become entire mountains that close our path to the Kingdom of heaven.[53]

Confessing our sins is much easier if we write down what we are going to say beforehand. By doing this, we won't forget to say something important, and reading down the list in order will stop us leaving out anything that might be embarrassing to admit to. St. Nicodemos of the Holy Mountain advises: 'If you wish to defeat the devil, who makes you feel shame, say first of all that sin which causes you the greatest shame.' In other words, start off with the 'worst' sin and move on from there.

It is important to remember that there is nothing new under the sun and most priests will have heard all kinds of embarrassing things from all kinds of people. In the *Ladder of Divine Ascent*, there is an account of a criminal who repented and wanted to join the monastery. The abbot in this account is referred to as a 'physician' emphasizing that we come to the Church to receive healing as we would from a doctor or physician:

As [the thief] lay on the ground, and moistened the floor with his tears, this wonderful physician, using all means for his salvation, and wishing to give to all an example of saving and effectual humility, again exhorted him, in the presence of all, to tell

---

[53] Metropolitan Cyprian, *Do You Have a Ticket?* (Etna: CTOS, 2007) p. 49.

in detail what he had done. And with terror he confessed, one
after another, all his sins which revolted every ear, not only sins
of the flesh, natural and unnatural, with rational beings and with
animals, but even poisoning, murder and many others, which it
is not lawful to hear or commit to writing.[54]

The above account should give us confidence that we can try and imitate this thief's repentance and confess our sins to obtain healing for our souls. In the words of St. John Chrysostom: 'There is no sin that is so great that it will overcome God's love for mankind, as long as we show repentance in good time and seek pardon.'

In addition to confessing deeds, we should also confess serious sinful thoughts that we have had. These 'thoughts' are not fleeting temptations or thoughts that we have had and quickly rejected, but those that we have engaged with or fantasized about. St. Nicodemos of the Holy Mountain explains:

You should confess, too, the evil thoughts that you have, if not all,
then at least those that bother you and prey on you most, because
just as the eggs of birds when they are hidden in the dung are giv-
en life and become chicks, so also evil thoughts when they are not
revealed to one's spiritual father are given life and become deeds.

These recurring thoughts that we have failed to confess are bound to manifest themselves in physical sins eventually. After all, sins are generally preceded by some kind of mental decision to agree with them in principle. Once we have agreed in thought to the sin, it is simply a matter of time for the right physical circumstances to present themselves which enable us to turn these thoughts into actions. St. Philotheos of Sinai says that 'the person who gives himself over to evil thoughts cannot keep his outer self free from sin; and if evil thoughts have not been uprooted from the heart, they are bound to manifest themselves in evil actions.'[55]

Confessing thoughts also trains us to recognize actions as wrong before starting them. Most temptations begin as thoughts and don't ap-

---

[54] St. John Climacus, *The Ladder of Divine Ascent* p. 24.
[55] *The Philokalia Vol. 3* (London: Faber & Faber, 1984) p. 29

pear to be wrong at first, and we can usually justify them some way or other. The practice of deciding what is Orthodox, and what is not, is known as 'discernment'. Spotting the beginning of sin needs the spiritual discernment that Archbishop Averky describes:

> Our nature is so damaged and maimed by sin, that we cannot assess our actions and conduct correctly; we could say that we are, in fact, completely blind, and unable to see ourselves as we really are. This is why in Great Lent we say the prayer of the great ascetic, and knower of the heart, Ephraim the Syrian: 'Grant me to see my own sins!' We do not see our own sins with the clearness that is necessary for fruitful repentance; we are incapable of the necessary criticism when it comes to ourselves, to our own emotional turmoil, because we are blinded by our passions. We even do not notice how our actions, which might seem to come from a pure idealistic inspiration, actually spring up from some secret passion or sinful inclination within us. When we follow this impure suggestion, we deceive ourselves, and we lead ourselves astray; we think that we are doing a good deed, when, in reality, we are acting according to this passion and are nourishing it and strengthening it instead of tearing it up by the roots.

St. John Chrysostom also teaches: 'the medicine of repentance is prepared at first from the knowing of our own sins.' Paying attention to our thoughts and rejecting ones that are sinful is one of the most challenging aspects of Orthodoxy, and everyone struggles to do it. Below, St. Evagrios the Solitary categorizes the different causes of these thoughts:

> We have learnt, after much observation, to recognize the difference between angelic thoughts, human thoughts, and thoughts that come from demons. Angelic thought is concerned with the true nature of things and with searching out their spiritual essences. For example, why was gold created and scattered like sand in the lower regions of the earth, to be found only with much toil and effort? Demonic thought, on the other hand, neither knows nor can know such things. It can only shamelessly suggest the acquisition of physical gold, looking forward to the wealth and

glory that will come from this. Finally, human thought neither seeks to acquire gold nor is concerned to know what it symbolizes, but brings before the mind simply the image of gold, without the passion of greed.[56]

Often, evil thoughts and images appear in our consciousness seemingly out of nowhere. These thoughts, according to the writings of St. Mark the Ascetic, are remembrances of previous sins that we have committed:

Involuntary thoughts arise from previous sin; voluntary ones from our free will. Thus the latter are the cause of the former. Evil thoughts which arise against our will are accompanied by remorse, and they soon disappear; but when they are freely chosen, they are accompanied by pleasure, and so they are hard to get rid of.[57]

These involuntary thoughts only become sinful when we start interacting with them and turning them over in our minds. We should ignore dreams the same as we do involuntary thoughts. These temptations or thoughts are the very ones that we pray to be delivered from in the 'Our Father'. If this fantasizing becomes ingrained and takes over our thoughts, we have become slaves to passion which St. John Climacus defines as follows:

Passion, they say, is preeminently that which for a long time nestles with persistence in the soul, forming therein a habit, as it were, by the soul's long-standing association with it, since the soul of its own free and proper choice clings to it.[58]

Passions can only be uprooted from the soul by spiritual struggle within the Church, and each of us must struggle as best we can against the particular passions that afflict us.

---

[56] *The Philokalia Vol.1* (London: Faber & Faber, 1979) p. 42.

[57] Ibid., p. 142.

[58] St. John Climacus, *The Ladder of Divine Ascent* p. 116

The Service of Confession

Although we have talked about confession as a service and an event in and of itself, in fact, the mystery of repentance is not a 'one off' event. Although our confession in words is a commitment in time, this confession is not an end but a beginning because through it we are reunited with the Church, through the action of the Holy Spirit.

Going to confession, therefore, is personal, but it is also a public profession of the faith and our desire to be united with the Orthodox Church. This uniting to the Church is performed by the bishops and priests through the grace of the Holy Spirit as St. Athanasius the Great teaches: 'as a man is baptized by a priest and is enlightened by the grace of the Holy Spirit, likewise he who confesses with repentance through the priest receives the forgiveness through the grace of Christ.'

This gift of the forgiving of sins is transmitted through the grace of consecration to Orthodox bishops. Those priests who have a blessing from the bishop to hear confessions act as the bishop's deputy when they perform this function. In the Russian Church, any priest can hear confessions; in the Greek usage, only priests experienced in the Orthodox spiritual life are given permission, by the bishop, to hear confessions.

The authority of the bishops, as the successors of the apostles, to forgive sins is clearly stated in the Gospels: '[Christ] breathed on them and He said to them: Receive ye the Holy Spirit. Whose sins you shall forgive, they are forgiven them; and whose sins you shall retain, they are retained' (John 20:22-23). Speaking to the apostles, Christ said: 'Truly I say unto you, whatsoever you shall bind on earth shall be bound in heaven: and whatsoever you shall loose on earth shall be loosed in heaven' (Matt. 18:18).

The practice of confessing sins is an ancient one, as we read in the first century collection of writings known as the Didache:

> On the Lord's Day gather together for the breaking of bread and giving thanks. However, you should first confess your sins so that your sacrifice may be pure; do not let anyone who is in a dispute with a neighbour join with you until they are reconciled so that your sacrifice may not be impure.

At the time the Didache was written, confessions were public, but the grace for the forgiving of sins, and the reuniting to the Church, was channelled through the bishop as St. Ignatius the God-bearer teaches:

> *The Lord forgives all who repent, if in repenting they return to the unity of God and the council of the bishop… Listen to the bishop, and to the priests and the deacons… Do nothing without the bishop; keep your bodies as the temples of God; love; avoid divisions; be the followers of Jesus Christ, even as He is of His Father. For as many as are of God and of Jesus Christ are also with the bishop. Those who truly repent and return to the unity of the Church, these, too, shall belong to God, that they may live according to Jesus Christ.*

The full service of confession is quite long, and today, due to the huge number of faithful compared to the number of priests available to hear confessions, a shortened form of the service is normally used. The confession service is held in front of the Gospel Book and the Cross; as we approach the Cross and the Gospel we venerate them, and the Priest reads the following prayer:

> **Behold my child, Christ standeth here invisibly and receiveth thy confession; wherefore be not ashamed, neither be afraid, and conceal thou nothing from me: but tell me, doubting not, all things which thou hast done; and so shalt thou have pardon from our Lord Jesus Christ. Lo, His holy image is before us; and I am but a witness, bearing testimony before Him of all the things which thou dost say to me. But if thou shalt conceal anything from me, thou shalt have the greater sin. Take heed, therefore, lest having come to the physician thou depart unhealed.**

We then start saying the sins that we have committed. Afterwards, unless the bishop or priest tells us not to receive Holy Communion for a particular reason he reads this prayer:

> **O Lord God of the salvation of Thy servants, merciful, compassionate and long-suffering, Who repentest concerning our evil deeds, and desirest not the death of the sinner, but rather that he should turn from his wickedness and live; Show Thy**

mercy now upon Thy servant [*Name*] and grant unto *him/her* an image of repentance, forgiveness of sins, and deliverance, pardoning all *his/her* sins whether voluntary or involuntary. Reconcile and unite *him/her* unto Thy holy Church through Jesus Christ our Lord, to Whom, with Thee, are due dominion and majesty, now, and ever, and unto the ages of ages. Amen.

The priest's role in the mystery of repentance is twofold. First, as we hear in the prayer at the beginning of the confession service, he is 'only a witness' before God of the things that we say in confession. Secondly, the priest, through the grace of the priesthood, is able to reunite us with the Church; at the same time, the sins that we have confessed are wiped away.

The role of the priest as confessor developed from the monastic life in which the disciples of an elder confess their thoughts and sins to him. It is for this reason that, in the Greek usage, confessors are usually from the monastic clergy, because they are experienced in the spiritual struggle. However, the grace of the Holy Spirit that we receive does not depend upon the personality or the talent of the priest for hearing confessions. The benefit that we receive from confession is not from the words of the priest (which may, or may not be helpful), but from our own repentance.

A priest will never disclose anything said in confession to anyone else, no matter what the circumstances; this confidentiality is a vital part of the trust between the priest and the person confessing to him. Because of this, if we want to discuss some issue not directly related to our sins, we should do this outside confession.

It is important in confession not to blame anyone else for our own sins or to justify our actions in any way. We should not mention other people by name, except perhaps when doing so reveals the seriousness of our sin.

Frequently Asked Questions

I went to confession and the priest told me off. I don't want to go to confession to him again. What should I do?

Most often, any upset we feel is a result of our pride and not the priest's over-zealousness. As in all disagreements, it is important to challenge ourselves and examine to what extent our spiritual state has caused it. We hear in the Book of Proverbs: 'reprove one that hath understanding, and he will understand knowledge' (Proverbs 19:25).

Society today teaches us to be self-centered and to perceive offence wherever we can find it. If we are told off, and we feel this is unfair, we ought to take to heart the words of the Apostle Peter:

> *Servants, be subject to your masters with all fear; not only to the good and gentle, but also to the harsh. For this is commendable if a man for conscience toward God endure grief, suffering wrongfully. For what credit is it, if, when you are beaten for your faults, you take it patiently? But when you do good, and suffer, if you take it patiently, this is commendable before God. For to this were you called, because Christ also suffered for us, leaving us an example, that ye should follow His steps, Who did no sin, nor was deceit found in his mouth; Who, when He was reviled, reviled not again; when He suffered, He threatened not, but committed Himself to Him that judgeth righteously; Who Himself bare our sins in His own Body on the tree, that we, being dead to sins, should live unto righteousness (1 Peter 2:18-24).*

We should not reveal what the priest has said to us in confession, and we should certainly never complain to others about the advice he has given. In doing this we will become guilty of putting a stumbling block in our brother's way (cf. Rom 14:13). Also, the priest can never reveal what we said in confession, so he will have no chance to offer an explanation.

What does 'conscience' mean in an Orthodox context?

Our conscience is the inner voice in us that cannot be removed, but it can be silenced by laziness in the spiritual life, eventually becoming atrophied and useless. Listening to our conscience is part of spiritual discernment. We need to discern the tricks of the demons that convince us to ignore our conscience and justify our sins. Our conscience is created and is a gift from God as St. John Chrysostom explains:

> *The loving Lord from on high, in forming human beings right from the beginning, implanted conscience in them as a tireless accuser, proof against dissuasion and deception at any time. Even if someone were able to escape the notice of all human beings in committing sin and perpetrating improper conduct, he could not escape that accuser.*[59]

The effects of this conscience can even be observed in people that are otherwise unrepentant. In a series of interviews with psychologists one infamous serial killer who had shown no remorse for his crimes, expressed regret for one particular aspect of one murder. It is evident on watching the video recording of the interview that, for a moment, he is troubled by his conscience, but he is able, almost visibly, to silence this voice within him.

What does the word 'epitimia' mean?

The Canons of the Church specify a period of time that we should refrain from taking Holy Communion if we have committed a serious sin: this is known as an *epitimia*. At first glance, this may seem harsh, but this framework is inseparable from the therapeutic, healing mission of the Church. It is not simply a punishment, but a means to help us understand the seriousness of our sin so we can receive healing for our souls.

An epitimia can only be set by a bishop or priest, and the Canons are guidelines for the clergy not inflexible rules; every person is dealt with individually, so in some cases, an epitimia might be appropriate and in others, it might not. Often, an epitimia might consist of number of prostrations, or an increased prayer rule, instead of a removal from Holy Communion.

---

[59] St. John Chrysostom, *Homilies on Genesis 1-17* (trans. Robert C. Hill) (Washington: CUA Press, 1985) p. 224.

Do dreams have a hidden meaning?

Even though the mystery of repentance forgives the sins that we confess, these sins, like medical operations on the body, leave scars on the soul as St. Cyril of Jerusalem teaches: 'The stains of sin also remain in the body; even if there has been a healing, the scar remains, so sin wounds both the soul and body, and the marks of its scars remain in all.' This spiritual scarring is the reason why we are troubled by the hurt that we have caused others even years after we have confessed the sin. It also explains why we are often troubled by dreams or thoughts relating to, or influenced by, our previous sins.

Often we dream about things we have thought about, or done, and this is normal. Sometimes we dream about random things, or have sexual dreams with disturbing content – this particularly applies to teenagers. We should reject all suggestions contained in dreams because we are all lacking in discernment which allows us to perceive the tricks of the demons. In Orthodox literature we often read of people having dreams or visions; in the unlikely event of any of us having a dream containing meaningful spiritual content we should consult our spiritual father before believing anything contained in it.

I go to confession regularly, but I still commit the same sins. What can I do about it?

We are more inclined to commit some sins than others. Some people are more inclined to anger than others, some are more jealous, some are more inclined to sins of a sexual nature. Whatever our disposition or spiritual state, going to confession is important even if we cannot see any immediate benefit. This is because by avoiding confession, we are going to add new sins in addition to our 'usual' ones.

The spiritual life is like learning to ride a bike. Falling off is part of the learning process; not getting back on is not going to make us better, but worse. It is the same with confession: not going because we always say the same things is not going to achieve anything at all. St. John Chrysostom compares the fight against sin to chopping down a tree with an axe; the tree is not cut down by one blow, but blow after blow of the axe eventually weakens the trunk and the tree falls. The blows we give to sins are those that we administer in confession. He also compares our spiritual state to that of an old crumbling rotten house: 'We remove the rotten parts from them and repair them. You have become old today because of sin. Renew yourself through repentance.'

Prayer is a powerful weapon against sin. We should try to fill our life with prayer; we should pray before meals, before work, before going to sleep. Saying a prayer before any action that we are doubtful about is a good way to guard against sin as this example from the life of Father Siluoan of Mount Athos shows:

> *On one of his train journeys he sat opposite a shopkeeper, who in a friendly gesture opened his silver cigarette-case and offered him a cigarette. Father Silouan thanked him but refused to take one. Then the shopkeeper began talking, asking, 'Are you refusing, Father, because you think it is a sin?…In the end Father Silouan made up his mind to say to him, 'Before you light up a cigarette, pray and repeat one "Our Father…"' To this the shopkeeper replied, 'Praying before having a smoke somehow doesn't work.' To this Silouan observed, 'So better not start anything which cannot be preceded by untroubled prayer'.*[60]

Saying prayers before actions is often difficult to remember, but the Orthodox Church has a short prayer which is ideal for these situations. The Jesus prayer, 'Lord Jesus Christ, Son of God, have mercy on me, a sinner,' expresses both Orthodox theology and the necessary acknowledgment that we are all sinners in the sight of God. Imagining that our sins are somehow going to decrease in time until we have nothing left to confess is not Orthodox, and not very realistic. As we grow in the spiritual life, we should have more to confess and not less, because we truly perceive our own sinfulness and our conscience is functioning properly.

What can we do if we have committed a serious sin?

When we commit a serious sin, there are two destructive consequences. The first, is that the sin hardens our heart, and we try to justify our actions by making excuses for ourselves. The second, and

---

[60] Archimandrite Sophrony, *St. Silouan the Athonite* (Tolleshunt Knights: Stavropegic Monastery of St. John the Baptist, 1991) p.70.

this often affects people of a more sensitive disposition, is that we lose heart because of the seriousness of our sin and fall into despair.

We are all tempted to make excuses for our sins, and these excuses come in numerous forms. For example, we might blame someone else for making us angry; we might fall into the trap of considering that, compared to other people, our sin is not that bad. Judging people, and assuming we are, in some way, 'better' than others because we have not committed certain sins, is a sure way to fall into these sins ourselves. In the case of young people, these sins can arise from judging parents and failing to honour and obey them. In monks and nuns, these types of falls are often caused by judging a superior or fellow monastics.

We should repent for our sins, but this sorrow must not lead us into depression or despair because we should never despair of God's mercy 'for godly sorrow produces repentance leading to salvation, not to be regretted; but the sorrow of the world produces death' (2 Cor. 7:10). St. Theognostos offers the following advice to those afflicted by despair:

> *If you drive off the dog of despair with the stone of hopefulness and supplicate boldly and insistently, your many sins will be forgiven you. Then, in the age to be, as a debtor you too will love the God who is beyond all goodness and yet has compassion for you.*[61]

Christ Himself said that He came not to call the righteous but sinners to repentance (Luke 5:32). We come to church, not because we are righteous, but because we are sinners and were 'conceived in iniquities' (Ps. 50). There is no need to despair on account of our sins because, as St. Cyril of Alexandria teaches, 'there is no sin which God cannot forgive for those who sincerely repent.'

---

[61] *The Philokalia Vol. 2* (London: Faber and Faber, 1982) p. 374.

7

Memorial Services

It is a holy and wholesome thought to pray for the dead, that they may be loosed from sins.

2 Maccabees 12:45

We are united within the Church with the souls of the departed, and we pray for those Orthodox who have died that their sins might be forgiven. The souls of the departed are helped by the prayers of the Church, and other acts of mercy performed in their memory as Metropolitan Kallistos (Ware) explains:

> *After death there is progress, in the sense of progress in self-knowledge. Once dead, the human person is not given a second chance, in the sense of being able to make a series of entirely new decisions, becoming an altogether different person from what he was in this life; but he can grow in self-awareness, realizing more and more clearly the significance of his past acts. Death, in other words, is the moment of truth.*[62]

It is only after the general resurrection and the Final Judgment that the souls of the righteous and sinners receive the full recompense of their deeds. This Final Judgment is the one spoken of by the Apostle Paul in his Second Epistle to the Corinthians: 'For we must all appear before the judgment seat of Christ; that every one may receive the things done in his body, according to that he hath done, whether it be good or bad' (2 Cor. 5:10).

When we die, we will be judged, but this judgment is not final and the sentence is not eternal. This partial judgment is often referred to as the 'Particular Judgment' and the time of the departure of the soul from the body is often referred to in the services of the Church. In the funeral service we chant the following hymn written by St. John of Damascus:

---

[62] K.Ware, 'One Body in Christ': Death and the Communion of Saints, *Sobornost* (1981) Vol.3 No.1 p. 183.

When the soul from the body is about to be rent with violence by angels dread, it forgets its family and friends and is troubled concerning its appearance before the judgment which shall come upon the things of vanity and much-toiling flesh.

The Particular Judgment is different in nature from a trial on earth for the simple reason that in earthly trials, the judge is trying to find out the truth. In the Particular Judgment, the judge is God, who knows the truth, so the trial serves only to make us aware of our actions. St. Maximus the Confessor explains:

Those who have not, however, wholly attained to perfection, but are liable for sins and falls, these will come before the great Judgment Seat – where, by the contrasting examination of the good and evil acts which they have performed, they are like those who are burning (by virtue of the examination of their consciences and thoughts); then, the scales being tipped by their good deeds, they will be cleansed and delivered from hell.[63]

After this judgment, the souls of the departed will receive a foretaste of heaven or hell. According to the teaching of St. Mark of Ephesus:

[Both the righteous and sinners] are in places proper to them, the righteous, in absolute repose and freedom are in heaven with the angels and have a foretaste of the Kingdom of Heaven, whereas sinners are shut in Hades, waiting with discomfort and inconsolable grief, like condemned men awaiting the Judge's sentence and foreseeing eternal torment.[64]

This foretaste of the eternal sentence should not be confused with the Roman Catholic doctrine of purgatory which the Orthodox Church has never accepted and which is discussed further on page 142.

We pray for the souls of the departed in the hope that they will receive mercy from God. Following the teaching of St. John of Damascus, we also give money to the needy in their memory:

---

[63] *The Evergetinos: A Complete Text Vol. 4* (trans. Archbishop Chrysostomos, Hieromonk Patapios), (Etna: CTOS, 2008) p. 362.

[64] Metropolitan Hierotheos, *Life after Death* (Levadia: Birth of the Theotokos Monastery, 1995) p. 168.

But who can number all of the testimonies found in the biographies of holy men, in the accounts of the lives of the holy martyrs and the divine revelations, which clearly indicate that even after death tremendous benefit is rendered to the departed by prayers, Liturgies and the distribution of alms for them. For nothing given to God perishes in return, but is rewarded by Him with the greatest interest.[65]

In addition to commemorating the departed at the Divine Liturgy and in our private prayers, we also pray for them by holding memorial services on the third, ninth and fortieth days after death. We calculate the day of these memorials by counting the day of death as 'day one'. In other words, if a person dies on a Sunday, the third day is Tuesday and not Wednesday.

These particular days are chosen because of their significance. Christ rose from the dead on the third day; we hope that the departed will find rest where the nine ranks of the Angels abide; we hope that the Lord, Who ascended into Heaven forty days after the Resurrection, will receive the departed into the radiant mansions of Paradise.

The souls of the Orthodox faithful departed are remembered during the Divine Liturgy at the following places:

- At the Service of Preparation in which particles of the prosphoron are removed and placed on the diskos.
- At the Litany of the Departed which is said on weekdays directly after the Litany of Fervent Supplication.
- In the Divine Liturgy, at the censing of the Gifts, when the hymn 'It is truly meet' is sung.

Memorial services are also held every year on the anniversary of death, showing that our love for the departed has not faded with the passage of time, but that it is renewed every year.

---

[65] Sisters of the Vladimir Icon Convent, 'The Church's Prayer for the Dead', *Orthodox Life* (1978) Vol. 28 No.1, p. 23.

Soul Sabbaths

In addition to days specific to each departed Orthodox Christian, the Church also has days dedicated to remembering all departed Orthodox Christians. These are known as 'Soul Sabbaths' or 'Forebears' Saturdays' and are kept on the following days:

Meat-fare Saturday

Meat-fare Saturday is the last Saturday before Great Lent that we can eat meat, and the day before 'Judgement Sunday' on which the hymns of the *Triodion* anticipate the Second Coming of Christ and the Last Judgment. We serve memorials on this Saturday as a reminder of the reality of the both the Particular, and the Final, Judgement.

The Second Third and Fourth Saturdays of Great Lent

The first Saturday of Great Lent is a commemoration of the miracle of St. Theodore the Tyro and not a Soul Sabbath. Kolyva is blessed in memory of the saint, but we do not commemorate the names of the Orthodox reposed. The next three Saturdays are held as Soul Sabbaths because the Litany for the Departed is not said during the weekday Presanctified Liturgy.

Saturday before Pentecost Sunday

On the Sunday of Pentecost we celebrate the descent of the Holy Spirit through which the redemption of the world was sealed. On the day before, we pray that the dead, as well as the living, will share this blessing.

The Saturday before St Demetrius' day (26th October)

The Russian Prince Dmitry Donskoi established this day as a remembrance of those killed in the battle of Kulikovo. Over the years, in the Slavic Churches, this day has become a Saturday of remembrance for all departed Orthodox Christians.

The Feast of the Beheading of St. John the Forerunner (August 29th/ September 11th)

On this feast, which is also a strict fast day on whatever day of the year it falls, many churches commemorate those Orthodox Christians who have fallen in battle.

The Tuesday after Thomas Sunday

In the Russian Church, this day is called '*Radonitsa*', which means the 'day of rejoicing' because it falls in the Paschal season during which we celebrate Christ's victory over death. This special memorial service begins with the paschal troparion 'Christ is Risen from the dead….' three times and then immediately the priest or deacon intones the Litany for the Departed.

The Panikhida and Lity

There are two common forms of memorial service used in the Orthodox Church. The longer service is called a *Pannychis* in Greek or *Panikhida* in Slavonic. The word *Pannychis* means 'vigil', and its use in this context derives from the vigils that the Christians used to keep at the tombs of the martyrs. The worshippers hold candles during a Panikhida to signify that they are praying that the soul of the departed may depart to the Eternal Light, Jesus Christ.

The Lity is shorter than the Panikhida and is sometimes referred to as the 'Trisagion Service' because after the priest's exclamation 'Blessed is our God…' the Trisagion sequence (Holy God to Our Father) is immediately read. After it, the choir sings the following Hymns for the Departed in Tone Four.

With the spirits of the righteous that have been perfected, give rest O our Saviour to the soul of Thy servant/handmaid preserving him/her for the blessed life with Thee O Friend of Man.

In the place of Thy rest, O Lord, where all Thy saints repose, do Thou grant rest also to the soul of Thy servant/handmaid for Thou alone art immortal.

Glory…

Thou art our God, Who didst descend into Hades, and didst dispel the pangs of those who were in fetters, do Thou grant rest also to the soul of Thy servant/handmaid.

Both now….

O thou only pure and undefiled virgin, who without seed conceived God in thy womb, pray thou that his/her soul be saved.

The text of the memorial services is identical for every lay person, but in every litany and exclamation the person is remembered by name; the personal pronoun is changed from 'his' to 'her' as appropriate. To make the text easier to read, we will omit these options from now on.

After these hymns, the Litany for the Departed is then intoned by the priest or deacon:

> **Have mercy on us, O God, according to Thy great mercy, we pray Thee hearken and have mercy.**
>
> **Again we pray for the repose of the soul of the departed servant of God [*Name*], and that Thou wilt pardon all his sins both voluntary and involuntary.**
>
> **That the Lord God will establish his soul where the righteous repose.**

The choir responds with a threefold 'Lord have mercy' to each of these petitions. The litany continues:

> *Deacon:* **The mercies of God, the kingdom of heaven, and the remission of his sins, we entreat of Christ, our Immortal King and our God.**
>
> *Choir* : Grant this O Lord
>
> *Deacon:* **Let us pray to the Lord**
>
> *Choir :* Lord have mercy

The priest then says the following prayer:

> **O God of spirits, and of all flesh, Who hast trampled down death and overthrown the devil, and given life to Thy world: Do Thou the same Lord, give rest to the soul of Thy departed servant [*Name*] in a place of brightness, a place of green pasture, a place of repose, from where all sickness, sorrow and sighing have fled away. Pardon every transgression which he has committed, whether by word, or deed or thought. For Thou art a good God, and lovest mankind, and there is no man who liveth and sinneth not: for Thou only art without sin, and Thy righteousness is an everlasting righteousness and Thy word is true. For Thou art the Resurrection and the Life, and the repose of thy departed servant [*Name*], O Christ our God, and to Thee do we send up glory, together with Thine**

unoriginate Father, and Thine all-holy, good and life-creating Spirit, now and ever, and unto the ages of ages.

When the memorial service is for young children, the prayer 'O God of spirits and of all flesh…' is replaced by the following:

O Lord, who watchest over little children in this present life, and in the life which is to come because of their simplicity of mind and innocence, comforting them in Abraham's bosom, and bringing them to brightly radiant places where the spirits of the righteous dwell: receive in peace the soul of Thy servant, the child [*Name*], for Thou Thyself hast said: Suffer the little children to come unto me, for of such is the kingdom of heaven.

The exclamation, 'for Thou art the Resurrection and the life…' then follows as usual. After the usual sequence between the deacon, choir and priest, the priest says the following dismissal:

May He Who hast authority over the living and the dead, as immortal King, and Who rose again from the dead, Christ our true God, through the prayers of His all-pure Mother; of the holy, glorious and all-famed apostles; of our holy and God-bearing Fathers, and of all the saints, establish in the dwelling-places of the righteous the soul of his servant [*Name*] who has been taken from us; give him rest in the bosom of Abraham, and number him with the righteous and have mercy upon us, in that He is good and the Friend of man.

Frequently Asked Questions

Why do we bless kolyva?

When commemorating the departed, we prepare a dish of sweetened boiled wheat grains called *kolyva* (pronounced kol-ee-va). Kolyva is blessed at a funeral or memorial service, and eaten as a sign of our brotherhood in Christ. Its sweetness represents the spiritual sweet-ness which awaits those who die in the Faith, and the wheat grain reminds us of our faith in the Resurrection; Christ says: 'except a corn of wheat fall into the ground and die, it abideth alone; but if it die, it bringeth forth much fruit' (John 12:24).

The practice of blessing kolyva dates back to the fourth century when the Emperor Julian the Apostate, a persecutor of Christians, ordered that the food in the markets be sprinkled with the blood of animals sacrificed to idols. He hoped by doing this to break the spirit of the Christians. The bishop was warned in a vision about this by the Great Martyr Theodore who told the bishop to order the Christians to boil wheat (called kolyva) as a replacement for the food in the markets. A simple recipe for kolyva is outlined below:

- Kolyva is made using whole wheat grain (not buckwheat).
- On the day before the kolyva is to be blessed, boil the wheat (500g of wheat grain is enough for about 30 people) until it is soft. Drain and dry it between paper towels overnight.
- On the next morning, mix the wheat with dried fruits, sugared peel, chopped nuts, glacé cherries, pomegranate seeds etc.
- Put the wheat and fruits in a suitable bowl, and sprinkle a little crushed biscuit on top of the wheat to absorb any moisture.
- Sieve icing sugar on top of the wheat to make a layer about 1cm thick. Press it down gently and decorate the top of the kolyva with nuts or glacé cherries in the form of a cross.
- Push a candle into the centre of the kolyva.

What can we do for non-Orthodox relatives that have died?

Only Orthodox Christians are commemorated during the Service of Preparation, and memorial services can only be served for Orthodox. By holding fast to this position, we proclaim our oneness in faith with our fellow Orthodox, and acknowledge that it is by this faith that we are saved.

The heterodox, in contrast, do not have this saving faith, so we cannot pray for them with the prayers of the Church. However, we must pray for them outside Church in our own prayers; the Holy Martyr Varus, in particular, is called upon to intercede for those that have died outside the Church. In addition, we can give money to the poor and to charity in remembrance of them.

8

The Tollhouse Controversy

For it is written, as I live, saith the Lord, every knee shall bow to me, and every tongue shall confess to God. So then, each of us will give an account of himself to God.

Romans 14:11-12

The fate of the soul after death, in which it is subject to the Particular Judgement, is often illustrated in Orthodox literature by describing the soul's passage through various tollhouses occupied by demons who have to be 'paid off' by the toll of good deeds. St. Macarius the Great, writing in the fourth century, describes the progress of the soul after death:

> *When the soul of man departs out of the body, a great mystery is there accomplished. If it is under the guilt of sins, there come bands of demons, and angels of the left hand, and powers of darkness take over that soul, and hold it fast on their side.*

According to Fr. Michael Pomazansky, 'the word "tollhouse" in itself does not indicate to us any particular religious significance. In patristic language it signifies that short period after death when the Christian soul must account for its moral state.'[66] The tollhouses may also be understood to depict the 'inward personal battle in the soul which has been separated from the body'.[67]

The tollhouse controversy erupted in the 1970s with the publication of Fr. Seraphim Rose's book *The Soul after Death* in which he used a variety of Orthodox and non-Orthodox sources to support the tollhouse teaching. The tollhouse debate erupts periodically on internet forums, and owing to the nature of the controversy, it is unlikely anyone will come up with a definitive answer that puts the argument to bed once and for all.

The evidence for actual 'tollhouses' in the services of the Church is not extensive. Tollhouses are not mentioned in the Orthodox burial

---

[66] M. Pomazansky, *Selected Essays* (Jordanville: Holy Trinity Monastery, 1996) p. 236.
[67] Ibid., p. 237.

service, but the ordeal of the soul after death certainly is; in the verses composed by St. John of Damascus we hear:

> *What manner of ordeal doth the soul endure when from the body it is parted! Woe is me! How many then are its tears; and there is none to show compassion! It stretches out its eyes to the angels; all unavailing is its prayer. It stretches out its hands to men; and finds none to help.*

There are many references in the Octoechos to the Particular Judgment, and a few mentions of the tollhouses specifically:

> *At the hour of mine end, O Virgin, rescue me from the hands of the demons, from condemnation and retribution, from dreadful trials and bitter tollhouses, and from the cruel prince and everlasting damnation, O Mother of God. (Tone 4, Friday Matins Ode 9).*

At the Particular Judgment we will receive a foretaste of our future life, according to God's righteous judgement as foretold by the Prophet Jeremias: 'I the Lord search the heart, I try the reins, even to give every man according to his ways, and according to the fruit of his doings' (Jer. 17:10). The examination by the demons is *not* this judgment because there is only one Lawgiver and Judge; the confrontation is a revealing of hidden sins and a bringing to awareness of them. Indeed, in the life of St. Basil the New we read that the demons have no record of confessed sins:

> *For whenever someone confesses his sins in that world below and thereafter devotes himself to repentance, God forgives him for the earlier sins he has confessed, and he is free thereafter, having invisibly received remission of them. For then the wicked demons in the tollhouses who have documentation of men's lawless acts noted in their ledgers, after quickly opening their foul records, cannot find even a trace in them of the sin they recorded there, for the Holy Spirit has invisibly erased them.*[68]

The ordeal of the soul after death is referred to in other lives of Orthodox saints. St. Peter the Publican's vision in which he saw his good

---

[68] *The Life of Saint Basil the Younger* (trans. D. F. Sullivan, A. M. Talbot, S. McGrath) (Washington: Dumbarton Oaks, 2014) p. 229.

and bad deeds being weighed on a balance, and the account of the death of St. Stephen of Sinai, below, are just two examples:

> *On the day before his death, he went into ecstasy of mind, and with open eyes he looked to the right and left of his bed and, as if he were being called to account by someone, in the hearing of all the bystanders, he said: 'Yes indeed, that is true, but that is why I fasted for so many years.' And then again: 'Yes, it is quite true; but I wept and served the brethren.' And again: 'No, you are slandering me.' And sometimes he would say: 'Yes, it is true. Yes, I do not know what to say to this. But in God there is mercy.' And it was truly an awful and horrible sight – this invisible and merciless inquisition. And what was most terrible, he was accused of what he had not done.*[69]

St. Macarius the Great refers to the demons as 'tax collectors' – a similar metaphor to that of the tollhouse:

> *Like tax-collectors sitting in the narrow ways, and laying hold upon the passers-by, so do the demons spy upon souls and lay hold of them; and when they pass out of the body, if they are not perfectly cleansed, they do not suffer them to mount up to the mansions of heaven and to meet their Lord, and they are driven down by the demons of the air.*

The 'Pro-' and 'Anti-' Tollhouse Arguments

The most complete account of the tollhouses is contained in the life of Saint Basil the New, but the number of tollhouses varies between different editions of the life: St. Demetrius of Rostov's *Life of St. Basil the New* describes twenty toll houses; the Moscow edition (in Greek) includes twenty-one, and the St. Petersburg Edition (1890) twenty-two. St. Cyril, the fifth century Patriarch of Alexandria, speaks of five tollhouses corresponding to the sins of the tongue and mouth (including gluttony and drunkenness), eyes, ears, nose and hand, but implies that there are others that deal with fornication, murder and sorcery:

---

[69] St. John Climacus *The Ladder Of Divine Ascent* p .77

The soul will be protected by the holy angels, as it makes its way forward and upward through the air, but it will discover toll stations, guarding and controlling the way, blocking the path of the souls that are trying to ascend. And each toll station deals with its own particular sins.[70]

The lack of consistency in the tollhouse accounts lends weight to Fr. Michael Pomazansky's assertion that the tollhouses are pedagogical tools to bring us to repentance rather than a definite, dogmatic system.

The *Soul after Death* is the foremost modern 'pro-tollhouse' work, but it remains controversial because of Fr. Seraphim's attempt to 'fill in the gaps' of Orthodox knowledge by resorting to non-Orthodox sources detailing various out-of-body and near-death experiences. Delving into the occult in order to prove the existence of tollhouses is dangerous because we are all, to a greater or lesser extent, lacking in discernment. The Church teaches the existence of the Particular and Final Judgements; how these occur is of no concern to us; our only concern should be that we not be condemned at them.

The 'anti-tollhouse' movement arose as a result of Fr. Seraphim's work and its main arguments can be summarised as follows:

- The tollhouse teaching is pagan or heretical in origin; it is not mentioned in Scripture
- It is too literal
- Outside the body the soul cannot function
- It is too similar to purgatory
- The demons appear to be judging the faithful
- The harshness of the tollhouse accounts might lead people to give up and despair.

Although the tollhouse debate itself is not spiritually profitable, it is perhaps worth considering the points raised by those opposed to the tollhouse teaching.

---

[70] Quoted in B. E. Daley, 'At the Hour of our Death: Mary's Dormition and Christian Dying in Late Patristic and Early Byzantine Literature' *Dumbarton Oaks Papers*, No. 55, 2001 pp. 71-89.

Firstly, the Church has often adapted terminology from pre-Christian writings in order to explain Her theology more clearly and to protect Orthodox beliefs from influence by heretics. An assertion that something is not mentioned in Scripture is not proof that it is not Orthodox. After all, the word 'Trinity' is not mentioned in Scripture either.

Some object to the literalism of the tollhouses with demons bearing ledgers with sins written in them, and bargains being made with 'spiritual gold'. Theses ledgers and gold, however, are not physical. How could they be when the demons themselves are incorporeal? The images of balances, scales, tollhouses are images that represent reality, but are not the reality itself.

These metaphors and images are instructive as guides for souls and aids to repentance. Moreover, the Church often uses such metaphors in Her services. For example, in the Sixth Hour during Great Lent we pray Christ to 'tear asunder the handwriting of our sins' – an obvious metaphor. This does not mean that the tollhouses are mythical, just that the reality of them is outside our understanding of time and space. Their reality does not concern us: it is how we transform our reality by repentance that is important for us.

The third point mentioned above is perhaps the most interesting. According to some opponents of the tollhouses, the soul cannot function outside the body. However, the Synod of the Russian Orthodox Church Outside Russia confirmed in 1981 that this belief is not in accordance with the mind of the Church.

> [This belief] is at variance with the teaching concerning the preaching of the Forerunner in Hades prior to the arrival of the Saviour there, as well as the possibility of the souls of the Old Testament personages of heeding the preaching of the Saviour in Hades or their going with Him to paradise….The very appearance of Moses on Mount Tabor reveals his soul as active and capable of taking part in a conversation with the Saviour concerning His redemption of the human race. The state and life of people beyond the grave are not all the same, but

depends upon the degree of sanctity or sinfulness of their life on earth.[71]

The tollhouses have only a superficial resemblance to the Roman Catholic doctrine of purgatory. The Orthodox Church has never accepted this doctrine according to which, to be cleansed from sin, a sinner needs to 'satisfy' God – to offer Him something to pay the debt for sin. The purgatorial fire is God's satisfaction. The idea behind purgatory is that repentance for sins is not necessarily sufficient for forgiveness of the debt that has been incurred. Those who are still in debt to God are required to spend the appointed time in purgatory.

There is no doubt that the tollhouse accounts could lend themselves to an interpretation based on this concept of satisfaction, but even as late as the fifteenth century, even the word 'satisfaction' itself was unknown to Byzantine theologians.[72] It is clear then, that the older tollhouse accounts were not influenced by this theory that is foreign to Orthodoxy.

In contrast, the Orthodox teaching on the Particular Judgement is not legalistic. This vision of the fourth century saint, Niphon of Constantiana, is characteristic:

> *Saint Niphon saw another soul being carried up belonging to a blasphemous and cruel man. The demons were accusing him, and reminding him, one-by-one, of the improper words and grave curses he had uttered. The angels said in rebuttal that he had a few claims to salvation. Often, for example, he would contemplate committing a sin, but then he would sigh bitterly and sometimes shed tears. Once in a while he would even give a little charity to the poor. Having this in mind, the angels of light claimed that God would have mercy on his soul. The demons, being angered, said: 'From his youth he committed unchristian acts. He polluted himself with numerous sins, and, indeed even sodomitic ones. How*

---

[71] Bishop Gregory, 'Extract from the Minutes of the Session of the Bishops of the Russian` Orthodox Church Outside of Russia' *Orthodox Life* (1981) Vol. 31 No.1 pp. 23-24.

[72] K. Hartnup, *On the beliefs of the Greeks: Leo Allatios and Popular Orthodoxy* (Leiden: Brill, 2004) p.211.

shall we describe his curses and his anger? What is worse, he even committed murder. If therefore he must be saved, then take the whole world and all the sinners of the earth and save them gratis; because we are labouring and troubling ourselves in vain!'

Some tollhouse accounts may seem overly harsh, but it is clear from the Gospels that we will have to give an account, not just for our deeds, but for every idle word we have spoken (cf. Matt 12:36). The confrontation with the demons described in the tollhouse accounts is not the judgment, but is a consequence of God's Judgement, a 'revelation of the righteous judgment of God Who will render to every man according to his deeds' (Romans 2: 5-6).

The demons are not judging our souls, but our souls are being faced with the due reward for our deeds (cf. Luke 23:41). The demons have no power over us, as we read in the Life of St. Anthony the Great: 'If the demons had no power even over the swine, much less have they any power over men formed in the image of God. So then we ought to fear God only, and despise the demons, and be in no fear of them.'

Even though the tollhouses are not literal 'houses in the sky' where the demons judge and condemn us, we should not ignore the Church's teaching on the Particular Judgement at which we will have to give an account of our deeds. The tollhouse debate may not be profitable in itself, but reflecting on the Judgement certainly is. We will be judged, not by the demons, but by God's merciful and just judgement. What we can say for certain is that the underlying message of the Church's teaching is not one of fear, but of the effectiveness of love – the love for our neighbour that will cover a multitude of sins (cf. 1 Peter 4:8).

Saint John of Damascus
The scroll contains the first verse of the burial Anthem.

9

The Mystery of Burial

We look not at the things which are seen, but at the things which are not seen: for the things which are seen are temporal; but the things which are not seen are eternal.

2 Corinthians 4:18

For most non-Orthodox Christians, death is a far off event which is only to be confronted out of necessity. Most modern heterodox funeral services concentrate on the person's experiences, likes and dislikes rather than praying for mercy and forgiveness; the soul's existence and the consequences of sin are glossed over or not even mentioned at all. Man, however, being a created being, has the attributes of 'createdness' – he has a concrete existence in both body and soul. Moreover, all Orthodox Christians have been reborn of water and the Holy Spirit and re-created in the baptismal font.

The mystery of burial is a celebration of the Resurrection; it is the Church on earth praying for the soul of a member of the Church who has gone to their rest before us, and provides an inspirational lesson on our own mortality and the need for repentance. St. Nicolas Cabasilas describes how, through this mystery, our grief at the death of a loved one can help us grieve for our sins:

> *It is indeed fitting that those who meditate on Christ's deeds mourn and weep. Were one to consider what novel things were accomplished for our salvation, what would happen to our indifference and the sleep which detains us? Whether we are grieved at the loss of things most precious, or constrained to weep by the memory of good things which we have lost, this is the way that we learn how great are the riches we possess, how it is possible to retain them, and how we may waste them.*[73]

Our faith in the Resurrection of Christ, and our belief in Christ's sacrificial death on the Cross, is the cornerstone of our personal response

[73] St. Nicolas Cabasilas, *The Life in Christ* (trans. C. J. Decatanzaro) (New York: St. Vladimir's Seminary Press, 1974) p.178.

to the death of our loved ones. When we die, we do so 'in the hope of eternal life' (Titus 1:2), and when we grieve, we do so enlightened by our faith in the Resurrection, but not like 'the rest who have no hope' (1 Thess. 4:13). In the Creed we say: 'I believe in the resurrection of the dead and in the life of the age to come'; the Resurrection of Christ has rendered death powerless as St. Athanasius the Great teaches:

> *If it is by the sign of the Cross and by faith in Christ that death is crushed, then it is clear, if truth is the judge, that it is none other than Christ Himself who has shown triumphs and victories over death and who has rendered it powerless. Death was formerly powerful and therefore to be feared, but is now despised after the coming of the Saviour and after the death and resurrection of His Body. Clearly it is by Christ Himself, Who ascended the Cross, that death has been destroyed and overcome.*[74]

In the words of St. Paul, we look for 'that blessed hope, and the glorious appearing of the great God and our Saviour Jesus Christ Who gave Himself for us, that He might redeem us from all iniquity' (Titus. 2:13). St. John Chrysostom describes the far-reaching consequences of Christ's sacrifice on the Cross:

> *You have observed His outstanding triumph, the splendid achievement of the Cross. Now let me tell you something even more remarkable, the manner in which He gained His victory, and you will marvel all the more. Christ conquered the devil using the same means and the same weapons that the devil had used to defeat us. Let me tell you how this occurred. The symbols of our fall were a virgin, a tree and death. The virgin was Eve (for she had not yet known man); then there was the tree, and death was Adam's penalty. And again these three tokens of our destruction, the virgin, the tree and death became tokens of our victory. Instead of Eve there was Mary; instead of the tree of knowledge of good and evil, the wood of the Cross; instead of Adam's death, the death of Christ.*

---

[74] St. Athanasius the Great, *Contra Gentes and De Incarnatione* (trans. R. W. Thomson) (Oxford: OUP, 1971) pp. 203-204.

Do you see that the devil was defeated by the very means he used to defeat us? By a tree the devil laid Adam low, and by a tree Christ defeated him. The first tree sent men to the world below, but the second called back those who had already descended. The first tree buried man, already naked and a captive; the second revealed to all the world the Victor naked. The first death condemned Adam's descendants, but the second death (Christ's) raised up even those who were born before Him.

Who shall tell of the mighty acts of the Lord? Though we were dead we became immortal. Such is the achievement of the Cross. Do you now understand the victory and the way it was won? Learn now how this victory was achieved without any labour or effort of our own. We bloodied no weapons, nor stood on the battle line, nor suffered any wounds, nor saw any fighting, and yet we won the victory. It was the Lord's battle, but the crown was ours. And since it is our victory, let us, like soldiers, raise joyous voices in praise of our achievement. Praising the Lord let us say: Death is swallowed up in victory. O death where is your victory? O death where is your sting?

All this was the glorious result of the Cross. The Cross is our trophy raised against the demons, our sword against sin and the sword Christ used to pierce the serpent. The Cross is the good will of the Father, the glory of the Only–begotten, the joy of the Spirit, the pride of the angels, the safeguard of the Church, Paul's boast, the bulwark of the saints, and the light of the entire world.

Preparations for Burial

As soon as someone has reposed, the Psalter is read over the body to comfort those who are mourning and to inspire them to pray for the departed at a time when prayers are especially needed. Any Orthodox Christian can, and should, read the Psalter at this time. The parish priest should be informed immediately so that the newly departed may be commemorated in the Divine Liturgy.

Traditionally, the funeral should take place on, or before, the third day, but this is not always possible. The most important thing to organise is to find a day for the funeral that is convenient for the priest. The funeral should, however, take place as soon as possible, and this requirement should be made clear to the funeral directors. There is no legal requirement in the UK to use an undertaker or funeral director, but it is simpler and safer to do so; collecting a body from a mortuary is not an easy task, nor is carrying a body from the church to the cemetery and lowering it into the grave. It is safer and easier to let the undertakers take care of all these arrangements.

In addition to informing the undertakers that the body should not be embalmed, they should be told that the coffin will be open during the burial service.

Funerals can be expensive to organise, but most of this expense is quite avoidable; there is no need for floral arrangements, limousines for the mourners, expensive caskets or splendid memorials. Many Orthodox families ask for donations to a nominated charity instead of flowers, and although this is a relatively modern custom, it is perfectly Orthodox.

Early Christians shunned the elaborate funeral rituals of the pagans. St. Jerome criticized the custom of depositing expensive personal possessions in the grave: 'The simplicity of the tomb of the Lord shames the pretensions of the wealthy who, even in their graves, cannot give up their riches.' A simple mourning was also preferred over the elaborate and emotional grieving process favoured by pagans. For St. Cyprian of Carthage, excessive mourning showed a lack of belief in the power of the Resurrection:

> We believe in God and live in hope, trusting that Christ suffered for us and rose again. We who abide in Christ and through Him, and will rise again in Him, why are we ourselves unwilling to depart from this life? Why do we bewail and grieve for our friends when they depart as if they were lost, when Christ Himself, our Lord and God, encourages us and says: 'I am the Resurrection and the Life: he that believeth in Me though he were dead, yet shall he live.' If we believe in Christ, let us have faith in His words and promises; and since we shall not die eternally, let us come with a happy assurance unto Christ, with Whom we are to conquer and to reign for ever.

The body is washed and, if the newly-departed was baptized into the Orthodox Church as an adult, clothed in his or her baptismal robe. The white robe from a pilgrimage to the River Jordan may be used instead. The white colour of the robe signifies the purity that should distinguish the soul of the Christian.

In addition, the body is covered in a large shroud decorated with a depiction of the burial of Christ and the words of the Trisagion hymn; in the Slavic Churches, the shroud is often replaced by a strip of paper or cloth placed around the forehead called a crown (below).

The crown signifies that the departed desires to be granted a heavenly crown, and that while on earth he struggled for Christ's righteousness. An icon of the Saviour (an icon of the patron saint can be used instead) is placed on the chest to signify that the reposed died in the faith of the Lord Jesus Christ.

If possible, the body is brought to church early in the morning before the Divine Liturgy so that the Bloodless Sacrifice may be offered for the forgiveness of sins of the newly departed and the mourners may partake of the healing Mysteries.

The body is carried into the Church as the choir sings the Trisagion hymn, signifying not only that the souls of the faithful departed are received by the angels, but also our desire that together with them we may ever hymn the Creator.

The coffin is placed in the centre of the church, facing the iconostasis, and four candles or candle stands are placed in crosswise fashion around it. In the Orthodox burial service the coffin is kept open, and although this practice has fallen out of fashion in most heterodox Churches, it is important to keep this theologically significant tradition that is often referred to in the burial service itself.

The Burial Service

So when this corruptible shall have put on incorruption, and this mortal shall have put on immortality, then shall be brought to pass the saying that is written, Death is swallowed up in victory. O death, where is thy sting? O grave, where is thy victory?

1 Corinthians 15: 54-55

During the burial service, we hold candles signifying the light of Christ and our own belief in the resurrection to eternal life. The burial service begins with **'Blessed is our God always now, and ever and unto the ages of ages'** followed by Psalm 90, which begins with the verse: 'He that dwelleth in the help of the Most High shall abide in the shelter of the God of heaven. He shall say unto the Lord: Thou art my helper and my refuge. He is my God, and I will hope in Him.'

Psalm 90 expresses the love God has for us, and that God is our only true refuge and protection. Commenting on the verse, 'with His shoulders will He overshadow thee, and under His wings shalt thou have hope,' St. Jerome says:

> *As an eagle, the Lord spreads His wings over us, His nestlings. There the Lord is compared to the eagle guarding its young. The simile, therefore, is appropriate that God protects us as a Father, and as a hen guarding her chicks lest they be snatched away by a hawk.*[75]

At the end of Psalm 90, the priest begins to read Psalm 118 (the seventeenth kathisma). Psalm 118 is also read during Saturday Matins which is the day on which special hymns are chanted for the dead. The Prophet David speaks in this psalm of the blessedness of the soul which has lived in accordance with God's commandments and of its hope in the mercy of God. The choir quietly sings 'Alleluia' during the reading of the first and third sections of the seventeenth kathisma and 'have mercy on Thy servant' during the second section. Between each section there is a Litany for the Departed to which the choir responds with 'Lord have mercy' (three times):

---

[75] St. Jerome, *The Homilies Vol. 1* (trans. M. L. Ewald) (Washington: CUA Press, 1964) p. 157.

Again we pray for the repose of the soul of the departed servant of God, [*Name*] and that Thou wilt pardon all his sins both voluntary and involuntary.

That the Lord God will establish his soul where the righteous repose.

The mercies of God, the kingdom of heaven, and the remission of his sins, we entreat of Christ our Immortal King and our God.

The priest's exclamation that follows emphasizes that it is the Resurrection of Christ that gives us hope that we may find rest with the saints in His Kingdom:

For Thou art the resurrection and the life, and the repose of Thy departed servant, [*Name*], O Christ our God, and to Thee do we send up glory, together with Thine unoriginate Father, and Thine all-holy, good and life-creating Spirit, now, and ever and unto the ages of ages.

The choir immediately begins the Evlogitaria of the Reposed at the end of Psalm 118.

The Evlogitaria of the Reposed

This hymn is sung in the same tone, and has the same refrain ('Blessed art Thou O Lord, teach me Thy statutes') as the Evlogitaria of the Resurrection that is sung on Sundays. The first verse alludes to the parable of the lost sheep (Luke 15: 3-7); a 'well-spring' is the source of a spring or stream, and in the services of the Church, Christ is referred to as the well-spring of life, miracles and healing.

The choir of Saints hath found the Well-spring of Life, and the Door of Paradise; I too, have found the way by means of repentance; I am the lamb that was lost. Call me back again, O Saviour, and save me.

Hymns to the martyrs are sung throughout the burial service because the martyrs, in confessing Christ unto death, are the perfect example of a Christian death, and because they struggled against sin, even unto blood (cf. Heb. 12:4). In the Evlogitaria, in particular, we commemorate the struggles of the martyrs:

Ye that preached the Lamb of God, and like lambs yourselves did suffer slaughter, and were translated to a life that ages not, O Saints, and is eternal; earnestly beseech Him, O martyrs, and implore that we be granted loosing from debts.

The Canon

The canon follows the normal structure for Matins except that the Magnificat is not sung after Ode Eight, and the Little Litany is replaced by the special Litany for the Departed. The irmoi of the canon are the same as those sung at Small Compline on Great Friday, providing another link between our burial and the commemoration of the burial of the God-man Jesus Christ; these irmoi are also sung on Sunday Matins of the Plagal Second Tone reminding us of our faith in the Resurrection.

In each of the odes we ask for the intercessions of the martyrs for the soul of the reposed. Our earthly life is also compared to a voyage across a stormy sea. Death for the Christian, on the other hand, is portrayed as a haven of quiet. After Ode Three, the choir sings the following hymns:

Truly, all things are vanity, and life is but a shadow and a dream. For in vain does every earth born man disquiet himself as saith the Scriptures. When we have acquired the world, then do we take up our abode in the grave, where kings and beggars lie down together. Wherefore, O Christ our God, grant rest to Thy departed servant since Thou art the Friend of Man.

O all-holy Theotokos disdain me not all the days of my life, and give me not over to the mediation of mortal man, but do thou thyself help me, and show mercy on me.

After Ode Six, the kontakion for the reposed is sung in the Plagal Fourth Tone:

With the Saints grant rest, O Christ, to the soul of Thy servant/handmaid where there is neither sickness, nor sorrow, nor sighing, but life everlasting.

During the singing of the kontakion the priest censes the body of the reposed, and ascends the soleas to cense the iconostasis and then the people. The Ikos is then read:

Thou only art Immortal, who hast created and fashioned man. For out of earth were we mortals made, and unto the earth shall we return as Thou didst command when Thou didst make me, saying unto me: Dust thou art and unto dust shalt thou return. Whither also, all we mortals make our way, singing as our funeral dirge the hymn: Alleluia, alleluia, alleluia.

The Anthem

The 'Anthem' chanted in the burial service was composed by St. John of Damascus and consists of eight verses in each of the eight tones. The verse sung in the fourth tone refers to the Prophet Job's lament after losing his family, wealth and health: 'He hath cast me into the mire, and I am become like dust and ashes' (Job 30:19):

I called to mind the Prophet who cried: 'I am earth and ashes'; and I looked again into the graves, and beheld the bones laid bare and I said: Who then is the king or the warrior, the rich man or the pauper, the upright or the sinner? Yet give rest, O Lord, with Thy Saints unto Thy servant.

The Anthem, and the other hymns of the burial service, often refer to the corruption that we undergo in the grave. Before the Fall, Adam and Eve were passionless and free from corruption, and we too will be resurrected before the Last Judgment in our bodies, raised from corruption to incorruption in accordance with the words of St. Paul:

So also is the resurrection of the dead. It is sown in corruption; it is raised in incorruption: It is sown in dishonour; it is raised in glory: it is sown in weakness; it is raised in power: It is sown a natural body; it is raised a spiritual body (1 Cor. 15: 42-4).

Christ appeared to His disciples after the Resurrection and talked and ate with them, but His Body was no longer confined by nature's laws as we hear in the Gospel when He appeared to the disciples although the doors were locked (John 20:19). Likewise, as St. Paul says, our resurrected bodies will be transformed:

Our conversation is in heaven; from whence also we look for the Saviour, the Lord Jesus Christ: Who shall change our vile body, that it may be fashioned like unto His glorious Body, according to the working whereby He is able even to subdue all things unto Himself (Phil. 3: 20-21).

The Beatitudes

The choir chants the Beatitudes immediately after the Anthem. Continuing the theme of repentance, the verses chanted refer to the good thief (Luke 23: 40-43).

> O Christ, who because of his repentance, didst pronounce in anticipation a citizen of Paradise the thief that upon the Cross cried to Thee: Remember me! Make me, a sinner, worthy of thy kingdom.

The Prokeimenon, Epistle and Gospel

The Gospel sequence begins with the reader and the choir chanting the prokeimenon: 'Blessed is the way in which thou shalt walk today, O soul, for a place of rest is prepared for thee.' This prokeimenon is unique in Orthodoxy because all other prokeimena are verses from the psalms. The Epistle reading is from the First Epistle of St. Paul to the Thessalonians (1 Thess. 4: 13-17).

> Brethren, we would not have you to be ignorant, concerning them which are asleep, that ye sorrow not, even as others which have no hope. For if we believe that Jesus died and rose again, even so them also which sleep in Jesus will God bring with Him. For this we say unto you by the word of the Lord, that we which are alive and remain unto the coming of the Lord shall not prevent them which are asleep. For the Lord Himself shall descend from heaven with a shout, with the voice of the archangel, and with the trump of God: and the dead in Christ shall rise first: then we which are alive and remain shall be caught up together with them in the clouds, to meet the Lord in the air: and so shall we ever be with the Lord.

The Gospel reading is from the Gospel of St. John the Theologian (John 5: 24-30) and reminds us of the Final Judgement, the resurrection of the dead and the rewards that will be given to the righteous and the punishments that sinners will have earned for themselves:

Amen, Amen, I say unto you, He that heareth My word, and believeth on Him that sent Me, hath everlasting life, and shall not come into condemnation, but is passed from death unto life. Amen, Amen, I say unto you; the hour is coming, and now is, when the dead shall hear the voice of the Son of God: and they that hear shall live. For as the Father hath life in Himself, so hath He given to the Son to have life in Himself; and hath given Him authority to execute judgment also, because He is the Son of man. Marvel not at this: for the hour is coming, in the which all that are in the graves shall hear His voice, and shall come forth; they that have done good, unto the resurrection of life; and they that have done evil, unto the resurrection of damnation. I can of Mine own self do nothing: as I hear, I judge, and My judgment is just; because I seek not Mine own will, but the will of the Father which hath sent Me.

The Prayer of Absolution

In the Slavic (and modern Greek use), the priest reads a prayer of absolution and places the sheet of paper on which the prayer is written in the right hand of the departed. This prayer is not found in older Greek service books.

The Verses for the Last Kiss

Before the coffin lid is sealed we come forward and the kiss the head and hand of the newly departed as the choir sings a number of hymns that call to mind our common mortality. This practice is an ancient one, as the writings of St. Dionysius the Areopagite confirm:

> *Coming forward, the godly hierarch offers sacred prayer over the deceased, and following this prayer, he kisses him, as do all the others in turn. The prayer is to the divine goodness, asking pardon for the deceased for all the sins caused by human weakness, begging that he be established in the light, in the land of the living, in the bosom of Abraham, Isaac and Jacob, where sickness and sorrow and sighing are fled away.*

The hymns of the Last Kiss are sung to the same melody that is used on Great Friday when the epitaphios is brought into the centre of the

Church. On hearing them, we call to mind the Burial of Christ and the sacrifice He made for the sins of all by willingly submitting to the Cross and death.

The doxasticon of the Last Kiss is sung to a longer melody in the Plagal Second Tone:

> As ye behold me lie before you all speechless and bereft of breath, weep for me, O friends and brethren, O kinsfolk and acquaintance. For but yesterday I talked with you, and suddenly there came upon me the dread hour of death. Come, all ye who loved me, and kiss me with the last kiss, for never again shall I walk or talk with you; for I go to the Judge with Whom there is no respect of persons. Slave and master stand together before him, king and warrior, the rich and the poor, in honour equal, and according to his deeds shall every man receive glory or be put to shame. But I beg and implore you all, that ye will pray without ceasing unto Christ God, that I be not doomed according to my sins, unto a place of torment, but that He will appoint unto me a place where is the light of life.

The Dismissal

The burial service ends with the priest giving the following dismissal:

> **May He Who hast authority over the living and the dead, as immortal King, and Who rose again from the dead, Christ our true God, through the prayers of His all-pure Mother; of the holy, glorious, and all-famed apostles; of our holy and God-bearing fathers, and of all the saints, establish in the dwelling-places of the righteous the soul of His servant [*Name*] who has been taken from us; give him rest in the bosom of Abraham, and number him with the righteous and have mercy upon us, in that He is good and the Friend of man.**

The phrase 'bosom of Abraham' indicates the comfort that the righteous shall receive, in much the same way that the Apostle John leaned on Christ's breast at the Mystical Supper. Abraham is not only an example of faith in God, but also of good actions as St. Ambrose of Milan explains:

The righteous are said to rest in the bosom of Abraham, for they rest in his grace, in his rest, in his calm peace, because they put on faith like unto his, and transformed one and the same will into good works.

Procession to the Grave

The body is carried to the grave as the choir sings the Trisagion hymn. The body is lowered into the grave as the choir sings the verses 'With the spirits of the righteous…' and the deacon intones the Litany for the Departed. This final part of the burial service is identical to the service of the Lity memorial service. The kolyva is blessed at this point.

After the dismissal, the priest takes a handful of dust and scatters it crosswise over the remains saying: '**The earth is the Lord's, and the fullness thereof, the world, and all that dwell therein.**' (Psalm 23:1) He then pours the ash from the censer over the coffin. In the Serbian and Bulgarian traditions, a bottle of wine is poured in crosswise form onto the grave. The modern Greek and Cypriot custom of the smashing of plates or other vessels into the grave is pagan in origin and should not be carried out.

Frequently Asked Questions

Why are Orthodox Christians buried facing east?

Orthodox Christians are buried facing east, where the sun rises, because 'Christ is the Dayspring from on high' (Luke 1: 78) and the 'Sun of righteousness' (Mal 4:2). This practice is particularly ancient and, as we shall discuss in the next chapter, an east-west orientation of graves is one way archeologists distinguish between Christian and pagan burials from the first centuries of Christianity. In the Russian usage, the cross is placed at the foot of the grave rather than at the head.

What is embalming?

Embalming is a procedure used to preserve the body after death in which the internal organs are punctured, the blood disposed of and replaced by a preserving solution. There are major environmental problems with embalming. The preserving solution contains the chemical formaldehyde which has been proved to cause cancer. In the USA alone, around seven million gallons of formaldehyde enter the soil each year through burial of embalmed remains.

Embalming is a desecration of the body, which is the 'temple of the Holy Spirit' (1 Cor. 6:19). The respect and honour we show to the body stems from our faith in the Resurrection, and in the power of the Holy Spirit which acts through the relics of the saints as St. John of Damascus teaches:

> *From the time when He that is Himself life and the Author of life was reckoned among the dead, we do not call those dead who have fallen asleep in the hope of the resurrection and in faith in Him. For how could a dead body work miracles? How, therefore, are demons driven off by them, diseases dispelled, sick persons made well, the blind restored to sight, lepers purified, temptations and troubles overcome, and how does every good gift from the Father of lights come down through them to those who pray with sure faith?*

Embalming should not be carried out unless the law expressly requires it; some countries, for example, require bodies to be embalmed if they are going to be transported across state or national borders. Orthodox Christians can be given an Orthodox funeral if they have been embalmed, but it should be avoided if at all possible.

10

The Orthodox Church and Cremation

Know ye not that your body is the temple of the Holy Spirit which is in you, which ye have of God, and ye are not your own? For ye are bought with a price: therefore glorify God in your body, and in your spirit, which are God's.

1 Corinthians 6: 19-20

Unlike heterodox churches, the Orthodox Church does not have an alternative funeral service in which the body is cremated rather than buried; Orthodox Christians who have chosen to be cremated are not permitted an Orthodox funeral. The only exception to this is the case of someone being cremated by relatives against his or her wishes; in this case a funeral service can be perfumed without the body present. Christians avoid cremation because burial is traditional: the actual act of fire consuming the body does not, of course, destroy or pollute the soul.

Cremation has become increasingly popular over the last hundred years, with over 75% of deaths in the UK, and 45% in the USA, resulting in cremation. During the cremation process the body is burned, together with the coffin, in a furnace for about an hour. The burned remains, consisting of teeth and larger pieces of bone, are loaded into a pulveriser and ground for around 30 seconds. The resulting powder is what is commonly referred to as 'ashes'.

Cremation is often promoted as an environmentally friendly alternative to traditional burial, but nothing could be further from the truth! A crematorium's furnace has to run at around 1000 °C per cremation – a massive use of fossil fuels. The atmospheric pollution emitted by crematoria chimneys is significant. In addition to the carbon dioxide released on burning the body and the fuel, cremation is also a significant source of atmospheric mercury pollution through the vaporization of dental fillings. In 2007, a UK government study showed that cremation accounted for around 16% of all atmospheric mercury pollution, a figure that was predicted to double by 2020 making cremation the biggest source of mercury pollution in the UK. In the UK, at least, efforts have been made by government to force crematoria to reduce mercury pollution by the installation of mercury abatement equipment.

Cremation is a fairly recent re-introduction into the West, and as a consequence there has been no universal pronouncement by the Orthodox Church on the issue. However, the bishops of the Russian Orthodox Church Outside Russia decreed in 1989:

> *The cremation of the bodies of the dead is contradictory to that which was established in the Christian Church from the very beginning. It also contradicts the content of the prayers contained in the Orthodox funeral rite in which the burial of the dead is taken as a fulfilment of the judgement God passed upon Adam: Dust thou art, and unto dust shalt thou return (Gen. 3:19).*[76]

There is no doubt that as Christianity spread, cremation died out in areas that had largely converted to Christianity. Archeologists generally use three indicators to identify Christian remains: burial, an east-west orientation of the grave and an absence of grave goods.

In general, the finding of cremated remains from antiquity and the early Middle Ages implies pagan beliefs on the part of the dead person or his family. The second century *Dialogue of Octavius,* between the pagan Caecilius Natalis and the Christian Octavius Januarius contains a discussion concerning cremation which is still relevant today:

> Caecilius Natalis: *I presume that is supposed to be why [Christians] abominate funeral pyres and condemn cremation. But of course every body, whether from the flames or not, is eventually reduced to earth in the course of the passing years; it makes no difference if it is torn apart by wild beasts or swallowed up by the sea or covered over with earth or taken away by flames. If corpses have sensation, any kind of interment causes them suffering; if they have none, speedy dispatch is the most salutary treatment.*
>
> Octavius Januarius: *And it is not true, as you believe, that we fear*

---

[76] M. Naumenko (trans.), 'On the Question of Cremation' *Orthodox Life* (1989) Vol.39 No. 3 p. 7.

to suffer any harm from cremation, but our practice is to adhere to the old, and the preferable custom of inhumation.

Burial is the traditional Orthodox practice. Cremation, on the other hand, with its destruction of the body by fire and the pulverizing of the burned remains by machinery is a wilful destruction of the temple of God referred to by St. Paul: 'If any man defile the temple of God, him shall God destroy; for the temple of God is holy, which temple ye are' (1 Cor. 3:17). Our bodies have been sanctified by the mysteries of the Church; we are baptized, chrismated and tonsured at our reception into the Orthodox Church; we receive the Body and Blood of Christ, and are anointed with the oil of unction.

Perhaps the most important argument against cremation is that it involves the destruction of the relics of the saints. As Orthodox Christians, we honour the relics of the saints as St. Gregory Palamas teaches:

> *You should venerate the holy shrines [of the saints] and any relic of their bones, for God's grace is not sundered from these things, even as the divinity was not sundered from Christ's venerable body at the time of His life-quickening death. By doing this and by glorifying those who glorified God – for through their actions they showed themselves to be perfect in their love for God – you too will be glorified together with them by God.*[77]

The relics of the saints have wrought miracles throughout history. The relics of the Prophet Elisseus raised a dead man to life (4 Kings 13:20-21), and even in our time, the bodies of Orthodox saints are often preserved incorrupt, giving off a sweet fragrance or even pouring forth myron.

Because of these miracles, the persecutors of Christians have consistently tried to destroy the relics of the saints. Writing in the fourth century, Eusebius describes how the bodies of the saints were left out for animals to destroy and how provision was taken to prevent the relics being venerated by the Christians. The destruction of the relics of the saints was also practised in the Ottoman Empire. For example,

---

[77] *The Philokalia Vol. 4* (London; Faber and Faber, 1995) p. 325.

the relics of the New Martyr George from Sofia (March 26th) were deliberately defiled and destroyed to prevent their veneration:

> *Then other materials were added, such as wood and resin, even the carcass of a dead goat. This was done on purpose as an insult to the Orthodox Christian faithful so they would not be able to identify George's relics and thus would be deprived of the grace that would emanate from them. The fire burned from 5.00 pm until the dawn of the next day. Meanwhile George's body in the main had become a pile of dust, which the Muslims gathered up and scattered to the four winds to prevent the Christians from collecting it.*[78]

It is significant that churches that reject the veneration of relics also accept cremation. Although the Roman Catholic Church has never formally abolished the veneration of relics, to all intents and purposes they have disappeared from modern Roman Catholicism. It is perhaps not surprising that the papacy recently lifted its ban on cremation: 'The [Roman Catholic] Church permits cremation, provided that it does not demonstrate a denial of faith in the resurrection of the body.'[79]

The position of the Orthodox Church on cremation is accurately summed up by Protopresbyter George Grabbe (later Bishop Gregory of Washington):

> *The order of burial which we have at present has been sanctified by ancient custom and, as such, is protected by the sacred Canons; it is consonant with the whole spirit of the Orthodox teaching concerning man, and is deeply edifying. On the contrary, cremation of bodies is unacceptable from the Church's point of view, as an innovation which has come from an infected source, which, in the case of its implementation, would deprive us of the incorrupt bodies of the holy saints of God.*[80]

---

[78] N.M. Vaporis, *Witnesses for Christ* (Crestwood: St. Vladimir's Seminary Press, 2000) p. 35.

[79] *Catechism of the Catholic Church* (London: Geoffrey Chapman, 1995) p. 495.

[80] G. Grabbe, Cremation *Orthodox Life* (1978) Vol. 28 No. 1 p. 36.

11

The Mystery of Monastic Tonsure

If any man will come after Me, let him deny himself, and take up his cross, and follow Me. For whosoever will save his life shall lose it: and whosoever will lose his life for My sake shall find it.

Matthew 16:24-25

The monastic life is simply the Gospel commandments lived to their fullest extent. Christ commands us: 'If thou wilt be perfect, go and sell that thou hast, and give to the poor, and thou shalt have treasure in heaven: and come and follow Me' (Matt 19:21). The Church Fathers call monasticism a 'higher calling' and a 'higher life'.

The monastic life is the prophetic and apostolic life. We see prefigurings of the monastic life in the Old Testament; the Prophets Elias the Thesbite and John the Forerunner were ascetics before the coming of Christ. The monastic life is the new life which the apostles preached to the world.

The Slavonic word for monk is *inok* which also means 'different' because, as St. Paisius Velichkovsky points out, the monk lives a different way of life: 'one that is spiritual and not fleshly; another activity, another age, another food, another garment, and another labour.' In Greek, the word for monk can be translated as 'alone', because monastics should strive to free themselves from the concerns of the world and seek after God alone. The ever-memorable Metropolitan Cyprian teaches:

> *Monks and nuns, driven by love into monasteries and deserts, are like sparrows alone upon the housetop, exiles wholly for the sake of God and inspired by Him. They struggle to be purified, to be released from the passions. In these places, they consume the devil and his passions with their prayer, making their hearts pure. In these places, they are illumined by the Holy Spirit, being made holy and coming into union with God.*[81]

---

[81] Metropolitan Cyprian, *The Monastic Life* (trans. Bishop Chrysostomos) (Etna: CTOS) p.40.

The monastic life is not an innovation as many Protestants assert. We hear in the Acts of the Apostles:

> The multitude of those who believed were of one heart and one soul; neither did anyone say that any of the things he possessed was his own, but they had all things in common. Nor was there anyone among them who lacked; for all who were possessors of lands or houses sold them, and brought the proceeds of the things that were sold, and laid them at the apostles' feet; and they distributed to each as anyone had need (Acts. 4:32, 34-35).

God desires 'all men to be saved and come to a knowledge of the truth' (1 Tim. 2:4) and lay people are not deprived of this opportunity of deification: their path however is different and in today's society, arguably more difficult. According to Archbishop Averky, it is for this union with God 'that all the monastic struggles are undertaken: renunciation of family life, keeping oneself in complete virginal purity, renunciation of all possessions, renunciation even of one's own will.'

The three fundamental pillars of the monastic life are virginity, non-possesiveness and obedience. The monastic life is therefore different in character from the worldly life as St. Maximus the Confessor makes clear:

> The achievements of the worldly man constitute the failings of the monk, and the achievements of the monk constitute the failings of the worldly man. For example, the achievements of the worldly man are wealth, fame, power, luxury, comfort, children and what is consequent upon all these things. But the monk is destroyed if he obtains any of them. His achievements are the total shedding of possessions, the rejection of esteem and power, self-control, hardship, and all that is consequent upon them. If a lover of the world obtains these against his will, he considers it a great calamity and is often in danger even of killing himself; some people have actually done this.[82]

In the Old Testament, the continuance of the family through having children was held in great regard. St. Elizabeth the mother of the

---

[82] The Philokalia Vol. 2 pp. 96-97.

Forerunner was reproached because she had not born children (cf. Luke 1:25), as was Rachel, the wife of Jacob the Patriarch and the mother of Joseph (Genesis 30:23). After the Incarnation, these reproaches for barrenness gave way to blessings for virgins. Christ says in the Gospel:

> *For there are some eunuchs, which were so born from their mother's womb: and there are some eunuchs, which were made eunuchs of men: and there be eunuchs, which have made themselves eunuchs for the kingdom of heaven's sake. He that is able to receive it, let him receive it (Matt. 19:11-12).*

Marriage is honourable, and the marriage bed undefiled (cf. Heb. 13:4). However, St. Paul also teaches that virginity for Christ is a higher calling:

> *I would have you without concern. He that is unmarried careth for the things that belong to the Lord, how he may please the Lord: But he that is married careth for the things that are of the world, how he may please his wife. There is difference also between a wife and a virgin. The unmarried woman careth for the things of the Lord, that she may be holy both in body and in spirit: but she that is married careth for the things of the world, how she may please her husband (1 Cor. 7:31-34).*

Monastics live the virgin life. For lay people, the monastic life of virginity is an example for them to follow: being faithful to their spouse, keeping the fasts, and living a chaste life. 'Chaste' in the Orthodox sense for married couples does not mean living a virgin life, but a married life in accordance to the teachings of the Church. It is for this reason that the Orthodox Church permits only two modes of living for clergymen: in marriage or monasticism.

Both marriage and monasticism are ways of living which, by their very nature, lead us to humble ourselves and to think of others rather than ourselves. 'He who leads the virgin life,' says St Cyril of Jerusalem, 'must not become proud before those who have entered into matrimony; for "marriage is honourable in all, and the bed undefiled", as the Apostle says. And you who maintain innocence, were you not born of marriage? Disdain not the silver, because you are gold.'

Monastics renounce their wealth in order to obey the words of Christ: 'If thou wouldst be perfect, go, sell all thou hast, and give to the poor.' Orthodox monastics give up 'treasure on earth in order to obtain the treasure of heaven' (cf. Matt. 6:19-21). However, nonpossessiveness is not simply being 'poor' because it is possible to be possessive and greedy even when poor. Conversely, married Orthodox Christians living in the world, whilst they might be unable to give all they have to the poor, have the opportunity to be generous and not to succumb to greed and possessiveness.

Our separation from God through the Fall occurred through pride and self-will and it is this trait that monastics strive to conquer above all through obedience. All Orthodox Christians are called to be obedient to the Orthodox Church as St. Paul teaches: 'Obey those who rule over you, and be submissive, for they watch out for your souls, as those who must give account. Let them do so with joy and not with grief, for that would be unprofitable for you' (Heb. 13:17).

Christ serves as the highest example of true obedience for, according to the words of the Apostle, 'being in the form of God… He humbled Himself, and became obedient unto death, even the death of the cross' (Phil. 2:6, 8), and He Himself says: 'I seek not my own will, but the will of the Father which hath sent me' (John 5:30).

The monastic life, in summary, is living the blessed life that Christ describes in the Beatitudes (Matt. 5:3-12). Monastics, in the words of St. Maximus the Confessor, give up the life of the world as a sacrifice:

> *Some of the things which we do for the sake of God are done in obedience to the commandments; others are done not in obedience to the commandments, but, so to speak, as a voluntary offering. For example, we are required by the commandments to love God and our neighbour, to love our enemies, not to commit adultery or murder and so on. And when we transgress these commandments, we are condemned. But we are not commanded to live as virgins, to abstain from marriage, to renounce possessions, to withdraw into solitude and so forth. These are of the nature of gifts, so that*

if through weakness we are unable to fulfil some of the command-ments, we may by these free gifts propitiate our blessed Master.[83]

The Monastic Ranks

All monastics are tonsured and the service is identical for monks and nuns. There are three ranks of monastics: Rasophore, Stavrophore and Great Schema. There is considerable variation in the naming of these ranks and the monastic clothing between various national churches. For example stavrophores are also known as monastics of the Little Schema.

Novices are given the cassock, soft hat and belt to wear, and they are permitted to leave the monastery because they are not tonsured. Ra-sophore monks and nuns are tonsured in a simple service in which their name is changed as a symbol of their renunciation of their for-mer life. Rasophore means 'rason wearer' and in the tonsure service the candidate is clothed in the rason and given the *kalymmavkion* (the monastic hat) and veil.

Tonsured monastics cannot leave the monastic life without epitemia. Some modernist churches allow priestmonks to leave monastic life, marry and continue as married priests. This practice is a clear violation of Church tradition according to St. Nicodemos of the Holy Mountain:

> *It follows, then, from what we have said, that as many as come to be Rasophores are no longer able to lay aside the Rason, and to marry. Of course not! For how shall they dare to do this at a time when they have shorn the hairs of their head? For this signi-fies that they have put out of the head every wordily thought, and have consecrated their life to God. How? When they have put on with a blessing the monastic Rason, and a Kalymmavkion, and have changed their name; and when two prayers have been said over them by the Priest, in which the priest thanks God because He has rescued them from the worldly life, and has called then to the solemn profession of monks; and in which he entreats God to receive them under His saving yoke?*[84]

---

[83] *The Philokalia Vol,2* p. 108.

[84] N.F. Robinson, *Monasticism in the Orthodox Churches* (London: Cope & Fenwick, 1916) p. 131.

Monks are always referred to as 'Father [*Name*]'. Nuns are always addressed as 'Mother [*Name*]'. Rasophore nuns are given the title 'Sister [*Name*]', although lay people often address them as 'Mother' out of respect.

Different monasteries and national Churches have different practices concerning when monastics are tonsured to the Great Schema. On Mount Athos, and in many Greek monasteries, all monks are tonsured to this rank after a period of time as novices or rasophores, but in the Slavic Churches monks and nuns are usually tonsured to the Great Schema only on their deathbed. Before the tonsure, the candidate goes to confession and makes a complete life confession. On the evening before the tonsure, the monastic garments are laid on the Holy Table.

Today, nearly all Orthodox monasteries follow the *coenobitic* system in which the monastics live together in a *coenobium*, eat and pray together and give up their personal possessions when they are tonsured. As monasticism became more established in Orthodox Christian countries, *idiorrhythmic* monasticism gradually began to supplant coenobitic as the dominant form. In the idiorrhythmic system, monastics keep their own possessions and money, eat separately and are not in obedience to anyone. They neither work for the monastery, nor are they required to attend church services. In earlier centuries, richer monastics employed poorer monks or nuns as servants.

By the end of the sixteenth century, all the monasteries on Mount Athos were idiorrhythmic and this remained the case until the late eighteenth century. The reasons for the rise of the idiorrhythmic system are numerous and complex, but this period of history was one of political and religious turmoil under the rule of the Ottoman Turks. It is only natural that many monks felt unwilling to surrender all their possessions to the monastery, when at any time the monastery's goods might be confiscated leaving the monk unable to help his family in times of need.

Unfortunately, the idiorrhythmic system created a vicious circle in which monasteries became poorer and poorer because the monks were not working to support them. As a result the monastic life on Mount Athos became increasingly lax as monks spent a large percentage of their time on personal business matters outside the monastery.

The idiorrhythmic system is based on a corruption of the ancient practice of Orthodox monastics living the solitary life as hermits. Today, hermits are rare because this is the most spiritually challenging form of monasticism; only rarely are experienced monastics permitted by their superior to live this life. By definition, the solitary life can lead to self-will if it is not practised with discernment.

On Mount Athos, all the main monasteries are now coenobitic, but there are also a large number of smaller monastic dwellings called 'cells' and 'sketes'. Monastic cells consist of two or three monks living together in a small building containing a chapel. The monks devote themselves to prayer and handiwork such as making incense, prayer ropes, or wood carving. An Athonite skete is most often a collection of buildings surrounding a small central chapel. Russian sketes are often really monasteries in all but name. Although those living in cells or sketes are more 'alone' than those in coenobitic monasteries, they live in obedience to their elder, they give up their possessions on becoming monks, and they eat and pray together.

The Service of Tonsure to the Schema

The tonsure service to the Little and Great Schema is much more complex and involves the taking of vows. Many of the hymns refer to the parable of the Prodigal Son because the tonsure service is a symbolical representation of the return of the Prodigal Son to his home and to the Father Who loves His children.

For the tonsure to the Great Schema, there is a special canon read at Matins the acrostic of which is: 'Grant to me O Christ, the happiness of a happy end.' After Ode Six of the canon the following hymn from the Sunday of the Prodigal Son is sung:

> Open unto me Thy fatherly embrace for as the Prodigal I have wasted my life. In the unfailing wealth of Thy mercy, O Saviour, reject not my impoverished heart. For unto Thee,

Monastic Clothing

Cassock, belt and prayer rope: All novices and monastics wear a black cassock (Greek: *anteri*; Slavonic: *podrasnik*), and a belt. Novices are also given a prayer rope (Gk. *komboschini*; Sl. *chotki*) when they are clothed in the cassock. Monks and novices have their heads covered at all times, and outside church, monks wear some form of soft black hat (Gk. *skoufos*). Nuns wear a black head-covering called an *epimandylion* in Greek and *apostolnik* in Slavonic. In the Russian church, a white apostolnik is often worn outside church, particularly in the summer.

Rason: The Greek rason (*exorason*) is worn in church services and when travelling. The Greek-style rason forms a cross when laid out flat (*right*); the Russian riassa is tailored, but retains the wide sleeves. Married deacons and priests also wear the rason.

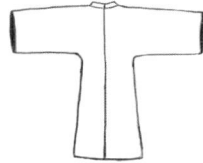

Hat and Veil: The monastic hat (*Gk. kalymmavchion*) is hard, and covered in felt; in the Greek church, married clergy wear a similar hat with a rim on top. Monastics wear a veil (Gk. *epikalymmavchion*) over the hat. In the Greek usage, this veil is removed during the Liturgy at the beginning of the Trisagion Hymn; in the Russian usage, the hat and veil are fastened together and are known as a *klobuk*.

Mantia: In the Russian usage, monks and nuns of the Little Schema wear a *mantia*: a long, flowing black cloak that represents the protecting power of God, and the wings of the angels. Bishops in the Russian church are vested in a purple mantia when they enter the church.

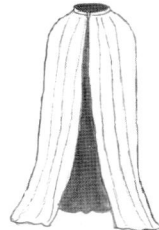

Paramandias: Monastics of the Little Schema wear the *paramandias* under their cassock which is embroidered with the symbols of the Crucifixion and the words: 'I bear the wounds of my Lord Jesus Christ upon my body'. Four tapes are sewn to the paramandias and are used to hold it in place with the aid of a wooden cross.

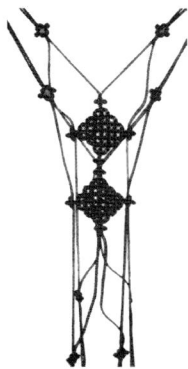

Analavos and Polystavrion: Monastics of the Great Schema wear the *analavos* (*right*) over the top of their cassock instead of the paramandias. The analavos is often referred to as the 'Schema' and is worn under the rason or mantia in church. In the Greek usage, a schema monk or nun also wear a web of cords called a *polystavrion (left)* over the analavos. The cords are plaited together so that they make numerous figures of the cross; 'polystavrion' means 'many crosses' in Greek.

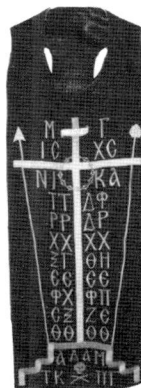

Koukoulion: In the Russian usage, monastics of the Great Schema wear a pointed veil called a *koukoulion* in church instead of the klobuk.

Right: A nineteenth century Russian hegumen wearing a mantia, koukoulion and the Russian style schema. which is longer than the Greek analavos.

> O Lord, I do cry out in compunction: Father, I have sinned against heaven, and before Thee.

The tonsure itself take places during the Divine Liturgy after the Little Entrance. At the beginning of the tonsure service, the candidate makes three prostrations to ask forgiveness of those present. Then he or she goes into the narthex and puts on a long white, or baptismal, robe signifying the complete laying aside of corrupt deeds, and he stands there in the entrance 'ungirded, barefooted and bareheaded'.

The hymn 'Open unto me Thy fatherly embrace…' is sung as the final kontakion in the sequence chanted after the Little Entrance. In the tonsure to the Great Schema, three penitential antiphons are then sung in Tone Four. The first hymn of the third antiphon is modelled on a hymn from the Anthem of the burial service:

> Where is the vain endeavour of the world? Where is the fleeting show of transitory things? Lo, do we not see that they are dust and ashes? Why, then, do we labour in vain? Why do we not renounce the world and follow Him who crieth: 'He that will come after Me, let him take up My Cross, and he shall inherit eternal life?'

The candidate is then led into the nave of the church by the monastics holding candles. He makes a prostration as he enters the church and another in the centre. Finally he lies flat on the ground in front of the ambon as the bishop or abbot says the following:

> **The kind-hearted God, as a father who loveth His children, beholding thy lowliness and true repentance, O child, receiveth thee in repentance as He did the Prodigal Son, as from thy very heart thou fallest down before Him.**

There now follows the questioning of the monastic who wishes to be clothed with the Great Schema. These questions and answers are, in many ways, analogous to those asked at baptism and marriage. The monk or nun confirms their desire to live the ascetic life and to live in obedience, poverty, chastity in the monastery until their death. To each of the abbot's questions, the candidate answers: 'Yes, God helping me, Reverend Father', a promise for which, as St. Symeon the New Theologian asserts, all monastics will have to give an account at the Judgment:

> *When Christ comes 'to repay every man for what he has done', then He will require of his monks, who have pledged themselves to Him 'in the presence of many witnesses', the vows they have promised to perform and observe before the holy altar and His holy angels. What are the questions to which we must reply? Is this not why we have approached the holy altar and this holy assembly? Is it with a desire for embracing the monastic life and the angelic way of living? And what do we answer to this question? 'Yes, reverend father.' The priest then says to us: 'You know brethren that inasmuch as you have come to be numbered with the servants of Christ the King you have prepared yourselves for trials. Know well then, that from now on especially the enemy will set in motion every device against you. You must therefore be hungry and thirsty and cold, be dishonoured and spat upon, be slapped in the face and be mocked, and endure all painful things that are in accordance with God.' What do we reply to these words? Do we not promise to suffer and endure all things, and pronounce the answer, 'Yes, reverend father', to every question about the endurance of afflictions? Do we not before God and the angels agree to observe self-control, vigils and prayers, and obedience till death to our superior and the whole community?*[85]

The abbot then reads three prayers in which he asks God to establish the new monk in His truth, to surround him by the power of the Holy Spirit, and grant him patience, so that he might freely follow the path of the monastic life and be included in the choir of the elect of God.

Before the cutting of the hair, the abbot, pointing to the scissors that are resting on the Gospel Book, says to the candidate: '**Take the scissors, and give them to me.**' This is repeated three times and on the third time the abbot says: '**Lo, from the hand of Christ thou receivest them. See to Whom thou approachest, to Whom thou dost promise, and whom thou dost renounce.**'

---

[85] St. Symeon the New Theologian, *The Discourses* pp. 63-64.

He tonsures the candidate in the form of a Cross, saying:

> **Our brother/sister [*Name*] is tonsured in the Name of the Father, and of the Son, and of the Holy Spirit.**

The new name, given at this point, is a sign that the newly-tonsured monastic has completely broken with his past life, and is beginning a completely new life, wholly dedicating himself to the service of God.

After the clothing, the abbot prays that the Lord will lead the newly tonsured monastic into His courts, and grant him 'unceasingly to dwell upon the good things, laid up for them that love God, and crucify himself to this life for the sake of the Kingdom of God.'

The Liturgy resumes with the chanting of 'All ye that in Christ have been baptized, Christ have ye put on. Alleluia,' and the same prokeimenon is read as at the mystery of baptism: 'The Lord is my light and my Saviour, whom then should I fear.'

The Epistle reading at the Liturgy is a special one for the tonsure service (Eph. 6: 10-17):

> Brethren, be strong in the Lord and in the power of His might. Put on the whole armour of God, that ye may be able to stand against the wiles of the devil. For we wrestle not against flesh and blood, but against principalities, against powers, against the rulers of the darkness of this age, against spiritual wickedness in high places. Therefore take up the whole armour of God, that ye may be able to withstand in the evil day, and having done all, to stand. Stand therefore, having your loins girt about with truth, having on the breastplate of righteousness, and your feet shod with the preparation of the gospel of peace; above all, taking the shield of faith, wherewith ye shall be able to quench all the fiery darts of the wicked one; and take the helmet of salvation, and the sword of the Spirit, which is the word of God.

The Gospel is from St. Matthew (Matt. 10:37-38;11: 28-30):

> He that loveth father or mother more than Me is not worthy of Me, and he that loveth son or daughter more than Me

is not worthy of Me. And he that taketh not his cross and followeth after Me, is not worthy of Me. Come unto Me, all ye that labour and are heavy laden, and I will give you rest. Take My yoke upon you and learn from Me, for I am meek and lowly in heart: and ye will find rest unto your souls. For My yoke is easy, and My burden is light.

After the dismissal, the newly-tonsured monastic stays for several days and nights in the church occupied in mental prayer, reading and spiritual reflection.

The Tonsure of St. Sergius of Radonezh

Frequently Asked Questions

Why don't monastics eat meat?

Monks and nuns are not vegetarians in the normal sense, because the Orthodox Church does not teach that eating meat is wrong. The monastic life developed from the example of the ascetics of the first centuries of Christianity who lived, like Saint John the Baptist, on the plants that they found in the wilderness. Orthodox monastics, following their example, refrain from eating meat. In addition, not eating meat is spiritually significant for monastics as St. Paisius Velichkovsky explains:

> *After the Flood, the Lord, because of human weakness, permitted the eating of meat, but the order of monastic life corresponds to life in Paradise, where there was no eating of meat. Although at the beginning of the monastic life there was in places a falling away from this order, especially in large cities, nevertheless St. Sabbas the Sanctified confirmed the non-eating of meat; and such has become the general order in all lands.*[86]

Some say that only monks and nuns need to keep the fasts. Is this right?

No. The fast days appointed by the Church should be kept by all Orthodox Christians. In many monasteries and convents, Monday is also kept as a fast day, but laypeople do not need to keep this particular fast. The idea that the canons of the Church only apply to monastics was particularly popular in nineteenth century Russia among the intelligentsia, but in fourth century Constantinople it must have been commonplace enough for St. John Chrysostom to comment:

> *You are deluded and in error if you think that one thing is demanded from the layman and another from the monk; the difference between the two is that one is married, and the other not. In everything else they have the same responsibilities… because all must rise to the same height. We turn the whole world upside down if we think that only the monk must live rigorously, while the rest are permitted to live a life of indolence… A man*

---

[86] Fr. Seraphim Rose (trans.), *Little Russian Philokalia Vol. 4* (Platina: St. Herman of Alaska Brotherhood, 1994) p. 145.

*is not defined by whether he is a monk or layman, but by the
way he thinks.*

All Orthodox Christians vow to 'renounce Satan, and all his works,
and all his angels, and all his service and all his pride' at their baptism. The monastic vows are an elaboration on, and a strengthening
of, these baptismal vows, but their existence does not give lay people
a licence to live in indifference to the teaching of the Church.

Why do people become monks or nuns?

The Orthodox monastic life attracts people from all backgrounds and
ages, and for many different reasons. In Greece, it is very common for
someone whose spouse has died to take up the monastic life as a result. Among younger people, some might have been raised in families
which encouraged their children to value and respect the monastic
life, but others might be struggling with some spiritual weakness. St.
Gregory of Nyssa gives the following advice:

> *We think it is beneficial for weaker Christians to take refuge in
> virginity, as in a secure fortress, and not to descend to the ordi-
> nary course of life. Otherwise they bring temptations upon them-
> selves and become entwined through the passion of the flesh with
> the things that are at war with the law of our mind. They should
> consider what is at stake in this life; not lands or wealth or some
> other earthly goal, but our preeminent hope.*[87]

The one thing that unites all monks and nuns is a love for the Orthodox Church and a desire to live according to the Gospel.

Why is the monastic life important?

The monastic life has always been held in great regard by traditional
Orthodox faithful because monastics, having giving up their own will
for Christ are the guardians of Orthodox doctrine and piety. There
have been periods of indifference to monasticism, but these, not sur-
prisingly, coincided with an indifference to Orthodoxy as a whole.
According to Archbishop Averky, when the monastic life is healthy
then the spiritual life of the Church will also be healthy:

---

[87] Kovcas, *1. Corinthians* pp. 127-128.

Monasticism was always a trustworthy indicator of the spiritual condition of the people, as if it were both a thermometer and barometer at one and the same time, showing its religious, moral level. The monastic life flourished, and this meant that the whole people were at a high in their Christian vocation; it falls, monasticism is wiped out, and this is a sign of a religious and moral decline, and the spiritual fall of a given people.

The monastic life is a light for lay people because it demonstrates the fruits of complete obedience. A layperson has elements of choice in their life that a monk does not have. A layperson can go on holiday when they want, eat when they want, go to church when they want, talk to whom they want etc. The discerning layperson can benefit by considering the implications of monastic obedience. Monks are called to be chaste, obedient, nonpossessive, but the same is expected of lay people albeit to a lesser extent. Saint Paul commands all Christians to 'obey them that have the rule over you, and submit yourselves' (Heb. 13:17).

Monastics try to fulfil the Gospel commandments, not in an abstract way, but by spiritual struggle in order to change themselves and the world around them. Metropolitan Anastassy, who was consecrated Bishop of Serpukhov in 1906, observes that not every Orthodox Christian perceives the importance of monastic spiritual struggle for the health of the Church as whole:

A monk, as is proven by the word itself (Greek: monos, one alone) is always and everywhere alone. He is separate from the elements of the world, even though he might live in the midst of a noisy city. The majority of humanity sees in him something of an alien quality which is unfamiliar to them. It is surprising that even those who are of the faith and evidently close to the Church often show a lack of understanding of the monastic ideal which for them remains inconsistent with their usual notions. They are ready to grasp and accept every act of service to the church – pastoral, missionary, philanthropic, educational, and all other paths of Christian life – except that of monastic asceticism.[88]

---

[88] Metropolitan Anastassy, A Defence of Monasticism (Jordanville: Holy Trinity Monastery, 1989) pp. 10-11.

Most Protestants object to monasticism because they envision Christianity as a social movement devoted to overcoming worldly problems, and they fail to understand how monastics can help the world by fleeing from it. Archbishop Averky answers this criticism succinctly:

> *Serving some sort of vague idea like humankind, is nothing more than an alluring dream, a self-deception. True love for people and the desire to serve them and profit them does not consist in empty dreams about the means of benefitting all of humankind, but in the genuine, heartfelt striving to do such good as is within one's power to those people with whom daily life places us in the closest and most immediate contact.*

How do Orthodox and Roman Catholic monasticism differ?

In Orthodoxy, there are no different 'religious orders' as there are in the Roman Catholic Church. Catholic religious orders have different aims and objectives. Benedictines, for example, live in communities and work to support the monastery; Franciscans, on the other hand, view personal poverty as of primary importance. Catholic religious orders can also be distinguished by their monastic clothing: Franciscans wear brown, Benedictines black and Carthusians wear white.

Celibate members of Roman Catholic orders often wear rings signifying that they are married to Christ, but this practice is unknown in Orthodoxy as are the various devotions that have developed in the Roman Catholic church since the split with Orthodoxy: the Franciscan veneration for *stigmata* (wounds that appear on the hands, wrists or feet) is just one example.

There are also major differences in how the two Churches view monasticism. The 'vows' in the Orthodox tonsure service are a confirmation of the candidate's willingness to continue in obedience in the struggle against possessiveness and the passions of the flesh. These questions and answers are quite different in character from the legalistic nature of most Roman Catholic profession services in which candidates sign a form of contract binding them to the life of his, or her, religious order.

Prophet Zacharias and Righteous Elizabeth, the parents of John the Forerunner and Baptist.

12

The Mystery of Marriage

For we are members of His body, of His flesh, and of His bones. For this cause shall a man leave his father and mother, and shall be joined unto his wife, and they two shall be one flesh.

Ephesians 5:31

An Orthodox marriage is a partnership between husband and wife in which they work, in synergy with the Holy Spirit, to purify themselves from the passions, guard their thoughts, and live in a spirit of repentance and mutual forgiveness so that they can be 'complete in Him, which is the head of all principality and power' (cf. Col. 2: 10). Spiritual struggle is central to Christian marriage. Through accepting the Gospel of Christ, the married couple seek to deny themselves, taking up their Cross and following Him (cf. Matt. 16:24) and to live for each other and not for themselves.

Marriage is not, as some assert, 'an end in itself' because, although we are made in God's image, we are called to become in God's likeness, and this likeness is without passion. In his commentary on Psalm 50, St. Athanasius the Great makes clear that sexual feelings are a result of the Fall:

> *God's original intention was that we give birth not through marriage and corruption; the violation of the commandment introduced marriage as a result of Adam's transgression, that is, as the result of falling away from the commandment given to him by God.*

Sexual relations between husband and wife are blessed by the mystery of marriage, and the mutual love between spouses is not only physical, but is inextricably linked and strengthened by their love for God and their obedience to the Orthodox Church as Hieromonk Gregorios explains:

> *Tbe wife sees Christ in her husband, and the husband loves his wife as Christ loved the Church. Christ is the loving bond of the husband and wife: and the love of Christ for the Church is the measure of the love the couple hopes to attain. The mystery of love*

*within marriage represents the mystery of the love of Christ for
the Church. Thus, those who are able to achieve true love within
marriage make Christ their own.*[89]

The Marriage Service

The marriage service is made up of two parts, the betrothal and the
crowning. In earlier centuries, the betrothal service was performed
separately and sometimes many years before the marriage. Today, the
betrothal is now performed just before the mystery of marriage.

Before the ceremony, the wedding rings are placed on the Holy Table
showing that the marriage has its beginning in Christ, and will end
in Christ. The priest blesses the couple and gives them each a lighted
candle, as a sign of their joy and of the hope that, through the kind-
heartedness of God, their life will be joyous and illumined.

The Betrothal

The service starts with the blessing by the priest: 'Blessed is our
God…' followed by the Great Litany to which special petitions are
added for the couple that are to be betrothed:

> For the servant of God, [*Name*], and for the handmaid of
> God, [*Name*] who plight each other their troth and for their
> salvation.
>
> That He will send down upon them perfect and peaceful love
> and help.
>
> That He will preserve them in oneness of mind, and in stead-
> fastness of faith.
>
> That He will bless them with a blameless life.
>
> That the Lord our God will grant unto them an honourable
> marriage, and a bed undefiled.

The priest then reads the prayer:

> O eternal God, Who has brought into unity those who were
> sundered, and hast ordained for them an indissoluble bond of

---

[89] Hieromonk Gregorios, *The Mystery of Marriage:A Fellowship of Love* (Columbia:
New Rome Press, 2013) p. 10.

love; Who didst bless Isaac and Rebecca, and didst make them heirs of Thy promise: Bless also these Thy servants [*Name*] and [*Name*], guiding them unto every good work…

The priest makes the sign of the Cross over the bridegroom with the ring of the bride, and over the bride with the ring of the bridegroom. The priest places the bride's ring on the groom's finger, and the groom's ring on the bride's. The couple then exchange the rings three times so that they end by wearing their own rings signifying that they are entering into this marriage of their own free will. The ring is worn on the right hand because it was the right hand of Moses which he stretched out over the water of the Red Sea: 'Thy right hand, O lord, is glorified in strength; thy right hand, O Lord, has shattered enemies' (Exodus 15:6).

The priest now joins their hands to show that it is Christ Himself who unites them as St. Gregory the Theologian says: 'I place the hand of the one in the other, and place both in the hand of God.' St. Symeon of Thessalonika writes: 'The priest entwines the fingers of their right hands, demonstrating by this that they have been joined together and become one, and that the man has received the woman from the hand of the Church, through the priest.'[90]

As the couple enter the nave of the church, the choir and the priest sing Psalm 127 with the refrain 'Glory to Thee O God, Glory to Thee' between the verses.

> Blessed are all they that fear the Lord, that walk in his ways. Thou shalt eat of the fruit of thy labours; blessed art thou, and well shall it be with thee.
> Thy wife shall be as a fruitful vine on the sides of thy house,
> Thy sons like young olive trees round about thy table.
> Behold, so shall the man be blessed that feareth the Lord.
> The Lord bless thee out of Sion, and mayest thou see the good things of Jerusalem all the days of thy life.
> And mayest thou see thy children's children; peace be upon Israel.

This psalm was sung in the Old Testament when the Levites entered the altar on holy days, and today this procession into the church sig-

---

[90] Gregorios, *The Mystery of Marriage: A Fellowship of Love* p. 37.

nifies the entrance of the couple into the Kingdom of Christ. In this psalm, 'Sion' is the 'temple of the body of Christ' (John 2:2); Jerusalem is the eternal city 'descending out of heaven from God' (Rev. 20:10); Israel is the new people of God – the Christians united together in the Church.

The Crowning

The crowning service begins with the blessing, 'Blessed is the Kingdom of the Father, and of the Son, and of the Holy Spirit.' The Litany of Peace is intoned and the following petitions are added.

> For the servants of God [*Name*] and [*Name*] who are now being united to each other in the community of marriage, and for their salvation.
>
> That He will bless this marriage, as He blessed that in Cana of Galilee.
>
> That He will grant unto them chastity, and of the fruit of the womb as is expedient for them.
>
> That He will make them glad with the sight of sons and daughters.
>
> That He will grant unto them procreation of virtuous offspring, and an upright life.
>
> That He will grant unto them, and to us, all our petitions which are unto salvation.

The priest then reads the following prayer which begins:

> O God most pure, the Creator of every living thing, Who didst transform the rib of our forefather Adam into a wife, because of Thy love towards mankind, Thou didst bless them, and say unto them: Increase, multiply, and have dominion over the earth, and didst make of them both one flesh. Because of this, a man shall leave his father and mother and cleave unto his wife, and the two shall be one flesh; what God hath joined together, let no man put asunder:

This prayer also commemorates the various righteous couples of the Old Testament. Abraham and Sarah; Isaac and Rebecca; Jacob and Rachel: Joseph and Asenath the daughter of Pharaoh; Zacharias and Elizabeth, the parents of the Forerunner. The betrothal of Rebecca to Isaac is a prefiguring of the joining of the nations to the Church, accomplished by baptism: Rebecca was chosen by the drawing of water from the well (Gen. 24:14) and we put on Christ by the water of baptism (Gal. 3:27).

In the second prayer, the Church calls upon the Lord to bless and preserve the couple, sending down grace from heaven upon them:

> **Preserve them O Lord our God as Thou didst preserve Noah in the ark; Preserve them O Lord our God, as Thou didst preserve Jonas in the belly of the whale; Preserve them O Lord our God, as Thou didst preserve the three holy children from the fire, sending down upon them dew from heaven. Let that gladness come upon them which the blessed Helen had when she found the precious Cross. Remember them O Lord our God as Thou didst remember Enoch, Shem, Elias. Remember them O Lord our God, as Thou didst remember Thy holy martyrs, sending down upon them crowns from heaven.**

The preservation of the three youths in the Babylonian furnace unharmed by the flame is a prefiguration of the ever-virginity of the Mother of God, and this reminds the couple that they should preserve themselves in purity for each other.

The crowns remind the couple of the 'prize of their high calling' which they strive for (cf. Phil. 3:14); and of the 'crown of righteousness' (2 Tim. 4:8) 'that fadeth not away' (1 Pet. 5:4). The practice of crowning a married couple is inspired by the wild-olive crowns awarded to the winners of athletic contests to which St. Paul refers below:

> *Know ye not that they which run in a race run all, but one receiveth the prize? So run, that ye may obtain. And every man that striveth for the mastery is temperate in all things. Now they do it to obtain a corruptible crown; but we an incorruptible (1 Cor. 9:24-25).*

The crowns remind the bride and bridegroom that they should strive to obey God's commandments in the race that they will run together, because crowns are only 'given to them that contest lawfully' (2. Tim 2:5). The crowns are also, as St. John Chrysostom teaches, 'a symbol of victory, signifying that the couple approach the marriage bed unconquered by pleasure'; St. Symeon of Thessalonika, echoing his words, asserts: 'crowns are placed on them because they are pure virgins up to the time of their wedding.' [91]

The wedding crowns are symbols of Christ as the Great High Priest, and the fact that the couple are both members of the Royal Priesthood. Crowns are also symbols of royalty and the husband and wife are king and queen within their home which is an extension of the church.

The priest, taking one of the crowns, says:

> **The servant of God, [Name] is crowned unto the handmaid of God, [Name] in the Name of the Father, and of the Son, and of the Holy Spirit.**

He then takes the second crown whilst saying:

> **The handmaid of God, [Name] is crowned unto the servant of God, [Name] in the Name of the Father, and of the Son, and of the Holy Spirit.**

In the Greek usage the crowns are often made from flowers and are taken home at the end of the ceremony and kept in the couple's icon corner. Because the crowns symbolize virginity, the crowning should be omitted if a person marries a second time.

The Prokeimenon and Epistle Reading

The Prokeimenon is taken from Psalm 20, but is slightly modified by changing the singular to the plural: for example 'his head' is changed to 'their heads'. This is done to show that both bridegroom and bride are being crowned as ones equal in honour:

> Thou has set upon their heads crowns of precious stone.
>
> Verse: They asked life of Thee and Thou gavest them length of days unto ages of ages.

The Epistle Reading is from St. Paul's Epistle to the Ephesians (Eph. 5: 20-33):

> Brethren, give thanks always for all things unto God and the Father in the Name of our Lord Jesus Christ; submitting

---

[91] Gregorios, *The Mystery of Marriage: A Fellowship of Love* p. 39.

yourselves one to another in the fear of God. Wives, submit yourselves unto your own husbands, as unto the Lord. For the husband is the head of the wife, even as Christ is the Head of the Church: and He is the Saviour of the body. Therefore as the Church is subject unto Christ, so let the wives be to their own husbands in everything. Husbands, love your wives, even as Christ also loved the Church, and gave Himself for it; That He might sanctify and cleanse it with the washing of water by the word, That He might present it to Himself a glorious Church, not having spot, or wrinkle, or any such thing; but that it should be holy and without blemish. So ought men to love their wives as their own bodies. He that loveth his wife loveth himself. For no man ever yet hated his own flesh; but nourisheth and cherisheth it, even as the Lord the Church: For we are members of His body, of His flesh, and of His bones. For this cause shall a man leave his father and mother, and shall be joined unto his wife, and they two shall be one flesh. This is a great mystery: but I speak concerning Christ and the Church. Nevertheless, let every one of you in particular so love his wife even as himself; and the wife see that she reverence her husband.

Many non-Orthodox Christians regard this reading as old-fashioned, but the traditional western understanding of marriage is very different to the Orthodox one. For example, in the traditional Church of England wedding service the husband is not given a ring; the ring that he places on his wife's finger serves as a sign of his rule over her, as does the vow of obedience that the wife makes to him.

Far from being servile, an Orthodox Christian wife, as St. John Chrysostom points out, is most often the driving force for piety within a marriage:

> *Nothing is more powerful than a pious and sensible woman to bring a man into proper order, and to mould his soul as she will. For he will not endure friends or teachers, or rulers, as he will his partner advising and counselling him, since the advice carries even some pleasure with it, because she who offers the advice is greatly loved.*

St. John Chrysostom addresses husbands with these words: 'never call your wife by her name alone, but with terms of endearment, with honour and with much love. For what if the wife be subject to us? It is a wife, as free, as equal in honour.'

The word 'obedience' is foreign to us today because we have become so used to being disobedient. Obedience has become something that we are forced to give, not something we give out of love and honour. The chief example of obedience and humility is Christ Himself who said: 'I do not mine own will, but the will of the Father who sent Me' (John 5:30) and Who humbled Himself by becoming obedient to death – even death on a cross (Phil. 2:8). When we hear in the Gospel that Christ was 'subject unto' Joseph and Mary, it means that He was obedient to them (cf. Luke 2:51).

The subjection of a wife to her husband and the duty of the husband to love and honour his wife are not motivated by fear, but out of love. St. John Chrysostom continues:

> Take upon yourself the same providential care of [your wife] as Christ takes upon Himself for the Church. And even if it becomes necessary for you to give your life for her, yes, and even to endure and undergo suffering of any kind – do not refuse it… for what sort of union is it, where the wife is afraid of her husband? And what sort of satisfaction will the husband have, if he lives with his wife as if he were living with a slave, and not with a woman by her own free will? Even though you would suffer anything on her account, do not chastise her, for neither did Christ do this.[92]

Orthodox marriage, therefore, is a synergy in which husband and wife humble themselves through their love for each other. Below, St. John Chrysostom describes how a good marriage is a perfect balance between husband and wife:

> The wife is a second authority; let not her then demand equality, for she is under the head; nor let him despise her as being in subjection for she is the body, for if the head despise the body, it will also perish. But let him bring love on his part as a counterweight to obedience on her part.

[92] J. Meyendorff, *Marriage: An Orthodox Perspective* (New York: SVS Press, 1975) p. 91.

Those who object to the Church's teaching on obedience and love cannot provide a viable alternative; if both husband and wife are always determined to have their own will, they will end up destroying one another. Our freedom of will must be exercised with care as Saint Paul makes clear:

> *Brethren, ye have been called unto liberty; only use not liberty for an occasion to the flesh, but by love serve one another. For all the law is fulfilled in one word, even in this; Thou shalt love thy neighbour as thyself. But if ye bite and devour one another, take heed that ye be not consumed one of another (Gal. 5:13-15).*

St. Paul commands that Christians submit themselves to each other (Eph. 5:21) because in doing so we are training ourselves to be subject to God. Our freedom is a direct result of the divine nature's freedom because man was created according to the image of God, and it is only by using this freedom wisely for the service of God that we can become like Him. Saint Maximus the Confessor explains this further:

> *All men are made in God's image, but to be in His likeness is granted only to those who through great love have brought their own freedom in subjection to God. For only when we do not belong to ourselves do we become like Him who through love has reconciled us to Himself.*[93]

The Gospel Reading

The Gospel reading (John 2:1-11) recounts the miracle at the marriage in Cana of Galilee:

> At that time, there was a marriage in Cana of Galilee; and the mother of Jesus was there: and both Jesus was called, and His disciples, to the marriage. And when they lacked wine, the mother of Jesus saith unto Him, They have no wine. Jesus saith unto her, Woman, what is that to Me and thee? Mine hour is not yet come. His mother saith unto the servants, Whatsoever He saith unto you, do it. And there were set there six waterpots of stone, after the manner of the purifying of the Jews,

---

[93] *The Philokalia Vol.1* p. 253

containing two or three firkins apiece. Jesus saith unto them, Fill the waterpots with water. And they filled them up to the brim. And He saith unto them, Draw out now, and take it unto the governor of the feast. And they took it. When the ruler of the feast had tasted the water that was made wine, and knew not whence it was: (but the servants which drew the water knew;) the governor of the feast called the bridegroom, and saith unto him, Every man at the beginning doth set forth good wine; and when men have well drunk, then that which is worse: but thou hast kept the good wine until now. This beginning of miracles did Jesus in Cana of Galilee, and manifested forth His glory; and his disciples believed on Him.

Litany, Lord's Prayer, Common Cup

A special Litany is read after the Gospel consisting of two parts joined together by the following prayer:

> O Lord our God, who in Thy saving dispensation didst vouchsafe by Thy presence in Cana of Galilee to declare marriage honourable; Do Thou, the same Lord, now also keep in peace and concord Thy servants [*Name*] and [*Name*] whom Thou hast been pleased to join together. Cause their marriage to be honourable. Preserve their bed undefiled. Mercifully grant that they may live together in purity and enable them to reach a ripe old age, walking in Thy commandments in purity of heart.

The Lord's Prayer is now read introduced by the exclamation 'and vouchsafe, O Lord, that with boldness…' that is used at the Divine Liturgy. The Liturgy, as St. Nicolas Cabasilas writes is a 'most-praised wedding' where we become flesh of Christ's flesh, and bone of His bones. In a reciprocal manner, the mystery of marriage is liturgical as the couple are lawfully joined together by grace and partake of the Body and Blood of Christ together. St. Symeon of Thessalonika teaches:

> *The Church is correct in preparing the Divine Gifts for the redemption and blessing of the bridal pair; for Christ Himself, Who gave us these Gifts and Who is the Gifts, came to the marriage (in Cana of Galilee) to bring to peaceful union and concord. So that those who get married must be worthy of Holy Communion; they*

must be united before God in a church, which is the house of God,
because they are children of God, in church where God is present
in the Gifts, where He is being offered to us and where He is seen
in the midst of us.[94]

The 'common cup' is a remnant of this older practice when the couple
would take Holy Communion at this point; in the Greek usage, the
choir still chants the communion hymn: 'I will take the cup of salvation
and I will call upon the name of the Lord.' The priest blesses the cup of
wine and the newly married couple share it, taking three sips each. The
sharing of the cup signifies that the couple are bound together forever,
that they will share everything in common, all their desires and inten-
tions, all their joys and their sorrows as St. John Chrysostom explains:

> *After marriage, you are no longer two, but have become one flesh,*
> *but you keep your possessions separate and do not share them? This*
> *love of money! You have both become one person, one living crea-*
> *ture, and you can still say 'my own'? That cursed and abominable*
> *phrase was brought in by the devil. Things that are far nearer and*
> *dearer to us than money that God has given us to share; should not*
> *these material possessions also be in common? We cannot say 'my*
> *own light, my own sun, my own water'; all our greater blessings are*
> *shared and why should not money be also?*

The Procession

The priest joins the hands of the newly-married couple and leads them
around the lectern three times to symbolize that Christ will lead them
into His Kingdom (cf. Gal 3:13). The priest holds a Cross in his hand
signifying that the married life, as well as being joyful, is a life of struggle because both husband and wife make sacrifices for each other. During the procession, the choir chants the following hymns which are
also sung during the threefold procession around the Holy Table during the ordination of a priest:

> Rejoice, O Esaias! A Virgin is with child, and shall bear a Son,
> Emmanuel, both God and man; Dayspring is His Name,
> and magnifying Him we call the Virgin blessed.

---

[94] Meyendorff, *Marriage: An Orthodox Perspective* p. 125.

O holy martyrs, who fought the good fight and have received your crowns, entreat ye the Lord that He will have mercy on our souls.

Glory to Thee, O Christ God, the boast of the apostles, and the joy of the martyrs, whose preaching was the Trinity one in essence.

The first hymn in this sequence refers to the Incarnation as foretold by the Prophet Esaias (Is. 7:14). The hymn to the martyrs acts as a reminder to the married couple that they too need to struggle against the temptations of life. The final hymn expresses the joy that the couple will enjoy together because their joy is Christ, and their faith Orthodox.

Final Prayers and Dismissal

After the procession, the crowns are removed and the priest greets the couple as they set out on the course of their life together with the words:

Be thou exalted, O Bridegroom, like unto Abraham; and be thou blessed like unto Isaac, and do thou multiply like unto Jacob, walking in peace, and keeping the commandments of God in righteousness.

And turning to the bride, the priest says:

And thou, O Bride, be thou exalted like unto Sarah; and exult thou like unto Rebecca; and do thou multiply like unto Rachel; and rejoice thou in thy husband, fulfilling the precepts of the law; for so it is well pleasing unto God.

After a final prayer, the priest gives the dismissal:

May He, who by His presence in Cana of Galilee declared marriage to be honourable, Christ our true God, through the prayers of His most pure Mother; of the holy, glorious and all-famed apostles; of the holy God-crowned sovereigns Constantine and Helena, the Equal to the apostles, of the holy Great Martyr Procopius and of all the saints: have mercy on us and save for He is good and the Friend of Man.

Saints Constantine and his mother Helena are commemorated in the dismissal because of their role in spreading the Christian faith. Within their family, the married couple will have a similar ministry to their children. St Procopius is commemorated because he encouraged twelve women to go to their death by martyrdom as if to a marriage feast.

Frequently Asked Questions

What impediments are there to marriage?

A marriage should only be performed between two Orthodox Christians; the non-Orthodox spouse must become Orthodox before the marriage service. The reason for this is spiritual and not merely cultural. In the mystery of marriage a couple are united together within the Church, and in earlier centuries they took Holy Communion together; in a mixed marriage one spouse has consciously rejected the importance of this mystery, and is not on the Orthodox path of true faith, asceticism, humility and the partaking of the mysteries.

This unwillingness to convert can cause stress within a mixed marriage, especially when it comes to bringing up the children as Orthodox Christians. It is not uncommon to hear of the non-Orthodox parent objecting to a child being Orthodox, or a husband trying to convert his children to heterodoxy. Mixed marriages have been performed regularly in the Russian Orthodox Church but this practice is an economy and not in strict accordance with the Church Canons.

In addition to the normal legal impediments concerning blood relatives, a couple cannot marry if they are brother and sister by baptism which is the case if either of the parents is a godparent to their prospective son-in-law or daughter-in-law.

In the case of second marriages, both bride and groom must have a civil and, if they have been married before in the Orthodox Church, a Church divorce. The latter is obtained by writing to the bishop of the diocese who will investigate the matter and decide whether there are justifiable grounds for divorce.

A married man or woman can become Orthodox even if their spouse does not wish to convert because, in the words of St. Paul, 'the unbelieving husband is consecrated through his wife, and the unbelieving wife is consecrated through her husband' (1. Cor. 7:14).

On which days are marriages not permitted?

We have discussed the spiritual purpose of marriage, but sexual relations are an important, although a lesser, part of marriage. Married couples do not have sexual intercourse on fast days, or on the night before receiving Holy Communion; on all these days spiritual, rather than physical, concerns should come first.

In addition, couples should try to abstain from sexual relations during the festive period between Christmas and Theophany and during Cheesefare week which is an icon of Paradise in which Adam and Eve did not have sexual relations with each other.

Sexual intercourse between husband and wife is blessed by the mystery of marriage, but we should not forget the vital role of purity of body coupled with spiritual struggle in Orthodox marriage. It is for this reason that married couples abstain from sexual intercourse on fast days; they should also refrain from unnatural sexual acts with each other.[95]

Abstinence from sexual relations within marriage needs to be a decision made by both husband and wife together as St. Paul teaches: 'Defraud ye not one the other, except it be with consent for a time, that ye may give yourselves to fasting and prayer; and come together again, that Satan tempt you not for your incontinency' (1 Cor. 7:5).

During the marriage service we pray that the couple will be blessed with children, so the mystery of marriage is always celebrated on days where the first night of the honeymoon is not within one of these periods where sexual relations are not permitted. Although there are some variations according to national custom, marriages should not be served:

- During the four fasts: Great Lent; Nativity Fast; Dormition Fast; Apostles Fast
- During Cheesefare Week
- On the Eve and on the day of Great Feasts
- On Tuesdays and Thursdays and Saturdays

---

[95] For example, engaging in oral or anal sex.

- Between Christmas Day and Theophany, and during Bright Week.
- On the Eve and on the day of the Feast of the Beheading of St. John the Baptist.

On what hand is the wedding ring worn?

Both husband and wife wear their wedding ring on the ring finger of their right hand. We read in the Prophecy of Jeremias that the Israelites wore a signet ring on their right hand (Jer. 22:24). Orthodox couples, following this example, wear their wedding ring on their right hand as a symbol of the power given to their union by the Holy Spirit. Additionally, the ring reminds them, every time they make the sign of the Cross, of the spiritual bond between them. The custom of wearing betrothal or wedding rings is an ancient one, and dates back at least to the second century. The custom of wearing wedding rings on the left hand was influenced by the belief, in the west, that a 'love vein' runs through this finger.

I am expecting a baby. Is there anything I should be aware of as an Orthodox Christian woman?

Pregnant and breast-feeding women are released from the strictness of the fasting regulations in order to ensure that the child receives adequate nourishment. Prayer, however, remains important particularly during pregnancy. Some parishes have a special prayer list to commemorate pregnant women at the Divine Liturgy, and there are prayers that can be read privately by the mother at home (*see overleaf*).

In the UK, women are encouraged to attend regular medical check-ups, but these need to be approached with care. Ultrasound scans have no medical side-effects and are perfectly acceptable from an Orthodox standpoint, but most doctors will also advise an amniocentesis (AFT) in order to test for various genetic conditions. The purpose of this test is to provide information to enable parents to decide whether or not to have an abortion. Amniocentesis causes miscarriages in a small number of mothers and the test is pointless for Orthodox Christians because abortion, for us, is not an option.

Prayers for a Woman with Child

O Sovereign Lord Jesus Christ our God, the source of life and immortality, I thank Thee, for in my marriage, Thou hast made me a recipient of Thy blessing and gift; for Thou, O Master, didst say: Be fruitful and multiply, and replenish the earth. Bless the fruit of my body that was given to me by Thee; favour him and animate him by Thy Holy Spirit, and let him grow a healthy and pure body, with well-formed limbs. Sanctify his body, mind, heart, and vitals, and grant this infant that is to be born an intelligent soul; establish him in the fear of Thee. Vouchsafe my child a faithful angel, a guardian of soul and body. Protect, keep, strengthen, and shelter him in my womb until the hour of his birth. But conceal him not in his mother's womb, for Thy hands have fashioned him, and Thou gavest him life and breath. Lord Jesus Christ, into Thine almighty and paternal hands do I entrust my child. Place him upon the right hand of Thy grace, and through Thy Holy Spirit sanctify him and renew him unto life everlasting, that he may be a communicant of Thy Heavenly Kingdom. Amen.

O All-Merciful Christ our God, look down and protect me, Thy handmaiden, from fear and from evil spirits that seek to destroy the work of Thy hands. And when my hour and time is come, deliver me by Thy grace. Look with compassionate eye and deliver me, Thy handmaiden, from pain. Lighten mine infirmity in the time of my travail and grant me fortitude and strength for birth giving, and hasten it by Thine almighty help. For this is Thy glorious work, the power of Thine omnipotence, the work of Thy grace and tenderheartedness. Amen.

My most gracious Queen, my hope, O Mother of God, the joy of those in sorrow, help me, for I am helpless; intercede thou and pray thy Son, Christ our God, that He lighten for me this season while I am with child, and that He ease the burden of heaviness of me, His unworthy handmaiden, and bestow His blessings upon the child to which I am giving birth. For I know no other help save thee, no other hope save thee, O Mother of God that will guard and protect me and my child. For by thine intercession and help we send up glory and thanksgiving for all things unto the One God in Trinity, the Creator of all, now and ever, and unto the ages of ages. Amen.

Miscarriages are, unfortunately, relatively common in the early stages of pregnancy and many women suffer an early miscarriage without even noticing that they are pregnant. If a miscarriage is known to have occurred, there is a special prayer to be read privately by the priest when the mother attends church. UK hospitals offer couples help in arranging a burial for the child, but non-baptized infants are not given an Orthodox funeral service because they have not been joined to the Church by baptism.

The Fathers, however, have never sought to dogmatize as to the eternal fate of these infants as St. Gregory of Nyssa makes clear:

> Certainly, in comparison with one who has lived all his life in sin, not only the innocent babe but even one who has never come into the world at all will be blessed. We learn as much too in the case of Judas, from the sentence pronounced upon him in the Gospels; namely, that when we think of such men, that which never existed is to be preferred to that which has existed in such sin.

There is no definitive answer to this problem, because as St. Gregory states, the issue is 'much greater than the human mind can grasp'; he goes on to quote the following words of the Apostle Paul: 'O the depth of the riches both of the wisdom and knowledge of God! How unsearchable are his judgments, and his ways past finding out!' (Rom. 11:33).

What does the Orthodox Church teach concerning sexual relations before marriage?

Having sexual relations before marriage is a serious sin, and one that has serious spiritual consequences. A man, for example, that has sexual intercourse before marriage is not able to be ordained to the diaconate or the priesthood. Living together as man and wife before marriage is now socially acceptable in the west, but it is not acceptable to the Church. The Orthodox Church does not permit couples that are in a sexual relationship outside marriage to receive Holy Communion, to be Godparents, or to be sponsors at weddings.

It is noticeable how many couples are content when they are living together, but when they marry they start to argue and often soon divorce. The act of regularizing a sexual relationship by marriage can lead to small issues, which before remained unnoticed, becoming big temptations. Although the couple have known each other carnally, it is clear that these sexual acts were, in fact, obscuring a deeper problem in their relationship. It is known from the writings of the Fathers that the demons do not tempt us so much when we are openly living in sin; it is only when we start to fight against temptation that we begin to engage them in warfare.

Secular advocates of sexual relations before marriage insist that it is sensible that couples get to know each other before marriage. The divorce rate among couples that live together before marriage fails to support this theory. Removing the sexual relationship from the equation allows us to see our relationship as it is – untarnished by lust.

In addition, having sexual relations before marriage can lead to the possibility of a woman choosing, or being coerced into having, an abortion. Having previous sexual partners can also cause problems of a psychological nature within the marriage especially when a couple are going through a difficult time. Finally, a lack of restraint before marriage also indicates a greater risk of adultery at some point in the future.

Is contraception permitted by the Orthodox Church?

This is a difficult subject, and one which both husband and wife have to discuss, pray about and ask the advice of their spiritual father. The purpose of sexual intercourse is for the conception of children as St. Maximus the Confessor, amongst others, has stated. Contraception therefore is not, strictly speaking, permitted. However the Church, understanding our weakness, tolerates contraception within marriage, but the couple may be given an epitimia to help them understand that their behaviour is not ideal.

Does the Orthodox Church allow divorce?

Although there is provision in the services of the Church for a second marriage, a Church divorce is necessary before any second marriage may be entered into. A Church divorce can only be granted by the bishop of the diocese or by an ecclesiastical court appointed by him. A divorce will usually only be granted if the marriage has irrevocably broken down due to adultery, abandonment, or if one of the spouses has apostatized from Orthodoxy; couples that have simply grown apart will be expected to try to mend their relationship with the help of the Church. Second marriages are relatively rare, and although a third marriage is permitted, a fourth is forbidden by the Canons of the Church.

Why does the Orthodox Church not permit same-sex marriages?

Unlike some heterodox churches, the Orthodox Church does not bless same-sex unions or carry out same-sex marriages. Marriage, by definition, involves sexual intercourse; the Church cannot bless a union whose foundation is 'contrary to sound doctrine' (1 Tim. 1:10).

The secular argument for same-sex marriage is based on the idea that two people of the same sex who love each other should be able to get married. However, in the Church the love we have for each other needs to be unto salvation, and not a carnal love or lust. Any love that involves acts that are contrary to the teaching of the Church is not saving. Sexual intercourse between man and wife is blessed in the mystery of marriage – sexual intercourse outside marriage cannot be sanctioned by the Church.

There are few supporters of same-sex marriage in Orthodoxy, but some have pointed to the example of the Byzantine *adelphopoiesis* (lit. brother-making) service as a support for Orthodox same-sex marriage. This rite, which was used for many hundreds of years, resembles the marriage service closely; the participants held candles, joined hands, processed around the icon-stand three times, and received Holy Communion together: they were, however, both men.

Prof. John Boswell's study of these rites concludes that they were 'same sex unions', but his scholarship, in this instance, has been widely discredited. Although there are elements common to the Orthodox marriage service, as its name suggests the 'brother-making' service joins two men together as spiritual brothers and is not a 'same-sex union' or marriage.

What happens if we are unable to have children?

Many couples are unable to conceive together for a lengthy period; some of these couples succeed in having children naturally, but others, unfortunately, are found to be infertile. We have mentioned earlier that the 'fruitful union' referred to in the marriage service does not solely involve conceiving children; it is primarily a spiritually fruitful union of faith and love. St. Paul says that women will be 'saved in child-bearing if they continue in faith and charity and holiness with sobriety' (1 Tim. 2:15); it is faith and the other virtues that saves; childbearing without faith is not saving. Some couples are unable to have children due to infertility, but this does not mean their marriage will be unfruitful. It is particularly important for couples struggling to conceive to observe the fasting periods set by the Church concerning sexual intercourse. The prayers of the Church, almsgiving and fasting are all important at this difficult time.

Any medical procedure that involves the wilful destruction of embryos is unacceptable to the Church. Most IVF protocols involve fertilizing multiple eggs and 'spare' embryos are discarded: this is abortion and is not permitted. It is possible to ask doctors to fertilize only two eggs so that the only possibility is twins and no embryos are killed, but IVF needs to be approached very carefully with much prayer.

Artificial insemination (AI) is used when a couple cannot conceive by regular sexual intercourse. This process involves the insertion of sperm directly into the womb. Because the sperm used is produced by masturbation some object to AI in principle, but most Orthodox have no objection as long as the sperm are from the husband; the use of sperm donors is not permitted.

Chemical fertility treatment is offered to women who are unable to ovulate naturally. It is acceptable to the Church as long as the rate of production of eggs is closely monitored because fertility treatment can be dangerous if too many eggs are released. Even with careful monitoring, multiple births are very common following fertility treatment, leading to the possibility of doctors offering a selective abortion (killing one or more of the babies in the womb).

13

The Mystery of Unction

Is any among you afflicted? Let him pray. Is any merry? Let him sing psalms. Is any sick among you? Let him call for the priests of the Church, and let them pray over him, anointing him with oil in the name of the Lord.

James 5: 13-14

Unction is the mystery during which, through being anointed with oil, Orthodox Christians receive the grace of God to heal their physical and spiritual infirmities and to strengthen their faith. Only in the Orthodox Church can we obtain true health of body and soul by changing our lives by repentance, by living the ascetic life of the Church.

Through the Fall, we inherited corruption, and we are, as St. Gregory of Nyssa teaches, clothed in an 'image that is of clay and mortal'. Christ came, as the Second Adam, to take upon Himself our nature and heal it, and the first stage in our personal healing is at our baptism when

Great Martyr and Unmercenary Healer Panteleimon

we are 'buried with Him by baptism unto death: that like as Christ was raised up from the dead by the glory of the Father, even so we also should walk in newness of life' (Rom. 6:4). This spiritual rebirth gives us the 'power to become sons of God' (John 1:12) and it is achieved by the Holy Spirit as St Paul teaches: 'For it is by grace you have been saved, through faith – and this is not from yourselves, it is the gift of God' (Eph. 2:8).

The cure for illness, therefore, does not come from within, but from without. We have received this gift of God, and to bring it to fruition we need to take up our cross (cf. Matt. 16:24) and embrace the

ascetical and mystical life of the Church. Every time we pray for the sick, when we anoint them with oil, we are carrying out the healing ministry of the Church. Indeed, when we keep the fasts, when we forgive, when we go to confession, when we receive the Body and Blood of Christ we are availing ourselves of the healing power of the Holy Spirit.

The mystery of unction can be held at any time of year, but in current practice is most often served on the Wednesday of Great Week. At this and other such 'general' unction services, every Orthodox Christian present can be anointed, not just those that are sick.

Preparation for the mystery

The mystery is served in the middle of the church where a table is set up on which are placed a Gospel Book and a bowl containing wheat, wine and oil. Seven candles and seven cotton buds or brushes are pushed into the wheat; a smaller bowl containing a mixture of wine and olive oil is placed in the centre of the wheat (right). The seven candles symbolize the seven gifts of the Holy Spirit. The grains of wheat are a symbol of new life because, although they appear dried up and lifeless, given the right conditions they will germinate and new life will come forth from them (cf. John 12:24).

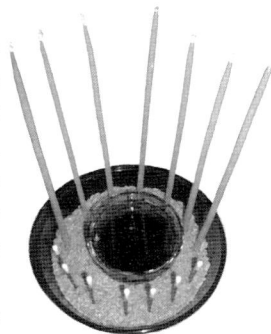

The olive oil is mixed with wine to commemorate the mercy shown by the Good Samaritan who poured oil and wine onto the wounds of the man beaten by thieves. St. John Chrysostom also likens St. Paul to a physician anointing us with the oil of his words:

> *Like a physician, he washes wounds, and through the laver of regeneration he wipes and cleanses them, and he applies stern words, like wine, in order that they may not be carried away by sins or vices committed in ignorance. And again, he heals through exhortation, anointing our souls, as it were, with oil; for he says: 'I beseech you therefore, brethren, by the mercies of God, that ye*

present your bodies a living sacrifice, holy, acceptable unto God, which is your reasonable service' (Rom. 12:1).[96]

St. John Chrysostom avers that the wine is a symbol of the Blood of Christ, and the olive oil a symbol of God's mercy:

What does it mean, that He mixed wine with oil? It means that He mingled Divinity with humanity, and compassion with salvation, and saved mankind. He mingled wine with oil, that is, He mingled the Holy Spirit with His own blood and imparted life to mankind. For, when the Lord's blood dripped from His side onto the earth, it washed away the handwriting of our sins…. If you wish to understand it in a different way, listen. He mixed wine with oil: He applied oil, the word of comfort, pouring in wine as an astringent, that teaching which gathers together the scattered man, as the Apostle says: 'reprove, rebuke, exhort'.(2 Tim 4:2)[97]

The Unction Service

There are seven Epistle readings, seven Gospel readings and seven anointings in the unction service. According to the service books, seven priests celebrate this mystery with each reading one Gospel and the sick person being anointed after each reading. This practice is rarely, if ever, carried out today due to the shortage of priests and the large numbers of faithful attending the service. In this chapter, we will assume that the unction is being carried out for a large number of faithful with one anointing towards the end of the service.

After the blessing by the priest, and the Holy God - Our Father sequence, the choir reads Psalm 142 which is followed by a Little Litany and the Alleluia sung together by the deacon and the choir. The psalm verses intoned by the deacon are specific to the Unction service.

The Alleluia in the Second Tone

> *Verse*: Lord, rebuke me not in Thine anger, nor chasten me in Thy wrath.

> *Verse*: Have mercy on me O Lord for I am weak

---

[96] St. John Chrysostom, 'On the Parable of the Man who fell among Thieves' (trans. Hieromonk Patapios), Orthodox Tradition (2001) Vol. 18 No. 1 p. 28.

[97] Ibid., p. 27.

The choir then sings the troparia of repentance:

> Have mercy on us, Lord have mercy on us; for lacking as we are in all defence , this supplication do we sinners offer unto Thee, as our Master: Have mercy on us.
>
> Glory…
>
> Lord, have mercy on us, for in Thee have we placed all our trust; be not wroth with us greatly, nor do Thou remember our iniquities; but look upon us even now, since Thou art compassionate, and do Thou redeem us from our enemies; for Thou art our God, and we Thy people; all are the works of Thy hands, and upon Thy Name have we called.
>
> Both now…
>
> Do Thou open the portal of compassion unto us, O most blessed Theotokos; for hoping in thee, let us not fail we pray; through thee may we be delivered from adversities, for thou art the salvation of the Christian race.[98]

After Psalm 50, the priest and choir together read the canon. The canon follows the usual structure, and makes special mention of both the olive tree and anointing with oil in the Old and New Testaments:

- The olive branch returned by the dove to Noah after the flood that indicated Noah's deliverance from the water (Gen. 8:11).
- The anointing with oil of King Saul by Prophet Samuel (1 Sam. 10:1).
- The Mother of God is the fruitful olive tree that we read of in the Psalms: 'But as for me, I am a fruitful olive tree in the house of the Lord; I have hoped in the mercy of God for ever, and unto the ages of ages' (Ps. 51.8).
- The anointing of Christ with perfume by the sinful woman (Luke 7: 37-48).

After the canon, following the normal structure of Matins, the choir sings the Exapostilarion:

> As we gather together in Thy holy temple to anoint Thy suffering Servants with Thy holy oil, look down upon our petitions, in Thy mercy O good One.

---

[98] Holy Transfiguration Monastery (trans.), *A Prayer Book for Orthodox Christians* p.299.

The choir then sings four verses appropriate to the unction followed by the following troparion in the Fourth Tone:

O Thou Who alone art a quick Helper O Christ, quickly visit from on high Thy sick servants; deliver them from disease and cruel suffering; raise them up to sing Thy praises and ceaselessly to glorify Thee, through the prayers of the Theotokos, O Thou who alone lovest mankind.

After this, the anointing service proper begins with the Litany of Peace, with the following petitions added:

That He will bless this oil through the power, operation, and descent of the Holy Spirit.

For the servants of God [*Names*] that God may visit them and that the grace of the Holy Spirit may come upon them.

After this Litany the priest reads the Prayer of the Oil secretly:

O Lord, who by Thy mercies and gifts, healest the afflictions of our souls and bodies: do Thou, the same Master, sanctify this oil, that it may bring healing to those who shall be anointed with it, relief from every passion, every sickness of flesh and spirit, and every evil; that by it Thy most Holy Name, of the Father, of the Son, and of the Holy Spirit may be glorified, now and ever and unto the ages of ages Amen.

While the priest is saying this prayer, the choir sings the following troparia:

- O Thou Who alone art a quick Helper O Christ (*see above*)
- Kontakion of the Sunday of the Blind Man (5th Sunday after Pascha)
- Kontakion of the Sunday of the Paralytic (3rd Sunday after Pascha)
- Dismissal Hymn of St. James the Brother of God (23rd October)
- Kontakion of St. James the Brother of God
- Kontakion of St. Nicholas of Myra (6th December)
- Dismissal Hymn of St. Demetrius (26th October)

- Dismissal Hymn of St. Panteleimon (27th July)
- Dismissal Hymn of the Holy Unmercenaries Cosmas and Damian (1st November)
- Kontakion of St. John the Theologian (26th September)
- Theotokion 'O Fervent Advocate…'[99]

In the seven Epistle and Gospel readings we hear of the miraculous cures performed by the Saviour and His apostles, and the power of faith in the Lord and love for our neighbour. The number seven is of great significance in this mystery. The seven readings and anointings signify the seven gifts of the Holy Spirit described by the Prophet Esaias:

> And there shall come forth a rod out of the root of Jesse, and a blossom shall come up from his root: and the Spirit of God shall rest upon him, the spirit of wisdom and understanding, the spirit of counsel and strength, the spirit of knowledge and piety shall fill him; the spirit of the fear of God. He shall not judge according to appearance, nor reprove according to report (Es. 11: 1-3).

St. Gregory the Great, Pope of Rome, likens these seven gifts (wisdom, understanding, counsel, strength, knowledge, piety and the fear of God) to sons that are born in us through the coming of the Spirit; those filled with these sevenfold gifts of the Spirit are made perfect through the Spirit and see God:

> Those whom the Spirit of sevenfold grace has filled, it makes perfect, and the Spirit imparts to them not merely the knowledge of the Trinity, but also the performance of the four virtues, that is, prudence, temperance, fortitude and justice… but the performance of the four virtues is received through the knowledge of the Trinity and by the performance of the four virtues, we attain the clear sight of the Trinity.

The number seven's importance is foreshadowed several times in the Old Testament. The Prophet Elias ended the great drought in the reign of King Ahab by his prayers which were answered the seventh time his servant looked out to sea for a rain cloud (1 Kings 18: 42-45); Naaman, the head of the Syrian army, was cured by dipping himself

---

[99] Holy Transfiguration Monastery (trans.), *A Prayer Book for Orthodox Christians* p.259.

seven times in the Jordan at the prayers of the Prophet Elisseus (2 Kings: 5: 9-14); Prophet Elisseus raised a child from the dead by bowing down upon him seven times:

> *Elisseus went into the house, and, behold, the dead child was laid upon his bed. And Elisseus went into the house, and shut the door upon themselves, the two, and prayed to the Lord. And he went up, and lay upon the child, and put his mouth upon his mouth, and his eyes upon his eyes, and his hands upon his hands; and bowed himself upon him, and the flesh of the child grew warm. And he returned, and walked up and down in the house: and he went up, and bowed himself on the child seven times; and the child opened his eyes. And Elisseus cried out to Giezi, and said, Call this Shunammite. So he called her, and she came in to him: and Elisseus said, Take thy son. And the woman went in, and fell at his feet, and did obeisance bowing to the ground; and she took her son, and went out (4 Kings 4:32-37).*

All seven readings follow a sequence identical to that used in the Divine Liturgy: Prokeimenon, Epistle Reading, Alleluia, Gospel Reading. To save space, we have not given the full text of all the readings; only the first sequence is reproduced in full, in order show the general structure of the service.

Prokeimenon in the First Tone

L et Thy mercy be upon us O Lord, according as we have put our trust in Thee.

Verse: Rejoice in the Lord O ye righteous. Praise is meet for the upright.

Epistle Reading: (James 5: 10-16).

B rethren, take the prophets, who have spoken in the Name of the Lord, for an example of suffering affliction, and of patience. Behold, we count them happy which endure. Ye have heard of the patience of Job, and have seen the end of the Lord; that the Lord is very pitiful, and of tender mercy. But above all things, my brethren, swear not, neither by heaven, neither by the earth, neither by any other oath: but let your yea be yea; and your nay, nay; lest ye fall into condemnation. Is any among you afflicted? Let him pray. Is any merry? Let him sing psalms. Is any sick among you? Let him call for the elders of the church; and let them pray over him, anointing him with oil in the Name of the Lord: And the prayer of faith shall save the sick, and the Lord shall raise him up; and if he have committed sins, they shall be forgiven him. Confess your faults one to another, and pray one for another, that ye may be healed. The effectual fervent prayer of a righteous man availeth much.

Alleluia in the Plagal Fourth Tone

Verse: Of mercy and judgment will I sing unto Thee, O Lord.

Gospel Reading: (Luke 10: 25-37)

At that time, a certain lawyer stood up, and tempted Him, saying, Master, what shall I do to inherit eternal life? He said unto him, What is written in the law? How readest thou? And he answering said, Thou shalt love the Lord thy God with all thy heart, and with all thy soul, and with all thy strength, and with all thy mind; and thy neighbour as thyself. And He said unto him, Thou hast answered right: this do, and thou shalt live. But he, willing to justify himself, said unto Jesus, And who is my neighbour? And Jesus answering said, A certain man went down from Jerusalem to Jericho, and fell among thieves, which stripped him of his raiment, and wounded him, and departed, leaving him half dead. And by chance there came down a certain priest that way: and when he saw him, he passed by on the other side. And likewise a Levite, when he was at the place, came and looked on him, and passed by on the other side. But a certain Samaritan, as he journeyed, came where he was: and when he saw him, he had compassion on him, And went to him, and bound up his wounds, pouring in oil and wine, and set him on his own beast, and brought him to an inn, and took care of him. And on the morrow when he departed, he took out two pence, and gave them to the host, and said unto him, Take care of him; and whatsoever thou spendest more, when I come again, I will repay thee. Which now of these three, thinkest thou, was neighbour unto him that fell among the thieves? And he said, He that shewed mercy on him. Then said Jesus unto him, Go, and do thou likewise.

After every Gospel, the deacon intones the following litany, and the choir answers each petition with 'Lord have Mercy' (three times).

> Have mercy on us, O God, according to Thy great mercy, we pray Thee, hearken and have mercy.
>
> Again we pray for mercy, life, peace, health, salvation and remission of sins of the servants of God [*Names*].
>
> That they may be pardoned every transgression, whether voluntary or involuntary.

The Prayer of the First Reading

After the usual introduction, 'Let us pray to the Lord'; 'Lord have mercy', the priest reads the appointed prayer. In this first prayer, the mystery of unction is explained in terms of the whole mystery of God the Word's *kenosis* and His providence for us. We have included the relevant Scripture references:

> O Thou who art without beginning, eternal, the Holy of Holies, who didst send down Thine only-begotten Son to heal every infirmity and every wound, both of our souls and bodies: send down Thy Holy Spirit and sanctify this oil; and cause it to be for Thy servants who are about to be anointed with it, unto perfect remission of their sins, and unto inheritance in the Kingdom of Heaven.
>
> For Thou art a great and marvellous God, who keepest Thy covenant and hast mercy towards them that love Thee, Who grantest forgiveness of sin through Thy holy Child, Jesus Christ; Who dost regenerate us from sin through holy baptism, and sanctifiest us with Thy Holy Spirit; Who givest light to the blind, who raisest up them that are cast down (Ps.144:15), Who lovest the righteous and showest mercy unto sinners, Who leadest us forth again out of darkness and the shadow of death (Ps. 106:14) and sayest unto them that are in captivity: 'Come forth'; and unto them that sit in dark-

ness: 'Be ye manifest' (Luke 1:79 Esaias 9:2). **For He shined in our hearts with the light of the knowledge of His presence (2 Cor. 4:6) when, for our sakes, He revealed Himself upon earth, and dwelt among men; and unto as many as accepted Him, to them He gave the power to become sons of God** (John 1:12), **granting us the adoption of sons** (Gal. 4:5) **through the washing of regeneration** (Titus 3:5), **and freeing us from the tyranny of the devil.**

And inasmuch as it hath not pleased Thee that we should be cleansed by blood, but by holy oil, Thou didst give unto us the image of His Cross, that we might become the flock of Christ, a royal priesthood, a holy nation (1. Pet. 2:9) **and didst purify us by water** (Eph. 5:26) **and sanctify us by the Holy Spirit.**

Do Thou, the same Master, O Lord, grant unto us grace in Thy ministry, as Thou didst grant it unto Moses, Thy servant, who found favour in Thy sight, and unto Samuel, beloved of Thee, and unto John, Thy chosen one, and unto all those who, from generation to generation, have been well pleasing unto Thee.

In like manner, make us also to be ministers of the new covenant of Thy Son (2. Cor. 3:6), **upon this oil which Thou hast acquired through the precious blood of Thy Christ; so that putting away earthly lusts, we may die unto sin, and live unto righteousness** (1. Pet. 2:24) **being clothed in Him through the anointing with the oil of sanctification which we are about to undergo.**

Let this oil, O Lord, become the oil of gladness, the oil of sanctification, a royal robe, an armour of might, the averting of every work of the devil, the seal of immunity from snares, the joy of the heart and an eternal rejoicing. Grant that they who are anointed with this oil of regeneration may be terrible to their adversaries, and may shine with the radiance of Thy saints, having neither spot nor wrinkle (Eph. 5:27), **and that they may attain unto rest everlasting and receive the prize of their high calling** (Phil. 3:14).

The other six readings and prayers are now read in order. The readings are listed below:

Reading	Epistle	Gospel
Second	Romans 15: 1-7	Luke 19: 1-10
Third	1 Corinthians 12:27-13:8	Matthew. 10: 1, 5-8
Fourth	2 Corinthians 6:16 – 7:1	Matthew 8: 14-23
Fifth	2 Corinthians 1: 8-12	Matthew 25: 1-13
Sixth	Galatians. 5:22-6:2	Matthew 15: 21-28
Seventh	1 Thessalonians. 5: 14-23	Matthew 9: 9-13

The Prayer of Absolution and General Anointing

After the seventh Gospel, the open Gospel Book is held over the head of the patient (text downwards), and the prayer of absolution 'O holy King, compassionate and all-merciful Lord Jesus Christ…' is read. When the service takes place in church, with only one anointing, the following prayer is now read:

O Holy Father, Physician of souls and bodies, Who didst send Thine Only-begotten Son, our Lord Jesus Christ, Who healeth every infirmity and delivereth from death: heal Thou also Thy servants from the ills of soul and body which afflict them and enliven them by the grace of Thy Christ, through the prayers of our All-holy Lady, the Theotokos and Ever-virgin Mary, through the intercession of the honourable, bodiless hosts of heaven; through the power of the precious and life-giving Cross; through the protection of the honourable, glorious Prophet, Forerunner, and Baptist John; of the holy, glorious and most blessed apostles, of the holy, glorious, victorious martyrs, of the venerable, God-bearing fathers; of the holy, unmercenary healers, Cosmas and Damian, Cyrus and John, Panteleimon and Hermolaus, Sampson, Diomedes, Photius and Anacetas; of the holy and righteous ancestors of God, Joachim and Anna, and of all the saints. For Thou art the Fountain of Healing, O Christ our God, and unto Thee do we send up glory to the Father,

and to the Son, and to the Holy Spirit, now and ever, and unto the ages of ages.

The anointing with oil now takes place. Each person is anointed, crosswise, on the forehead, eyelids, nose, cheeks, lips, the chest and both sides of the hands. After the anointing, the oil is wiped off using paper towels which should then be left in the receptacle provided. The anointed areas of the body should not be washed that night.

The Dismissal

In the dismissal of the mystery of unction, the priest commemorates St. James, the Brother of God, primarily because of the importance of his teaching on the healing effects of unction:

> **May Christ our true God, through the intercessions of His most pure Mother, by the power of the precious and life-giving Cross, of the holy, glorious and all praised Apostle James, the Brother of God, the first Bishop of Jerusalem, and of all the saints, save us and have mercy on us in that He is good and the Friend of Man.**

St. James was St. Joseph the Betrothed's son from a previous marriage. The title 'Brother of God' is theologically significant. Even though St. James never used this title himself, the Orthodox Church honours him with it, to confirm our faith that Christ is truly God and Man.

Frequently Asked Questions

May non-Orthodox be anointed with unction?

Only Orthodox Christians can be anointed with the oil of unction. The unction service can be served at home, at hospital or the oil may be brought from the church. However, the most commonly used anointing service that is used for the sick in hospital is not the unction service, but a short service of prayer followed by anointing with oil from a vigil lamp. Non-Orthodox Christians may be anointed with this oil.

May any Orthodox Christian be anointed, or only the extremely sick?

Until relatively recently in the Russian Church, only the extremely sick were anointed with the oil of unction. The service for general anointing found in earlier Slavonic service books had been replaced in the seventeenth century by a service which closely resembled the Roman Catholic service of 'extreme unction': a final anointing for those in danger of death. It was widely assumed in the nineteenth century Russian Church that someone had to be unconscious or near death before the mystery of unction could be served for them. Moreover, it was thought that a patient who recovered after anointing had to become a monastic or spend the rest of their life in repentance and fasting.[100] General unction services, following a similar structure to that used today, were served at the Church of the Dormition in Moscow, but this was the exception at this time, and not the rule.

Why do we have to go to confession before unction?

The mystery of unction presupposes that those being anointed are Orthodox Christians in good standing with the Church, that they are following the path of repentance by going to confession regularly, by keeping the fasts and saying their prayers. It is not necessary that we go to confession just before the service in some vain attempt to avoid sin before being anointed. Conscientious Orthodox Christians should be going to confession regularly, and it is this regular confession that is necessary before being anointed in the mystery of unction.

Should we fast from midnight before receiving Holy Unction?

No. However, it goes without saying that those who wish to receive anointing should have been trying to keep the fast days appointed by the Church; this is especially important considering that unction services are often held during Great Week.

---

[100] D. Sokolof, *A Manual of the Orthodox Church's Divine Services* (Jordanville: Holy Trinity Monastery, 2001) p. 158.

Saint Philaret of New York

14

Orthodoxy and Medicine

Take heed lest by any means this liberty of yours become a stumbling block to them that are weak. For if any man see thee who hast knowledge eating in the idol's temple, shall not the conscience of him who is weak be encouraged to eat those things which are offered to idols? So shall this weak brother, for whom Christ died, perish through thy knowledge.

1 Corinthians 8: 9-11

The Orthodox Church works with medical professionals to provide the best care for the sick by combining medical treatment with prayer; this is why we visit the sick in hospital and ask the prayers of the Church before undergoing medical procedures. There are, however, a few medical procedures that are always unacceptable to the Church, and we will discuss these below together with a selection of procedures which are acceptable to, and encouraged by, the Church.

Euthanasia

The word 'euthanasia' means 'good death' and is used to describe the killing of someone who is terminally ill and in pain. At the moment, voluntary euthanasia is permitted in certain European countries; people opt to be killed for a number of reasons, including not wanting to grow old and, most infamously, for having 'lost sparkle'. Sometimes euthanasia is carried out by relatives of terminally ill patients and this is usually termed 'mercy killing' by the press.

The Orthodox Church views all forms of euthanasia as unacceptable, regarding them as either murder or suicide. Suffering and illness are part of our fallen condition, but are not worthless because, as St. Maximus the Confessor confirms, those whom divine providence is leading toward holiness are tested by bodily sufferings. Christ Himself says: 'in your patience possess ye your souls' (Luke 21:19).

This is not to say that suffering needs to be prolonged unnecessarily; there is a prayer appointed to be read by the priest in the event of prolonged suffering to hasten the hour of death. There is also a special canon to be read at the departure of the soul which may be read by any Orthodox Christian. In all these prayers, the Church prays that the soul may be granted the mercy of God even though we are all held under the yoke of our sins which causes our strength to fail (cf. Lam. 1:14).

Euthanasia by medical intervention is illegal in the UK, but hospitals have, in the past, performed it by withdrawing feeding to patients that were capable of eating and drinking; this practice is euthanasia and is not permitted by the Church.

On the other hand, many patients with advanced cancer are, in effect, killed by their medical treatment because the painkillers that they are prescribed eventually suppress the respiratory system. This is not euthanasia, but merely a side effect of the drugs needed to keep the patient comfortable. In addition, medical staff may decide that if a patient has no hope of recovery, it is not in their best interest to commence painful and distressing life-support treatment. The issues surrounding withdrawal of medical treatment, however, are more complicated.

Seriously ill patients who are unable to breathe unaided are placed on a machine called a ventilator which breathes for them. The ventilator provides a vital life support system for the patient, but in certain cases doctors may advise that this life support be withdrawn. The Orthodox Church would not consider this sinful, but in making this decision we need to combine the advice of the doctors with prayer because the issue is far from straightforward. For example, some patients suffering from 'locked-in syndrome' or in a deep coma have made a full recovery after families refused to remove life support.

Medical staff may advise removing intravenous or naso-gastral feeding if they think that a paralysed patient who is able to breathe unaided has no hope of recovery. This is a more complex problem than allowing the removal of artificial ventilation because in making this decision doctors are denying the patient nutrition. However, although artificial feeding supports life, the Church does not demand that we prolong life by every means. Indeed, artificially feeding a terminally ill patient that is unable to eat actually increases suffering by causing a number of painful medical complications. Removing artificial feeding allows a natural death so it does not amount to euthanasia.

Today, in the UK, an emphasis is placed on allowing a patient to die peacefully and with dignity, and patients are able to choose what level of care they require by making what is called an 'Advanced Decision' indicating, for example, whether they want to be resuscitated or placed on a ventilator. An Advanced Decision, often called a 'living will', provides doctors with a legal basis not to intervene and prolong life by artificial ventilation or feeding. Even without the legal force of an Advanced Decision, medical staff in general are pleased to accommodate the wishes of terminally ill patients that want to die peacefully, and they appreciate the support of the patient's family at this time.

Orthodox Christians understand that death is inevitable and we need to be prepared for it and provide the necessary support to the medical staff and ensure that we pray for, and care for, our relative. However, taking a decision regarding withdrawal of life support or artificial feeding on behalf of a dying relative is, by its very nature, a difficult one and needs to be taken after discussion with a spiritual father.

Organ transplants from heart-beating donors

Most organs used for transplants are taken from donors while their hearts are still beating: a procedure called 'organ harvesting' or 'organ recovery'. The first recorded instance of an organ being taken from a 'heart-beating' (HB) donor occurred on June 3rd 1963 when Guy Alexandre removed a kidney from a patient in Louvain, Belgium. The recipient died a month later from septicaemia.[101]

Heart-beating donation is preferred over donation from those who have died for many reasons. Keeping blood flowing through the organs as long as possible improves the success of transplants, and allows the transplant team to assemble and for the recipients to be notified and prepared for operation.

The removal of organs from 'heart-beating' donors is always unacceptable to the Orthodox Church because it is a deliberate medical

[101] C. Machado, *Brain Death: a Reappraisal* (New York: Springer Science, 2007) p. 21.

intervention to end life; cutting out a vital organ while the heart is still beating is euthanasia in all but name.

Organs may legally only be recovered from the 'dead', and the definition of death needed for HB transplants is a complete absence of brain stem activity commonly referred to as 'brain death'. This definition of death was invented solely to provide HB donors for transplants, but the definition is flawed because it relies on the brain being the only source of control in the body; according to Dr. Alan Shewmon, the 'brain's role is more modulatory than constitutive, enhancing the quality and survival potential of a presupposedly living organism.'[102]

To illustrate this point, at the Third International Symposium on Coma and Death (Havana, 2000), Dr. Shewmon showed a video of a patient referred to as 'TK' who had been 'brain dead' since the age of four. This diagnosis had been confirmed by repeated clinical tests, including EEG's and MRI angiograms to check for brain blood flow. TK's heart was still beating unaided twenty years later, and he was cared for at home for six years.[103]

Patient TK eventually died of heart failure and an autopsy showed that his brain had been completely destroyed.[104] Amazingly, the Diabetes Insipidus from which TK suffered had spontaneously resolved during his period of 'brain death' despite him having no functioning brain tissue.

In TK's case, and in other patients whose bodies continue to function without any brain-stem activity, a host of biological processes continue to support life without any direction from the brain. As well as the heart beating, nutrients are assimilated and wastes eliminated, thousands of complex proteins and ions are maintained at the correct levels essential for life, infections are overcome and wounds heal,

[102] D. A. Shewmon, The Brain and Somatic Integration: Insights Into the Standard Biological Rationale for Equating "Brain Death" With Death. *Journal of Medicine and Philosophy* (2001) Vol. 26, No. 5, p. 457.

[103] D.A. Shewmon, Chronic 'brain death' meta-analysis and conceptual consequences. *Neurology* (December 1998) Vol. 51, No. 6, pp.1538-1545.

[104] S. Repertinger et al., Long Survival Following Bacterial Meningitis-Associated Brain Destruction. *Journal of Child Neurology* (2006)Vol. 21, Issue 7, pp. 591-595.

hormones are produced and their levels adjusted by complex feed-back responses. Indeed Dr. Shewmon reports that a 13-year-old boy whom he had examined began puberty while brain-dead.[105]

The processes by which cells communicate with each other to coordinate bodily response are still poorly understood, but it is known that cell signalling occurs without direct input from the brain. For example, all cells in the body are programmed to die and are kept alive by signals from other cells: a phenomenon known as apoptosis.

Defining death by an absence of brain stem activity is far from an exact science. Overdoses of barbiturates, excess alcohol and hypothermia may all cause a cessation of brain activity which could be classified as 'brain death'. For example, in 2009, Coleen Burns woke up the day before doctors were due to 'harvest' her organs after declaring her 'brain dead'. Defenders of organ transplantation would say protocols were not followed correctly in this case, but it is evident that patients with a complete absence of brain stem activity are not actually 'dead'.

Alternatives to the current definition of an absence of brain stem activity as 'death' have been proposed. One definition is that of a loss of 'being' indicated by a lack of self-awareness, an absence of intentional behaviour and sociality etc. This definition is unacceptable because it would leave the permanently unconscious and the severely disabled in danger of having their organs harvested.

Death also cannot be certified simply on the basis that the brain is no longer able to control the body. For example, there is a strong biological correlation between the symptoms of a high spinal transection and the criteria used for determining brain death. The former condition is a complete severing of the spinal cord resulting in tetraplegia and, in severe cases, an inability to breathe unaided. In both cases the brain does not function in integrating the organism, but paralysis or tetraplegia certainly does not imply 'brain death' or a lack of sentient being.

The only reliable method of certifying death is the older cardiores-

---

[105] D.A. Shewmon, *Neurology* (December 1998) Vol. 51, No. 6, pp. 1538-1545.

piratory criterion in which death is defined as an absence of heart-beat and breathing. This definition, as Professor Ian Kerridge argues, avoids re-defining death solely because of the needs of the transplant lobby:

> *The danger is that death is defined on the basis of providing use-ful organs for transplant. We argue that the definition of death should not be related to organ transplantation and that it is bio-logically, philosophically, and socioculturally more accurate to re-gard 'brain death' as a state separate from death.*[106]

In other words, an absence of brain stem activity does not indicate death, but is rather a prognosis of immediate death; a patient who is 'brain dead' will die if life support is removed and is in a state of permanent irreversible unconsciousness. An absence of brain stem activity thus moves from being the starting-gun for organ removal to a diagnostic tool useful for medical staff and relatives alike. The latter can prepare themselves for the imminent death of their loved one (once life support is removed) and medical staff have a strong basis for advising against continuation of ventilation and intensive care support.

Professor Ian Kerridge argues that the current portrayal of how trans-plants are carried out is both scientifically inaccurate and dishonest.

> *Rather than redefining those who are 'brain dead' as 'dead' it may be more honest to acknowledge that such individuals are not dead and that removing their organs is in fact killing them. Such an ac-tion is undeniably morally troubling; it may, however, be morally justifiable in precisely defined circumstances such as where recov-ery is impossible and personal identity is lost. It may also be less morally objectionable than the creation of a fiction (the redefini-tion of death) which is the only alternative. The long term viabil-ity of transplantation programmes is likely to be better served by telling the truth than trading in fictions.*[107]

---

[106] C. Machado, I. Kerridge et al., A definition of human death should not be related to organ transplants. *Journal of Medical Ethics* (2003) Vol. 29, No. 3 pp. 201-202.

[107] I. H. Kerridge et al., Death, dying and donation: organ transplantation and the diagnosis of death. *Journal of Medical Ethics* (2002) Vol. 28, No. 2, pp. 89-94.

Prof. Kerridge's view that certain circumstances could justify killing a patient to recover their organs is not shared by traditionalist Orthodox Christians. The Church's objection to HB donors is not about rejecting scientific progress, but about protecting those who are least able to protect themselves as Alan Shewmon explains:

> To admit that many brain-dead patients are deeply comatose, severely disabled, living human beings is progress, not regress. It will force a refinement in our understanding and diagnosis of death, a clarification in our fundamental philosophical principles regarding human life, and realignment between our understanding and our consciences in dealing with these most vulnerable human lives.[108]

To avoid being involved in heart-beating transplants, Orthodox Christians should not sign up to organ donor registers, and take steps to opt out of donating if they live in countries where consent for donation is assumed. Orthodox Christians should also refuse all organs obtained from HB donors.

Organ transplants from non-heart-beating donors

Transplant centres in the UK are currently looking at expanding the use of organs from donors whose heart has stopped, a practice known as asystolic organ transplantation or non-heart-beating (NHB) donation. Generally, the heart is required to stop for ten minutes before the organs are removed although different countries have different NHB protocols.

Organs from NHB donors still provide only a small proportion of total transplants, but kidneys, liver, pancreas, lung and cornea transplants from NHB donors are all carried out regularly in the UK and survival rates are just as good when compared with beating-heart transplants.[109]

NHB remains unpopular because of the difficulty in preventing the organs deteriorating outside the body. However, a number of centres

---

[108] D. A. Shewmon, Mental disconnect: 'physiological decapitation' as a heuristic for understanding 'brain death'. Chapter in M. Sánchez Sorondo (Ed.), *The Signs of Death* (Vatican City: Pontifical Academy of Sciences, 2007) p. 326.

[109] E. Chaib, Non Heart-Beating Donors in England. *Clinics* (2008) Vol. 63, No. 1 pp. 121–134.

in the UK have developed a mix of surgical techniques and pumping machines to prevent organs deteriorating before transplant.

Non-heart-beating donation is compatible with Orthodoxy, but signing up to an organ donation register inevitably means granting permission to become a heart-beating donor which, as we have discussed above, is not permissible for Orthodox Christians. Organs can be donated after death via NHB donation, even without the donor having signed a donor register, as long as the next of kin give permission.

Heart transplants

Heart transplants are not acceptable to the Church, because the hearts are obtained from HB donors. In addition, reliable evidence exists of recipients receiving aspects of the donor's personality following heart transplants; these changes are not simply psychosomatic, because they occur when the identity of the donor is unknown to the recipient. This evidence supports the Orthodox belief that our heart is central to our existence and not merely a biological pump that can be changed when it is worn out. St. Philaret of New York explains the Church's view on heart transplants:

> *The heart is the centre, the mid-point of man's existence. And not only in the spiritual sense, where heart is the term for the centre of one's spiritual person, one's "I"; in physical life, too, the physical heart is the chief organ and central point of the organism, being mysteriously and indissolubly connected with the experiences of one's soul. It is well known to all how a man's purely psychical and nervous experiences, joy, anger, fright, etc.,—are reflected immediately in the action of the heart, and conversely how an unhealthy condition of the heart acts oppressively on the psyche and consciousness... Yes, here the bond is indissoluble—and if, instead of the continuation of a man's personal spiritual-bodily life, concentrated in his own heart, there is imposed on him a strange heart and some kind of strange life, until then totally unknown to him—then what is this if not a counterfeit of his departing life; what is this if not the annihilation of his spiritual-bodily life, his individuality, his personal "I"?*[110]

[110] *The Orthodox Word* (May-June 1968), Vol. 4, No. 3, pp. 134-137.

Heart transplants are promoted as saving lives but they are, from an Orthodox point of view, doing no such thing. Even on a purely medical level, organ rejection is relatively common and every recipient needs lifelong medication to suppress the immune system and prevent the organ being rejected. In the end, around half of recipients die within ten years of receiving a donated heart.

Living donation

Becoming a 'living donor' by donating bone marrow, a kidney or a lobe of the liver is completely acceptable to the Church and a practical demonstration of Christian love. Although relatives normally provide the most likely match for living donations, it is also possible to donate to non-relatives. Donating organs for money is, of course, immoral and unacceptable.

Blood transfusions

Donating blood or bone marrow is actively encouraged by the Orthodox Church. In May 2016, the Orthodox Metropolis of Oropos and Fili established a blood bank supplied by donations from monks, nuns and pilgrims.[111] Any major operation, particularly those following severe trauma, uses tremendous amounts of blood, and it is only right that if we are willing to receive blood we should also donate it.

Abortion

The deliberate killing of a baby in the womb is a serious sin whether it is carried out by surgical intervention or by taking drugs to induce a miscarriage. The Orthodox Church has always believed that life begins at conception (fertilization) and therefore has always considered abortion to be a serious sin.

In exceptionally rare cases, a baby may start to develop outside the womb or otherwise put the mother in danger of death. In this case, to save the mother's life, the embryo must be removed and will unfortunately die as a result. This would not be classed as an abortion. More commonly, abortion drugs are used to remove a baby that has died in the womb. This traumatic event is not an abortion, but a miscarriage.

[111] http://www.hsir.org/pdfs/2016/05/24 E20160524bAimodosia05-16.pdf

The Roman Catholic Church's opposition to abortion is relatively new, but it tends to be extremely dogmatic. The Orthodox Church has always opposed abortion, but takes a much more compassionate attitude to these issues. If a child has an abortion following a rape, for example, the Church would look to support the victim and her family rather than publicly excommunicate them as the Roman Catholic Church has done in the past. The Orthodox Church does not publicly humiliate people in this fashion, especially after such a traumatic experience. An epitimia is, by nature, a private matter and an aid to repentance not a punishment.

The opposition of the Orthodox Church to abortion is born out by several recent studies. A 2004 study of almost 80,000 women carried out at Oxford University found that women who had an abortion were significantly more likely to suffer from breast cancer than those who had not. A meta-analysis published in 2011 in the British Journal of Psychiatry studied data from more than 870,000 women and found that those who had an abortion were at an increased risk of anxiety disorders, depression, drug abuse and suicidal behaviour. According to the same study, nearly 10% of all mental health problems in women can be attributed directly to abortion.

Embryo screening and genetic modification

In Chapter Twelve we discussed the problems associated with IVF as a remedy for infertility. IVF is also used to create designer embryos such as the so-called 'saviour siblings' that are screened for diseases and designed to provide blood or bone marrow, when they grow up, for a sick brother or sister. It is also used to produce embryos by pronuclear transfer (commonly called a 'three parent baby'). All these procedures are completely unacceptable to the Orthodox Church.

Alternative medicine

Acupuncture, homeopathy and crystal healing are all forms of alternative medicine. The term 'complementary medicine' refers to alternative medical treatments than can be used in conjunction with mainstream medicine. Both alternative and complementary medicine claim to be 'holistic' treatments - the word 'holistic' means considering the 'whole system'; holistic medicine, therefore, is concerned with curing both the body and the soul.

Illness, according to the tenets of alternative medicine, is caused by the body's 'energy flow' being in some way affected. This theory is found in many alternative medical practices influenced by eastern religions. In Ayurvedic medicine it is known as 'prana' and in acupuncture as 'Qi'. Practitioners of homeopathy refer to it as 'vital force'. Alternative medical practitioners believe that their 'success' is due to the realigning or liberation of the 'energy flow' to release the body's energy.

There is no doubt that physical symptoms, and even healings and miracles can be caused by demonic forces. We should not seek healing of the soul and body via alternative medicine, because, by seeking healing for our souls outside the Church, we are laying ourselves open to demonic assault. Even if we get better, is this 'healing' unto our salvation or our condemnation?

Any treatment that has spiritual or 'pseudo-spiritual' content must be avoided no matter how Orthodox this treatment claims to be. This warning also applies to those medicines, readily available in health shops, that boast of being able to cure emotional or spiritual problems. In general, any form of medicine or treatment that has any spiritual basis should be avoided; drinking herbal teas, taking vitamin supplements etc. are obviously acceptable because they are natural pharmaceutical remedies – they do not form part of a spiritual treatment or claim to treat illness of the soul.

Alternative medicine might claim to be able to cure spiritual illness, but this can only be cured through spiritual struggle and partaking of the mysteries of the Church. Until we come to the conclusion that the problem with our life is not our disordered 'energy flow' but our sins, we will never be able to start on the path of repentance. We should run to Christ as the Physician of our souls and bodies; we should trust in the Church from whom we receive, as St. Ignatius of Antioch teaches, the true 'Medicine of Immortality'.

Saint Mark of Ephesus

15

The Mystery of Ordination

See that you all follow the bishop, even as Jesus Christ does the Father, and the priests as you would the apostles; and reverence the deacons, as being the institution of God.

St. Ignatius of Antioch

By our baptism and chrismation, all Orthodox Christians are members of the Body of Christ and we comprise 'a royal priesthood, a holy nation' (1 Peter 2:5). We are set apart and called to become gods by grace. However, only some members of this royal priesthood are set by apart, by ordination, to become ministers of the mysteries of the Church.

The grace needed to celebrate the mysteries is given in the mystery of ordination. Deacons are ordained in order to assist at the mysteries which bishops or priests celebrate through the grace of their ordination. The mystery of ordination to the episcopate (often called consecration) confers, on the bishop, the grace to ordain deacons and priests, and also to participate in the consecration of other bishops.

The bishop is the source of the life-giving mysteries of the Church, and the shepherd of the rational flock (cf. John 10: 14) by the grace of the Holy Spirit. St. Ignatius of Antioch is clear that the 'rational flock' of Christians should never separate themselves from their shepherd, the bishop, as long as he proclaims Orthodoxy:

> *Let no man do anything connected with the Church without the bishop…Wherever the bishop shall appear, there let the multitude [of the people] also be; even as, wherever Jesus Christ is, there is the Catholic Church.*

The bishop is our guide, our protector and our example. Most importantly, without the bishop, the faithful cannot partake of the life-giving mysteries because all the mysteries have their source in the Orthodox faith of the bishop. When a priest serves the Divine Liturgy, or any other mystery, he is doing so as the bishop's representative. This is why a priest cannot celebrate the mysteries in another diocese without the permission of the bishop of that diocese. When a priest is serving in his own parish he does not need to ask the bishop's permission before each service, but his permission is needed before any exercise of economy. In addition, a married priest cannot tonsure monastics nor should a married priest hear the confessions of his family members.

The first degree of the priesthood is that of the reader; to emphasize this, during the service for the setting apart of readers, the candidate wears a short *phelonion*. Readers are tonsured and wear a cassock in church and a *sticharion* when serving in the altar.

The ministry of subdeacon is the next degree after reader. Subdeacons are ordained to serve in the altar, and as a sign of this ministry, the newly ordained subdeacon washes the bishop's hands at his ordination; the candidate remains standing before the iconostasis holding the jug, bowl and towel until the Great Entrance. Subdeacons wear a sticharion with an *orarion* crossed over it. In the Russian Church, readers and layman are sometimes allowed to wear an orarion in the same manner as a subdeacon; this practice is not found in the Greek Church.

The diaconate is the final degree before the priesthood. Unlike readers and subdeacons, deacons are always addressed as 'Father [*Name*]' and receive Holy Communion in the altar. In many western denominations the diaconate is merely a stepping stone to the priesthood; the Orthodox diaconate, however, is an important ministry in its own right. Deacons assist bishops and priests at the Divine Liturgy and at other mysteries as Saint Symeon of Thessalonika explains:

> *The deacon is called 'liturgic' and 'cathartic' (a purifier) because he has the order of assistant, and can do nothing without the priest. This function pertains to the last of the angelic orders. He purifies those who approach, guiding them and opening their minds in order that they may receive the mysteries.' Let us attend', he says and 'Wisdom! Upright!' and 'With fear of God and faith draw near'; and he incites them to prayer, crying out, 'In peace let*

us pray to the Lord', and, 'let us pray to the Lord,' and, 'Let us bow our heads to the Lord.' These things purify the listeners and lead them to enlightenment.[112]

Through the mystery of ordination we are all given new life, because the priests regenerate us through the mystery of baptism and forgive our sins in the mystery of repentance. Below, St. John Chrysostom compares the priesthood with parenthood:

God has given greater power to priests than to natural parents, not only in disciplining, but also in helping. The difference between the two is as great as that between the present and the future life. Parents bring us into this life; priests into the life to come. Parents cannot stop bodily death or drive away the start of disease; priests have often saved the soul that is sick and at the point of death, by making the punishment milder for some, and preventing others from ever incurring it, not only through instruction and warning, but also through helping them through prayer. Priests have authority to remit sins, not only when they regenerate us, but afterwards too.

Deacons are ordained after the consecration of the Holy Gifts, and priests are ordained after the Cherubic Hymn so that they can participate in the consecration. Bishops are consecrated after the singing of the Trisagion Hymn.

The Ordination of a Deacon

The candidate to be ordained a deacon must already have been tonsured a reader and ordained a subdeacon. He is brought forward and makes three bows as he is led up towards the Royal Doors. The bringing forward of the candidate indicates that he is not putting himself forward to be ordained but is being put forward by the Church. The bishop makes the sign of the cross over the candidate, and he is led around the Holy Table three times whilst the clergy and choir sing:

O holy martyrs, who fought the good fight and have received your crowns, entreat ye the Lord that He will have mercy on our souls.

---

[112] Adapted from St. Symeon of Thessalonika, *The Liturgical Commentaries* p. 99.

The Vestments of the Deacon

The deacon wears a long vestment called a *sticharion* (*right*) over his cassock. The sticharion is also worn by altar servers and readers, but the deacon's sticharion is slit up the sides and the two halves are held together by buttons. The deacon wears a pair of cloth cuffs (*left*) made from the same material as his sticharion; each has a long cord attached which is used to tie the cuffs in place when they are worn. The cuffs recall the power and grace of the Holy Spirit through which the deacon assists in serving the holy mysteries. They also represent the bonds with which the Saviour was tied with when He was brought before Pilate.

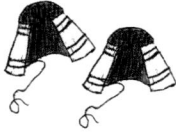

The characteristic vestment of the deacon is the *orarion* (*left*) which is fastened to the left shoulder of the sticharion and hangs down loosely. Subdeacons also wear the orarion, but they always wear it wrapped around their chests in the form of a cross (*right*). The deacon wears his orarion in this fashion during the Divine Liturgy from the Lord's Prayer to after the distribution of Holy Communion. When the deacon intones litanies, or makes any other exclamation he holds the orarion in his right hand and lifts it up.

In the ordination service, the deacon is given a liturgical fan (*ripidion*) to hold on which is painted an icon of a six-winged seraphim. A pair of these fans are kept behind the Holy Table and are carried by altar servers during the Little and Great Entrances. These fans are rarely used today by the deacon except during the Liturgy of St. James.

Glory to Thee, O Christ God, the boast of the apostles, the joy of the martyrs, whose preaching was the Trinity One in Essence.

Rejoice, O Esaias! A Virgin is with child, and shall bear a Son, Emmanuel, both God and man; Dayspring is His Name, and magnifying Him we call the Virgin blessed.

After the procession, the subdeacon that is to be ordained kneels on one knee and places his forehead on the Holy Table and the bishop puts his stole on the subdeacon's head, and signs him three time with the sign of the cross. Laying his hand on the candidate's head, he then reads this prayer in a loud voice:

The grace divine which always heals that which is infirm, and completes that which is lacking, elevates through the laying on of hands [*Name*], the most devout subdeacon, to be a deacon. Wherefore, let us pray for him, that the grace of the All-holy Spirit may come upon him.

Whilst the priest and the choir sings 'Lord have mercy' twelve times the bishop reads the following prayer quietly:

O Lord our God, who in Thy foreknowledge dost send down the fullness of the Holy Spirit upon those who are ordained by Thine incomprehensible power to be Thy servants, and to celebrate Thy pure mysteries, do Thou, O Sovereign Master preserve this man, whom Thou hast been pleased to ordain through me, by the laying on of hands, to the service of the diaconate, in soberness of life, and to hold the mystery of the faith with a pure conscience. Grant unto him the grace which Thou didst grant unto the Protomartyr Stephen, whom Thou didst call to be the first worker in this ministry. Make him worthy to please Thee in serving in the office which Thou hast bestowed upon him in Thy goodness, for they who minister well prepare for themselves a good reward; show him forth as completely Thy servant.

The senior deacon present then says the Great Litany quietly in the altar adding three petitions that are specific to the mystery of Ordination. Whilst this litany is being said, the bishop reads a prayer quietly

The Vestments of the Priest

Sticharion: The priest's cuffs are identical to those of the deacon, but his sticharion differs in that it is made of lighter material and has narrow sleeves fitted with cords. The sticharion represents the shining raiment of the angels and in particular that of the angel who appeared to the myrrh-bearing women at the Tomb of Christ after the Resurrection. It also represents the purity that the priest needs to preserve, and the illumination that he ministers to the faithful through the mysteries and the preaching of the Gospel. In the Slavic usage, the sticharion is always white, but in the Greek usage it is often coloured.

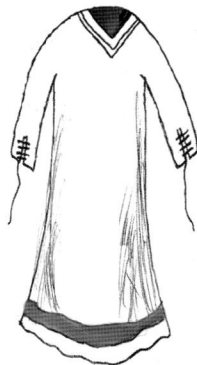

Epitrachelion: Also called a 'stole', the epitrachelion is the characteristic vestment of the priest, and he wears it when celebrating any mystery or prayer service. The epitrachelion is derived from the deacon's orarion, but it is worn over both shoulders and not one, signifying the double grace of the priesthood. For convenience, the two halves of the epitrachelion are fastened together by buttons.

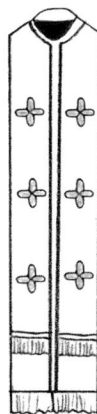

The epitrachelion represents the enlightening divine grace that descends from the Father of lights, through the incarnate Son, in the Holy Spirit. Because the priest puts on the epitrachelion over his head and wears it around his neck, it also represents that the priest is subject to Christ and must perform the services of the Church in obedience to the Master Christ, and to submit to Christ's yoke in humility.

Zone: The zone is worn over the sticharion and epitrachelion and is fastened with cords at the back. It signifies the strength that the priest receives from the Holy Spirit, his readiness to serve the Lord and the divine power that strengthens him during the course of his serving. The zone also recalls the towel with which the Saviour washed the disciples' feet at the Mystical Supper.

Phelonion: The phelonion is worn during the Liturgy, when a Gospel is read, and when a priest enters through the Royal Doors. The phelonion represents the power and illumination of the Holy Spirit and because it does not have sleeves it also represents the all-embracing and all-encompassing power of God. In addition, the phelonion reminds the priests of the garment of righteousness with which they must be vested as servants of Christ (Is. 61:10). Russian phelonions are usually made from stiffer material and have a higher back than in the Greek and Romanian traditions.

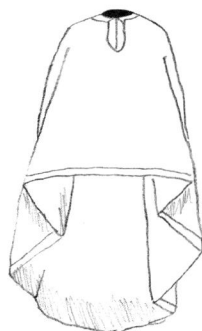

Epigonation: Senior priests wear the epigonation (Slavonic: *palitsa*) a square piece of stiffened cloth that hangs down on the priest's right side. The wearing of the epigonation, in the Greek usage, signifies that the priest has a blessing from the bishop to hear confessions. In the Russian usage, some priests are given the *nabedrennik* by the bishop as a sign of their long-service to the Church. The nabedrennik is larger than the palitsa and rectangular in shape, and the priest wears it on his left-hand side; it is not worn in the Greek Church.

ending with the exclamation: 'For Thou art our God, and unto Thee do we send up glory to the Father, and to the Son, and to the Holy Spirit, now and ever and unto the ages of ages.'

The newly-ordained deacon is raised up and his crossed-over stole is taken off and fastened onto his left shoulder as the bishop exclaims 'Axios!'; the clergy inside the altar answer 'Axios, Axios, Axios!' and the people and the choir reply 'Axios, Axios, Axios!' The bishop gives the deacon a pair of cuffs and one of the ceremonial fans (*ripidion*), in the same manner. When this is completed the newly-ordained deacon enters the altar through the Royal Doors and fans the Holy Gifts.

The Ordination of a Priest

The candidate is led by the senior deacon into the altar, in the same manner as in the ordination of a deacon. He kisses the hand of the bishop who is seated at the front right-hand corner of the Holy Table, and he is led around the Holy Table three times whilst the choir sing the same troparia as in the ordination of a deacon.

After the procession, the candidate kneels on both knees and places his forehead on the Holy Table and the bishop puts his hand on the deacon's head, and signs him three time with the sign of the cross. He then reads this prayer in a loud voice:

> **The grace divine which always heals that which is infirm, and completes that which is lacking, elevates through the laying on of hands [*Name*], the most devout deacon, to the office of priest. Wherefore, let us pray for him, that the grace of the All-holy Spirit may come upon him.**

Whilst the priest and the choir sings 'Lord have mercy' twelve times, the bishop reads a prayer quietly asking that the Holy Spirit come down through the laying on hands. After this prayer, the senior priest quietly reads a shortened Litany of Peace containing special petitions relevant to the mystery, whilst the bishop reads this prayer quietly:

> O God, great in might and incomprehensible in wisdom, marvellous in counsel above the sons of men; do Thou, the same Lord, fill with the gift of Thy Holy Spirit this man whom thou

hast been pleased to advance to the office of priest. Grant that he may be worthy to stand in innocence before Thine altar, to proclaim the Gospel of Thy Kingdom, to minister the word of thy truth, to offer unto Thee spiritual gifts and sacrifices, to renew Thy people through the bath of regeneration. Grant that when he shall go to meet Thee at the Second Coming of our Great God and Saviour Jesus Christ, Thine Only-begotten Son, he may receive the reward of the good steward in the office committed unto him, through the plenitude of Thy goodness.

The newly-ordained priest is now raised up and the deacon's stole removed from him. The bishop gives him the epitrachelion as he exclaims, 'Axios!'; the clergy respond by saying, 'Axios, Axios, Axios!' and the faithful signify their agreement by repeating this threefold acclamation. The bishop gives the priest the zone, phelonion and priests' service book exclaiming 'Axios!' each time to which the clergy and the faithful respond as before. The newly ordained priest, now vested in priest's vestments, re-enters the altar and takes his place among the priests. After the consecration of the Holy Gifts, the bishop hands the newly-ordained priest the consecrated Lamb and says: 'Receive thou this pledge, and preserve it whole and unharmed until thy last breath, because thou shalt be held to an account in the second and dread Coming of our Great Lord, God, and Saviour, Jesus Christ.'

The priest, holding the Lamb in his hand, stands at the Holy Table facing west until just before the exclamation, 'the Holies are for the holy.'

The Consecration of a Bishop

The service for the consecration of a bishop is substantially different from the ordinations of deacon and priest. Although it is rarely seen, we will discuss this service in some detail as it contains a wealth of information on the Orthodox Faith.

In the episcopal consecration, the bishop-elect is questioned about his beliefs and affirms to the whole Church his Orthodox Confession of Faith. Priests and deacons do not have to do this, because the bishop who ordains them guarantees their Orthodoxy of Faith, having previously examined them closely. Today, bishops in traditional Orthodox churches are chosen from the monastic clergy but unmarried laymen were sometimes chosen in earlier centuries. Most often, the candidate is an hegumen (abbot) or an archimandrite, which is a higher rank in the monastic priesthood. In this section we will refer to the monastic priest that is to be consecrated as the 'bishop-elect'.

A new bishop is elected by the existing bishops of the Synod, and this normally takes place some weeks before the actual consecration service. A consecration is preceded by an All-night Vigil service on the previous evening at which the bishop-elect makes a public confession of the Orthodox Faith.

The bishop-elect is led into the middle of the church holding in his hands the Orthodox Confession of Faith. The senior bishop questions him about his beliefs and the bishop-elect replies by reciting the Nicene Creed. He is then questioned further: **Tell us, in particular, what dost thou believe concerning the properties of the three Persons of the ineffable Godhead, and concerning the Incarnation of the Person of the Son and Word of God?**

The bishop-elect answers by reciting a Second Confession of Faith summarizing the Orthodox doctrine concerning the Trinity, the incarnation, the Resurrection, and the veneration of icons. This confession is essentially a summary of the decisions of the Seven Oecumenical Councils.

In the first part of this confession, the bishop-elect affirms his Orthodoxy and refutes the teachings of Arius (who taught that Christ is not God), and Macedonius (who taught that the Holy Spirit is not God). Arianism was condemned at the First Oecumenical Council, and Macedonianism at the Second:

> **I believe in one God, the Father Almighty, Maker of Heaven and earth, and of all things visible and invisible; For He is without beginning, unbegotten and without cause, but is Himself the natural beginning and cause of the Son and of the Spirit. And I believe in his Only-begotten Son, without change and outside time, begotten of Him, being of one es-**

sence with Him by whom all things were made. And I believe in the Holy Spirit, who proceeds from the same Father, and with Him is glorified as co-eternal, being of one essence with Him, and equal in glory, and enthroned together with Him, the author of creation.

I believe that one of the same super-substantial and life-giving Trinity, the Only-begotten Word, came down from heaven, for us men, and for our salvation, and was incarnate by the Holy Spirit of the Virgin Mary and became man; that is to say, was made perfect man, yet remaining God, and in nowise changing His divine essence by His participation in the flesh, neither being transmuted into anything else; but without change assuming human nature. He endured suffering and death in His human nature, being free in His Divine nature from every suffering.

And on the third day He rose again from the dead; and ascended into heaven, and sitteth on the right hand of God and the Father. And I believe those traditions and narrations concerning the One Catholic and Apostolic Church which we have received from God and the God-bearing Fathers. I acknowledge one baptism for the remission of sins. I look for the resurrection of the dead and the life of the world to come.

In the next section, he affirms his belief in the decision of the Fourth and Fifth Oecumenical Councils which condemned the heresy of the Monophysites who taught that Christ's human nature was dissolved in His divine nature, and those who believe that the union of the two natures in Christ produced a new, third, composite divine-human nature.

In addition, I confess the one person, the Word made flesh; and I believe and proclaim that Christ is one and the same in two natures after His incarnation, preserving those things which were in them and from them.

He then confesses that each of the two natures of Christ has a will and an energy, thereby opposing the heresies of Monothelitism and Monoenergism that were condemned by the Sixth Oecumenical Council.

The Vestments of the Bishop

Omophorion: The characteristic vestment of the bishop is the omophorion which is worn across the shoulders to represent the lost sheep and the bishop's role as the shepherd of his flock. The bishop wears the omophorion when he conducts any service in church. The great omophorion is worn during the Divine Liturgy and resembles the deacon's orarion in shape but is wider and wound around the shoulders. The small omophorion (*right*) is worn outside the Liturgy, for example, when the bishop hears confessions.

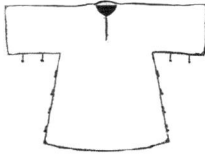

Sakkos: During the Divine Liturgy, the bishop wears a vestment with short sleeves called a *sakkos* (*left*) inspired by the garment worn by the Byzantine Emperors. The word *sakkos* means 'sackcloth' reminding the bishop that he must govern his diocese with humility, and it is fitted with twelve bells symbolizing that the bishop preaches the same faith as the apostles and to recall the bells attached to the vestments of the Old Testament priests (Ex. 28: 33-34). During the Divine Liturgy, the bishop wears the great omophorion and all the vestments of the priest except the phelonion. The epitrachelion is worn under the sakkos and the great omophorion over it.

Enkolpion. Both inside and outside church, the bishop wears an *enkolpion* with an icon mounted in the centre. The word *enkolpion* means 'on the chest' and hangs from a chain around the neck. Because this icon portrays the Mother of God, the enkolpion is more commonly known as a *panagia* which means 'all holy', a term used by the Church to honour the Mother of God. In church services, many bishops also wear a cross as well as a panagia.

Mitre: The bishop wears a mitre during the Liturgy recalling the mitre of the Old Testament priesthood (Ex. 39:31) and symbolising his obedience to the Orthodox Church. In the Russian Church, mitres are also worn by archimandrites and some archpriests.

Staff: The bishop's staff symbolizes his role as a shepherd of his flock. The head of the staff is decorated with two snake heads separated by an emblem of the Cross. The snakes recall the command of God to Moses to make a bronze serpent and place it on a staff (Numb. 21:8-9) in order that those bitten by snakes might look on it and be saved. When the bishop is not holding his staff, it rests on the iconostasis by the icon of Christ. Outside church, the bishop carries a plain staff as a symbol of his authority.

Eagle Symbol: In church, the bishop stands on the symbol of an eagle flying above a city to remind him that he should soar above the cares of the world and should inspire his flock to ascend from earth to heaven. In Greek churches, the eagle symbol often takes the form of a mosaic set in the floor; in the Slavic churches, the eagle is embroidered on a rug called an *orlets*.

Dikirion and Trikirion: When the bishop blesses the people during the Divine Liturgy, he holds a three branched candlestick (*trikirion*) in his right hand and a two branched candlestick (*dikirion*) in his left. The trikirion represents the three Persons of the Trinity, one in essence, and the dikirion the two natures of Christ: God and Man.

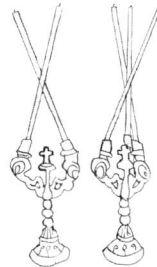

> **Therefore also I adore two wills, in that each nature retains its own unique will and its own energy.**

The bishop-elect now affirms his support for the veneration for icons, as decreed by the Seventh Oecumenical Council. In doing so, he confirms the teaching of the Orthodox Church that the honour shown to an icon of Christ, for example, redounds to the prototype (Christ).

> **I reverence, relatively, but not in the way of worship, the images divine and worthy of adoration of Christ Himself, and of the all-undefiled Mother of God, and of all the saints, addressing to their prototypes the honour shown to them. I reject as ill-advised those who think otherwise.**

This Confession of Faith ends with the bishop-elect affirming his belief that the Son of God became flesh from the Theotokos thus refuting the heresies of Arius and Nestorius which were condemned at the First and Third Ecumenical Councils:

> **And I literally and truly confess our Sovereign Lady, Mary the Theotokos, as having borne in the flesh One of the Trinity, even Christ our God. And may the same be my helper, protector, and defender all the days of my life. Amen.**

He is now questioned on his beliefs in the Orthodox Church as expressed by Her Canons and by the writing of the Holy Fathers. He replies:

> **In this my confession of the holy faith, I promise to observe the Canons of the holy apostles, and of the Seven Ecumenical Councils, and of the pious Local Councils, the traditions of the Church, and the decrees, orders and regulations of the Holy Fathers. And all things whatsoever they have accepted I also accept; and whatsoever things they have rejected I also reject.**

The bishop-elect next affirms his loyalty to his Patriarch or Synod, and promises to uphold the good order of the Church. Specifically, he promises to treat the opponents of the Church with gentleness, and to withstand any efforts to corrupt him by money or offers of power. He presents his written confession of faith to the senior bishop who confirms his election.

On the next day, after the chanting of the Trisagion at the Divine Liturgy, the bishop-elect is led forward through the Royal Doors into the altar. At least three bishops are needed to consecrate a new bishop. He kneels on both knees and the bishops present take the Gospel Book and hold it, writing downwards on his head. St. Nicodemos of the Holy Mountain explains that this action reminds the bishops that:

> *Even though they have become the leaders of others, they are themselves under the authority of the laws of the Gospel. St. John Chrysostom has noted that a bishop who is the head of the people of God is himself under another authority (for it is unbearable to have uncontrolled authority). By having the token of authority over his head, it is indicated that he is led by law. It is ordered that the head be not bare, but covered in order to teach the head of the people that He [i.e. Christ] too has authority over him.*[113]

The senior bishop then exclaims in a loud voice:

> **By the election and approval of the most God-loving bishops, and of all the consecrated Synod, the grace divine, which healeth that which is infirm, and completeth that which is lacking, through the laying on hands elevateth thee, the most God-loving Hieromonk duly elected to be the Bishop of the God-saved diocese of [*Name*].**

Whilst the other bishops keep hold of the Gospel book, the senior bishop makes the sign of the cross three times over the head of the bishop-elect while saying the appointed prayer quietly. At the end of this prayer, one of the bishops reads the Litany of Peace with extra petitions relevant to the consecration. The senior bishop then reads this final prayer quietly:

> O Lord our God who, because it is impossible for the nature of man to endure the essence of the Godhead, in Thy providence for us hast appointed teachers of like nature with ourselves, to serve at Thine altar, that they may offer unto Thee sacrifice and oblation for all Thy people; Do Thou, the same Lord, make this man also, who has been proclaimed a steward of the episcopal

---

[113] St. Nicodemos of the Holy Mountain, *A Handbook of Spiritual Counsel* (trans. P. Chamberas) (Mahwah: Paulist Press, 1989) p. 193.

grace, to be an imitator of Thee, the true Shepherd Who didst lay down Thy life for Thy sheep; to be a leader of the blind, a light to those in darkness, a reprover of the unwise, a teacher of the young, a lamp to the world: that, having perfected the souls entrusted unto him in this present life, he may stand unashamed before Thy throne, and receive the great reward which Thou has prepared for those who have contended valiantly, for the preaching of the Gospel.

The newly-consecrated bishop is then vested in the sakkos and the omophorion. The omophorion that he wears across his shoulders represents the lost sheep. The bishop, acting as a true icon of Christ, is called to be a good shepherd of the flock of rational sheep entrusted to him. The omophorion is decorated with crosses because the bishop has willingly taken the Cross of Christ upon his shoulders.

Frequently Asked Questions

Is it true that the Orthodox Church used to ordain deaconesses?

Female deaconesses were ordained in the first few centuries of Christianity, and they continued to serve in convents after this. The ordination service for deacons and deaconesses was very similar, and deaconesses were given Holy Communion in the altar in the same way as deacons. Deaconesses assisted at the baptism of female converts, and distributed Holy Communion in convents, but their role was unique: they were not 'women deacons'. The practice of ordaining deaconesses died out, but was never outlawed; St. Nectarios of Pentapolis (1846-1920), for example, ordained deaconesses to minister to the nuns in convents that were under his supervision.

Can priests marry after their ordination?

Subdeacons, deacons and priests cannot marry after their ordination according to the Sixth Canon of the Quinisext Oecumenical Council which states:

> *No subdeacon, nor deacon, nor presbyter, should in any ways be at liberty to arrange for himself a matrimonial union after his ordination; if he dares to do this, he shall be deposed.*

If anyone entering the clergy desires to be joined in law to a woman, he shall do this before his ordination as subdeacon or deacon or presbyter.[114]

In addition, anyone that has been twice married, or has had sex before marriage cannot be ordained. The 17th Apostolic Canon states that 'he who has been twice married after baptism, or who has had a concubine, cannot become a bishop, presbyter, or deacon, or any other of the sacerdotal list.' There are also a number of other restrictions on who can be ordained; these are in place for spiritual reasons. Men are not allowed to be ordained if their wife is not a practising Orthodox Christian, or if she has been divorced. On the other hand, divorce is no impediment to ordination if it took place before Orthodox baptism, because deeds or sins before baptism are washed away in the font.

---

[114] Nedungatt, Featherstone, *The Council in Trullo Revisited* pp. 75-76.

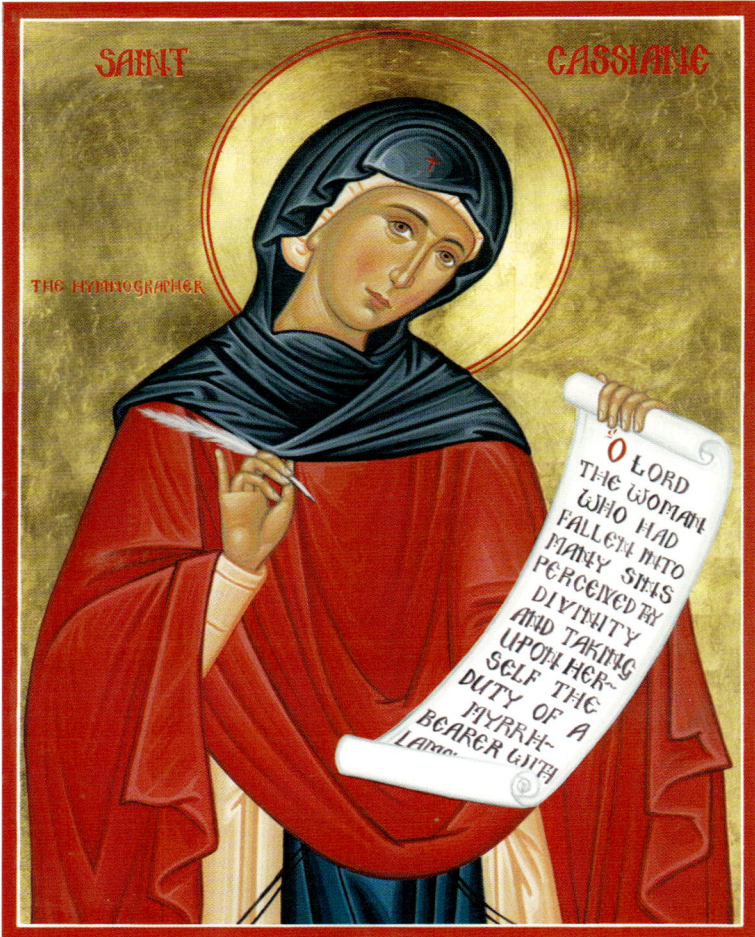

Venerable Cassiane the Hymnographer

The scroll contains her most famous composition, the 'Hymn of Cassiane', which is chanted in Great Week.

16

Orthodox Women and the Priesthood

As many of you as have been baptized into Christ have put on Christ. There is neither Jew nor Greek, there is neither slave nor free, there is neither male nor female: for ye are all one in Christ Jesus.

Galatians 3:27-28

In Orthodoxy, the differences between the genders are not as important as the mystery that makes us equal – our baptism. We are all born as a result of sexual union between man and woman, and we are born, die and will be judged in our bodies. However, in this life, we are all seeking to be 'delivered from this body of death' (Rom. 7:24) and to attain eternal life, in which our bodies will be transformed and we will live like the angels of God (cf. Matt 22:30).

We attain real equality in the Church by being united to each other by faith, although our responsibilities and gifts are different as St. Paul teaches: 'Now there are diversities of gifts, but the same Spirit. And there are differences of administrations, but the same Lord. And there are diversities of operations, but it is the same God who worketh all in all' (1 Cor. 12: 4-6).

The biological differences caused by gender are inherent in human nature, but we should remember that we have been reborn of 'water and the Spirit' (John 3:5). The links between us as brothers and sisters in Christ are much stronger than those between us and the members of our gender who are not in the Church. Orthodox Christians are members (body parts) of the Body of Christ, and members 'one of another' (Eph. 4:5).

However, in proclaiming our oneness in faith, we do not abolish the order of creation, or promote some form of New Age unity, because as St. Gregory Palamas teaches, the created has nothing in common with the uncreated:

Every created nature is far removed from and completely foreign to the Divine nature. For if God is nature, other things are not nature; but if every other thing is nature, He is not a nature, just as He is not a being if all other things are beings. And if He is a being, then all other things are not beings.

We are all one in Christ and in the Church 'there is neither Jew nor Greek, there is neither slave nor free, there is neither male nor female' (Gal. 3:28). Our equality is not a logical equality which does away with physical differences, or an equality based on rights.

In Orthodoxy, men do not have the 'right' to become priests simply because they are male. Men are chosen by the Church to become priests because of their Orthodox faith and the uprightness of their life. Our equality in the Church is spiritual because our ultimate goal, as men or women, is to attain the Kingdom of Heaven. St. Basil the Great says that 'the virtue of man and woman is the same; creation is equally honoured in both, therefore there is the same reward for both.'

Despite this equality of reward, historically only pagan and heretical sects had priestesses; it was unthinkable to the Church to even consider the ordination of women priests. The fourth century saint, Epiphanius of Cyprus, writes: 'Since the beginning of time a woman has never served God as a priest… God has never appointed a single woman upon the earth to this ministry.'

The Orthodox Church does not ordain women to the priesthood, because She has never done so. We accept this tradition, and all other Church traditions, because by doing so we reject the disease of error and the poison of self-will. Keeping Orthodox traditions is not a matter of pick and choose, but part of our Christian struggle to purify our souls by repentance and humility.

However, this argument from tradition is perhaps overstated by heterodox opponents of the ordination of women; there are important theological reasons why the Orthodox priesthood is only male and these reasons give us an insight into the role of the priesthood itself.

The priest's presence in the mysteries renders Christ present. This Orthodox understanding of the priesthood is quite different from the Roman Catholic one. The latter believe that the grace of the priesthood is created and given to the priest personally, so when a Roman Catholic priest performs the sacraments, *he* is performing them. In contrast, the sacrifice in the Orthodox Eucharist is not carried out by the priest, but by Christ; according to St. John Chrysostom, the words are spoken *through* the priest and not *by* him:

> It is not a man who causes the sacrificial gifts to become the Body and Blood of Christ: this is done by Christ Himself who was crucified for our sakes. The priest stands there carrying out the action, but the power and grace are from God.

An Orthodox bishop is reminded of this principle when he is consecrated. A bishop is called to be an imitator of Christ the True Shepherd, and a priest is called to imitate both Christ and his bishop. St. Theodore the Studite describes a priest as an 'icon of Christ' not simply because the priest resembles Christ in appearance, but because Christ Himself is the Great High Priest, and became man to save mankind. Christ did not become human, He became a man. This is why the priest, as an icon of Christ, is male. This symbolism, according to Metropolitan Kallistos (Ware), is an integral part of the worship of the Church and cannot be divorced from it:

> The priest is an icon of Christ; and since the incarnate Christ became not only man but a male – since, furthermore, in the order of nature the roles of male and female are not interchangeable – it is necessary that the priest should be male. Those western Christians who do not regard the priest as an icon are not, however, creating women priests but dispensing with priesthood altogether.[115]

This misunderstanding of the priesthood among the heterodox has elevated the priesthood into the 'holy grail' for women – a position of status and power: the only one that 'counts' in serving God. However, the Orthodox priesthood is a service and not a position, and the ordained ministry is only one of the ways in which men and women can perform a service to the Church.

We have mentioned the central role of monasticism in the Orthodox Church. In addition, laymen and women can build, repair, sing, bake

---

[115] P. Moore (Ed.), *Man, Woman, and Priesthood* (London: SPCK, 1978) p. 83.

prosphoras, clean, cook, sew vestments, and teach Orthodoxy to the children of the parish. The most influential layperson in the congregation, moreover, is not a man, but the priest's wife who is referred to as 'Presbytera' in Greek, or 'Matushka' in Russian, as a token of honour and as a sign of her importance to the parish. Metropolitan Kallistos (Ware) explains:

> *If the woman in the home acts as giver and protector of life, the priest's wife is called to do this throughout the parish. Just as the priest is father not to his own children solely but of the entire community, so the priest's wife is called to be mother alike in her own family and in the parochial family as a whole. Yet she is not ordained for this task, but is simply realizing in a particular manner the royal priesthood that is the common inheritance of all. Her maternal vocation has to be exercised with the utmost discretion, not so much through anything she says, or does, as through what she is.*[116]

What then, is the role of women in the Orthodox Church? This question presupposes a grouping together of individuals into one collective based on gender: this in itself is not Orthodox. What women? Some women will undertake the monastic life, some will get married, and some might never get married. Our role, as members of the Church is not to struggle for the rights of our gender but to heal ourselves in the Church, changing the world around us.

Some women believe that the Orthodox Church discriminates against them. Some men, equally erroneously, believe that Orthodox women are second-class citizens in the Church and that this status can be justified in the historical record. For example, Patrick Mitchell, in his book *The Scandal of Gender*, fails to consider the significant achievements of Saints Irene, Theodora and Pulcheria the Byzantine Empresses, when he states: 'on very rare occasions in its thousand year history Byzantium was ruled by a woman.' He then goes on to say: 'Russia was not ruled by a woman until its westernization by Peter the Great.'[117] Unfortunately,

---

[116] Ibid., p. 86.

[117] P. Mitchell, *The Scandal of Gender* (Salisbury: Regina Orthodox Press, 1988) p. 135.

Mitchell forgets to mention that St. Olga of Russia ruled as regent from 945-963 and is commemorated as the Enlightener of the Russian land and Equal of the Apostles.

It is true that upper-class Byzantine women lived in secluded quarters where men were forbidden to enter, but this seclusion was one way: the women, if they wished, could exit, but men could not enter. Working-class and middle-class women, on the other hand, were a constant feature of life in the streets of Constantinople. The city was a crowded place; the twelfth century Byzantine poet John Tzetzes, for example, lived underneath a priest's family who kept pigs (and numerous children) in their apartment. Only the rich could afford to offer their daughters the privacy such as Anna Komnene (1083-1153) enjoyed, being taught by visiting tutors. This tutoring obviously paid off as Anna took charge of a ten-thousand-bed hospital at which she taught medicine.

The eminent Byzantinologist Professor Judith Herrin paints a rather different picture to Mitchell of life for women in the Orthodox Byzantine Empire:

> *A combination of factors, specific to the early medieval Byzantine empire, allowed women to break through the silence of the historical record to a remarkable degree, one not matched by their sisters in the Muslim, Jewish, and Western Christian worlds of the time. Among these factors the acceptance of female heads of state in a world overwhelmingly dominated by male authority deserves emphasis.*[118]

This level of freedom for women was unmatched in western countries of the same period. Orthodox Byzantine women could buy and sell property and daughters had the right to inherit property and dispose of it as they wished. In contrast, it was only in the late nineteenth century that married British women were allowed to own or inherit property. It was not until 1925 that the eldest daughter in a family could inherit property from her parents; previously, the daughter was passed over in favour of her younger brother.

[118] J. Herrin, *Unrivalled Influence: Women and Empire in Byzantium* (Princeton: Princeton University Press, 2013) p. 31.

The unparalleled equality of women in Orthodox Byzantium was a result of Orthodox theology which, far from viewing women as 'second-class', rejoices in their exaltation through the Incarnation of Christ. Saint Proclus of Constantinople teaches:

> *Through Mary all women are blessed. The female can no longer be held accursed, for the rank of this sex surpasses even the angels in glory. Now Eve is healed, the Egyptian woman passed over in silence. Delilah is sealed in a tomb. Jezebel given to oblivion. Even Herodias herself is no longer mentioned. Now behold the catalogue of admirable women: All praise Sarah, the fertile field of the people. Rebecca is honoured, a capable provider of blessings, and Leah too they admire as mother of the ancestor in the flesh. Deborah wins praise because she led in battle despite her sex. Elizabeth also they call happy, for she carried the Forerunner in her body, and he leaped in delight at the approach of grace.*[119]

Men and women are equal in the Church and the concept of 'rights' is foreign to Her; the concept itself is just thinly disguised disobedience. Christ calls us to be humble (cf. Matt. 11:29); and obedience, as St. Diodochos of Photiki explains, leads to true humility:

> *It is well known that obedience is the chief among the initiatory virtues, for first it displaces presumption and then it engenders humility within us. Thus it becomes, for those who willingly embrace it, a door leading to the love of God. It was because he rejected humility that Adam fell into the lowest depths of Hades. It was because He loved humility that the Lord, in accordance with the divine purpose, was obedient to the Father even to the Cross and death, although He was in no way inferior to the Father; and so through His own obedience He has freed mankind from the crime of disobedience and leads back to the blessedness of eternal life all who live in obedience.*[120]

Campaigning for the ordination of women and other 'womens' rights' leads to gross distortions of Orthodox Tradition. For example,

---

[119] Adapted from K.G. Holum, *Theodosian Empresses* (Berkeley: University of California Press, 1982) p. 141.

[120] *The Philokalia Vol.1* p.265.

Leonie Liveris complains that 'the Church, often aided and abetted by women, has demanded certain behaviours by women concerning menstruation, child-bearing, birth control, abortion, sexuality, virginity and celibacy.'[121] Surely, no conscientious Orthodox Christian can support abortion or promote promiscuity? Having sexual relations outside marriage is a serious sin for both men and women; men who have had sexual intercourse before marriage, for example, cannot be ordained to the clergy.

Liveris continues: 'In recent years the practice of female circumcision has been revealed as customary in some Orthodox communities.' Nothing could be further from the truth. Female Genital Mutilation (FGM) has its origins in paganism and is widely practiced in Islam and among members of the Coptic, Ethiopian and Eritrean Churches. Although they refer to themselves as Orthodox, all these Churches reject the Fourth Oecumenical Council, and as a result they are outside Orthodoxy, being more properly called 'non-Chalcedonian' or 'Monophysite' Churches. There is no tradition of FGM in Orthodox Churches.

Liveris also complains that 'the teachings of her "otherness" are with women [sic] from the first days after her birth to the time of her funeral,' but as we have discussed in previous chapters, all the mysteries, including baptism and burial, are identical for men and women. The only service that is performed solely for women are the prayers relating to childbirth.

Finally, she advocates that 'these are issues for feminist Christians to challenge the Church.' This point demonstrates the dangers of allowing feminism, or chauvinism, to infect Orthodoxy because as, Saint Basil the Great explains, Orthodox tradition is central to our faith:

> From the dogmas and preaching preserved in the Church, we have some in doctrine set forth in writing, and others, which have come down to us from apostolic tradition, we have received in secret, both of which have equal force as regards piety. Accordingly, no one contradicts these, at least no one that has any experience at

---

[121] L.B. Liveris, *Ancient Taboos and Gender Prejudice* (Aldershot: Ashgate Publishing, 2005) p. 112.

all in ecclesiastical matters. For if we should undertake to discard the customs not set forth in the Scriptures, as though they had no great force, we would unwittingly do damage to that which is most important in the Gospel, and would turn our preaching into empty words.

Rejecting Church tradition will ultimately lead to complete atheism, because if we accept that the Church has taught wrongly for centuries on certain topics, why would She be right on others? Although individual members of the Church make mistakes, the Orthodox Church does not, because She is the Body of Christ. The only issue we need to challenge within the Church is our own behaviour.

There are, however, some issues concerning women that might seem discriminatory to someone who does not fully understand how the Orthodox Church functions, and what the purpose of the Church is. The six subjects that we discuss below were raised by Verna Harrison in her article 'Reflections and Concerns on Women's Roles in Orthodox Churches'.[122]

1) The Churching of women

A mother does not enter the church for a period of forty days after giving birth. On the fortieth day after childbirth a prayer is read over the new mother and she re-enters the Church. Christ Himself fulfilled the ordinances of the law when He was circumcised on the eighth day; on the fortieth day He was brought to the Temple and received by the Elder Symeon. The prayers read on the fortieth day commemorate this event.

The 'bodily uncleanness' that is referred to in this service is a result of the Fall. We inherited death from Adam, and also certain bodily functions that are considered by the Church to be sufficient to prevent us from partaking of the Body and Blood of Christ in the Eucharist. For men, these are emissions of semen; for women, the time of their monthly period and the time after childbirth. In addition, married couples cannot receive Holy Communion if they have had sexual intercourse the night before.

---

[122] V. Harrison, *Sourozh* (1988) 33, pp. 43-49.

Some may wonder why male babies are taken around the altar during the churching service, but female babies are not. The procession through the altar is meant to be a prefiguring of the boy's possible future service as a member of the clergy. In earlier centuries when female deaconesses were still ordained, female children were indeed taken around the altar as St. Symeon of Thessalonika indicates. As the role of deaconesses has fallen into disuse, so has the practice of carrying female babies into the altar.

2) Women entering the altar

No one is permitted to enter the altar unless they are ordained, or they have a blessing from the bishop or priest to do so. In practice, this means that women do not enter the altar because the Orthodox Church no longer ordains deaconesses. In convents, however, nuns are appointed by the bishop to enter the altar and change the covers on the Holy Table. In contrast, no layman is ever permitted to touch the Holy Table.

3) Head coverings

Women cover their heads in Church because they wish to follow the traditions of the Church (cf. 1 Cor. 11:5) and to honour the angels (cf. 1. Cor. 11:10); they choose to place themselves under the light yoke of obedience to Christ which actually grants freedom. Head coverings do not signify inferiority – monks, nuns and bishops all have their heads covered in church. The monastics cover their heads as a sign of their obedience to their superior, and the bishop's mitre symbolizes both his role as high priest and his obedience to the Church.

A covered head expresses the desire of a woman to be in obedience to God and the Church, not her inferiority to men – for, in the words of St. Paul, 'we are all one in Christ Jesus' (Gal. 3:28). This oneness is a result of our transformation within the Church, but it does not obliterate or distort the natural order as Metropolitan Kallistos explains:

> *[Men and women] are created in God's image; the subordination of woman to man and her exploitation reflect not the order of the nature created by God, but the contra-natural conditions resulting from original sin. Equal yet different according to the order*

of nature, man and woman complete each other through their free co-operation; and this complementarity is to be respected on every level – when at home in the circle of the family, when out at work, and not least in the life of the Church, which blesses and transforms the natural order but does not obliterate it.[123]

We confess both the order of creation and conform to the order that the Church has established by dressing appropriately in church. This order applies to both men and women; laymen are not allowed to cover their heads in Church, or braid or plait their hair (a common practice among men in ancient Greece and Rome).

4) Women reading in church

Verna Harrison highlights the apparent contradiction between the 'great talent' that women have for reading and singing and the fact they are denied a 'chance to read' in church. However, the issue here is not one of 'talent', because reading in church is not an artistic performance. Everything in the church should be done 'decently and in order' (1 Corinthians 14:40), so the various roles in the church are only carried out by those chosen, tonsured or ordained to serve them. Women are permitted to read and sing in church if they are appointed; in convents, nuns read and sing all the services. St. Paul's admonition, 'Let your women keep silence in the churches: for it is not permitted unto them to speak' (1 Cor. 14:34), served to regulate the prayers and prophesies of the Christian Corinthian women, and is not a blanket ban.

5) Inclusive language

Harrison objects that Orthodox services end with the phrase: 'through the prayers of our holy fathers…'. This ending is monastic in origin, because the services that we hear today in the Orthodox Church developed from the monastic usage, and the word 'fathers' in this sense means the 'holy fathers' among the monastics present. When a bishop is present this final phrase is replaced by: 'Through the prayers of our holy master [i.e. the bishop], Lord Jesus Christ have mercy on us.'

Having said that, every dismissal, of every service, asks the prayers of

[123] Moore, *Man, Woman, and Priesthood* p. 85.

the Mother of God before those of any saints. Overall, the language of the Church is already inclusive because when we say 'man' (*anthropos*), we mean 'mankind' which includes men and women. For example, the phrase 'Thou art the Friend of man,' does not mean that Christ is the Friend of men and not women! A more accurate, but less poetic translation would be 'Thou art the Friend of human beings.'

Man is only truly complete, a true human being, when he is completed by Christ in Whom dwells the fullness of the Godhead (Col 2:9-10). This 'perfect human being' is what we are striving for in the words of St. Paul: 'Until we all come in the unity of the faith, and of the knowledge of the Son of God, unto a perfect man, unto the measure of the stature of the fullness of Christ' (Ephesians 4:13). It is this completeness we are struggling for within the Orthodox Church rather than for a meaningless linguistic equality.

Harrison's suggestion that the ending should be changed to 'through the prayers of our holy fathers and mothers…' seems harmless, but tampering with Church traditions in a vain quest for linguistic equality will inevitably lead to the use of blasphemous constructions such as 'Our Mother' instead of 'Our Father'.

6) Communing during menstruation

Orthodox women refrain from communing during their period, and this practice is confirmed by the Second Canon of St. Dionysius which rules that those who approach Holy Communion should be 'wholly clean in soul and body'. This also applies to men who have had a nocturnal emission. Both these bodily functions remind us of our fallen state, but as Archbishop Chrysostomos explains:

> The Eucharist is a direct participation in perfect manhood through the partaking of Christ, the Perfect God and Perfect Man… and this oneness with Christ serves the function of moving us continually away from the world and mortal flesh to the life in Christ.[124]

The priest exclaims 'the holies are for the holy', during the Divine Liturgy because we are called to take Holy Communion in a spirit of re-

---

[124] Archbishop Chrysostomos, Bishop Auxentios, Archimandrite Akakios, *Orthodox Insights Vol.2* (CTOS: Etna, 2009) p. 26.

pentance, bodily purity and in a good spiritual state. Women, at this time, are not in an ideal physical state which makes even everyday life difficult. Although menstruation is not sinful, it is inextricably linked to our fallen state, being naturally associated with child-bearing and sexual intercourse. The same can be said of men's nocturnal emissions.

The feminist Leonie Liveris objects to the Church tradition on menstruation by highlighting what she perceives to be a contradictory position on men's nocturnal emissions:

> *One has yet to hear men willingly speak aloud of their acceptance of this 'unclean state', or obviously absent themselves from communion, particularly at those time when most of the community expect to take communion – at Easter and following the fast of the Theotokos in August.*[125]

As we have discussed above, the position of the Church on these bodily functions is clear and unambiguous. Men should not receive Holy Communion after a nocturnal emission, or after having sexual intercourse. Perhaps Liveris has yet to hear of men absenting themselves from Holy Communion on these grounds, but it certainly does occur in contemporary traditional Orthodoxy. By their nature, these things are private and it is no surprise that Orthodox Christians decline to discuss these things in public.

[125] Liveris, *Ancient Taboos and Gender Prejudice* p.148.

17

Further Reading

All these books are available from Orthodox bookstores such as the Eastern Christian Supply Company and Saint Nectarios Press generally at much lower prices than from secular bookstores.

Service Books and Explanations of the Services

L.C.L. Brenton (trans.), *Septuagint with Apocrypha.* ISBN 978-0913573440

Holy Transfiguration Monastery (trans.), *Prayerbook for Orthodox Christians.* ISBN 978-0943405018

Holy Transfiguration Monastery (trans.), *The Great Horologion.* ISBN 978-0943405087

Holy Transfiguration Monastery (trans.), *The Holy Psalter* ISBN 978-0943405009

D. Sokolof, *A Manual of the Orthodox Church's Divine Services.* ISBN 978-0884650676

Mother Mary, Archimandrite Kallistos Ware, *The Festal Menaion.* ISBN 978-1878997005

Mother Mary, Archimandrite Kallistos Ware, *The Lenten Triodion.* ISBN 978-1878997517

Commentaries on the Mysteries

Protopresbyter George D. Metallinos, *I Confess One Baptism.* ISBN 978-9608554207

Hieromonk Gregorios, *The Divine Liturgy: A Commentary in the Light of the Fathers.* ISBN 978-9608906792

St. Symeon of Thessalonika, *The Liturgical Commentaries.* S. Hawkes-Teeples (trans.). ISBN 978-0888444233

N.Cabasilas, *A Commentary on the Divine Liturgy.* ISBN 978-0913836378

St. Germanus of Constantinople, *On the Divine Liturgy.* P. Meyendorff (trans.). ISBN 978-0881410389

Metropolitan Cyprian, *Do You Have a Ticket? Concerning Repentance and Confession.* ISBN 978-0911165234

C. Carvarnos, *The Future Life According to Orthodox Teaching.* ISBN 978-0911165067

Metropolitan Cyprian, *The Monastic Life.* ISBN 978-0911165111

Hieromonk Gregorios, *The Mystery of Marriage – A Fellowship of Love.* ISBN 978-1939028150

Orthodox Theology

Archbishop Chrysostomos, *God made Man and Man made God.* ISBN 978-1884729928

Bishop Chrysostomos, Bishop Auxentios, *Scripture and Tradition.* ISBN 978-0911165043

Archimandrite Akakios, *Fasting in the Orthodox Church.* ISBN 978-0911165166

Ecumenism

Saint Edward Brotherhood, *Christian Union? An Orthodox Christian's Guide to Ecumenism: Past, Present and Future.* ISBN 978-0947935030

Christian Life and the Modern World

T. Rasophore, A. Holden, *The Ark of Salvation – A Young Adult's Guide to the Orthodox Church.* ISBN 978-0947935016

D. Cownie, J. Cownie, *A Guide to Orthodox Life: Some Beliefs, Customs, and Traditions of the Church.* ISBN 978-0911165227

18

Glossary

Aer: An embroidered cloth which is used to cover the chalice and *diskos*.

Afterfeast: The days following a Great Feast in which hymns to the Feast are combined with those of the saint.

Altar: The area behind the iconostasis. Often also called the sanctuary.

Ambon: The raised area in front of the Royal Doors.

Amen: A Hebrew word which is translated as 'so be it' or 'this is right.'

Antidoron: Literally 'instead of the gifts'. Antidoron is bread that is blessed at the Liturgy and given to those Orthodox Christians who have not taken Holy Communion.

Antimension: A cloth printed with an icon of the burial of Christ, and in which small relics of the saints are contained. The antimension is kept on the Holy Table and the Divine Liturgy is served on it.

Apodosis: Also called 'leave-taking'. The last day of a festal period on which the hymns of the feast are chanted again.

Aposticha: Literally 'on the verses'. The aposticha consists of hymns separated by verses from the psalms.

Archimandrite: Orginally, an abbot in charge of a number of monasteries, but today this title is awarded to senior hieromonks.

Artoklasia: The service of the blessing of five loaves, wheat, wine and oil at the All-night Vigil.

Artophorion: Also called a 'tabernacle'. The artophorion is kept on the Holy Table and contains the Holy Communion that is kept back, or reserved, for the sick.

Asceticism: From the Greek word meaning 'training'. Fasting, standing for prayer and prostrations are all forms of asceticism.

Asterisk: Placed on top of the diskos representing the Star of Bethlehem. It also serves a practical purpose of keeping the chalice veil from touching the Lamb.

Canon: (1) A section of Matins that consists of verses punctuated by refrains and based on the nine Old Testament odes. (2) A ruling of an Oecumenical or local Council.

Catechumen: Literally 'a hearer'. Someone who is being taught the Orthodox Faith with the aim of converting.

Chalice Veils: Special cloths that are used to cover the chalice and *diskos* during the Liturgy. They can be seen clearly at the Great Entrance.

Coenobium: A monastery in which monastics renounce their possessions, live, work and pray together.

Communion Hymn: A short verse from the psalms chanted during the communion of the clergy.

Deification: (Greek: *theosis*) Becoming gods by grace.

Dikirion: A two-branched candlestick held by the bishop.

Diskos: A round metal plate fixed on top of a small stand. The Lamb which is to become the Body of Christ is placed on the diskos.

Dismissal Hymn (Greek: *apolytikion*) Also known as the 'troparion of the feast', a dismissal hymn is a short hymn sung at the end of Vespers, the beginning and end of Matins and at the Little Entrance.

Doctrine: See 'dogma'.

Dogma: The theological definitions of the Church (see Acts 16:4).

Dogmaticon: A hymn to the Theotokos which also encapsulates the dogma of the Incarnation. Also known as a 'Dogmatic Theotokion'.

Doxasticon: Literally 'glory verse'. A sticheron sung after 'Glory to the Father….'

Epitaphios: (Slavonic: *plashchanitsa)* A cloth embroidered with an icon of the burial of Christ. It is kept on the Holy Table from Pascha to the Ascension.

Epitimia: A period of time without receiving Holy Communion, or some other discipline given by the Church as an aid to repentance.

Epitrachelion: Literally 'around the neck'. The priest's stole that he wears at every service.

Evlogitaria: A hymn with the refrain 'Blessed art Thou O Lord teach me Thy statutes.' Derived from the Greek '*evlogitos*' which means 'blessed'.

Exapostilarion: after the Greek word for 'dismissal'. A hymn sung at the end of the canon of matins after the Little Litany.

Forefeast: The days before a Great Feast on which hymns are sung in anticipation of the feast.

Grace: The uncreated energies of God are called the grace of God.

Great Entrance: The procession in which the chalice and *diskos* are brought out of the altar into the centre of the church and then placed on the Holy Table.

Hegumen: An abbot of a monastery.

Heresy: Derived from the Greek verb 'to choose'. A belief that is different from Orthodoxy. In Orthodoxy the word does not have the same derogatory character as in the West.

Heterodox: Literally 'different belief' as opposed to 'Orthodox' which means 'right belief'. Equivalent to 'non-Orthodox'.

Hierarch: A bishop. The word 'hierarchy' is often used in Orthodoxy as an alternative to 'episcopate'.

Hieromonk: A monk who is also a priest. A hierodeacon is a monk who is also a deacon.

High Place: The raised area behind the Holy Table.

Holy Table: The table in the middle of the altar on which the Divine Liturgy is celebrated, often called the 'altar table' or 'altar'.

Hypakoe: from the Greek for 'hearken'. A short hymn sung before the Hymns of Ascent on Sunday, or after Ode Three of the canon on Great Feasts.

Hypostasis: Often translated as 'person'.

Iconostasis: The screen separating the altar from the rest of the church.

Idiomelon: A type of sticheron sung to its own, long, melody.

Ikos: A stanza read after the kontakion during the Matins canon.

Incarnation: A word used to describe the Son of God taking on flesh and becoming man. From the Latin word *carnis* which means 'flesh'.

Incorporeal: Often rendered as 'bodiless' in many translations, the word 'incorporeal' is used to describe the angels who have existence but no physical form.

Irmos: (pl. *irmoi*) The first hymn in the ode of the canon. Normally the irmos is sung by the choir, and the troparia following are read.

Katavasia: The final hymn in the ode of the canon, sung by the choir. Great Feasts often have their own special *katavasia* relating to the Feast.

Kathisma: The Orthodox Psalter is divided into twenty chapters called 'kathismas'. The word kathisma means 'sitting' in Greek so we sit down when a kathisma is read.

Kenosis: A Greek word meaning 'self-emptying' and used to describe the whole mystery of the Son of God's incarnation and His dispensation.

Kolyva: A dish of sweetened, boiled wheat prepared for blessing at memorial services.

Kontakion: Originally a part of a long poem, a kontakion is a short hymn sung after Ode Six of the Matins canon. Kontakia are also sung at the Little Entrance and read during the Hours just before the forty-fold 'Lord have mercy'.

Lamb: The central portion of the prosphoron that is cut out during the Service of Preparation (see diagram on p.76). The Lamb becomes the Body of Christ.

Little Entrance: The procession in which the Gospel Book is brought out of the altar.

Lity: (1) The section of the All-night Vigil between Vespers and Matins that is served in the narthex. (2) The Trisagion memorial service for the Departed.

Matins: The morning service of the Orthodox Church.

Menaion: A set of twelve books containing the services of the Church for every day in all the months of the year.

Moleben: A prayer service of thanksgiving or petition.

Narthex*:* The area at the back of the church separated from the nave by a wall or partition.

Octoechos: From the Greek for 'eight tones'. Contains the text for the Sunday and weekday services of the Church.

Oecumenical Council: A gathering of bishops from all over the world that proclaims the Orthodox Faith and condemns heresy.

Orarion: The long band of cloth worn by subdeacons and deacons.

Panikhida (Greek: *Pannychis*): A memorial service for the reposed.

Pascha: The feast of the Resurrection of Christ. The word 'Pascha' is derived from the Hebrew word for Passover.

Passion: (1) From the Latin word for 'suffering'. The Passion of Christ describes His suffering and death on the Cross. (2) A passion is a sin that has become deeply rooted in us.

Phelonion: A cloak-like vestment worn by the priest.

Presbytera: A priest's wife is addressed as Presbytera [*Name*] in the Greek church. The Russian equivalent is 'Matushka' and the Romanian 'Preoteasă'.

Proskomedia: Literally 'offering'. The Service of Preparation in which bread and wine are offered and prepared.

Prosomion: A special melody to which other hymns are sung to.

Prosphoron: A round bread which is stamped with a special seal and is used for the Divine Liturgy.

Prothesis Table: A table, situated in the north-east corner of the altar, that is used in the Service of Preparation.

Ripidion: A liturgical fan. A pair of ripidi, decorated with icons of seraphim, can be seen behind the Holy Table.

Royal Doors: The doors in the middle of the iconostasis. These are more correctly called the Beautiful Gates.

Sabbath: The Hebrew word for Saturday. The Sabbath is not Sunday.

Sessional Hymn: Sometimes called 'sitting hymns' because sessional hymns are sung after reading of the kathisma at Matins.

Soleas: The raised area in front of the iconostasis. See also *ambon*.

Stasis: A section of a kathisma.

Sticharion: Long robe worn by the clergy when serving in the altar.

Sticheron: (pl. *stichera*) Hymns to a saint or feast often separated by verses from the psalms.

Theanthropos: Usually translated as 'God-man'. Christ is the *Theanthropos*.

Theophany: The feast of the baptism of Christ in the Jordan celebrated on the 6th January.

Theosis: Often translated as 'deification'. The ultimate aim of all Orthodox Christians is *theosis* – to 'become a god by grace'.

Theotokos: A Greek word meaning 'Mother of God'.

Theotokion: A hymn to the Theotokos chanted after 'both now and ever…'.

Trikirion: The three-branched candlestick held by the bishop.

Triodion: In Great Lent a weekday canon is made up of only three odes, which is why the service book of Great Lent is called the Triodion (lit. 'three odes').

Typica: A short service read instead of the Divine Liturgy; the Typica consists of the Typical Psalms and Beatitudes, the Creed, the kontakion of the day and Psalm 33.

Typicon: The regulations concerning the content and order of the services are contained in the typicon. Also, the rules and practices of a monastery are called its 'typicon'.

Unction: Literally 'anointing'. The oil sanctified in the mystery of unction is itself referred to as 'unction'.

Vespers: The first evening service of the Orthodox Church.

Index